ACKNOWLEDGMENTS

I want to thank the many, many folks whose collaboration made
this book possible. Stacy V. Frizzle, John Gable, R. Neil Laughlin,
Jane M. Connors, Judy Michaud, Lori Harris, Pat Naberezny,
Gladys Szabo, Wilma Sarna, Elaine Thibeault, and Kathy Muench.

Most-special thanks go to Dottie Moody, whose attention to detail
and dogged determination to "Get it done, Frank." made all the
difference.

DEDICATION

I'm pleased to dedicate this work to Sigurd A."Sig" Knudsen Jr, whose energy, heart and imagination picked up the Brunswick Community Center for Senior Citizens all those years ago, and transformed it to the unique Center that builds community that People Plus is today.

Also to Jane A. Marriner Connors, whose energy, heart and imagination took on a socially-wounded paratrooper all those years ago, and made me what I am today.

And finally to my grandsons Jadon and Silas. Two boys filled with promise, who give their "Grumpy Frank" another good reason to get up in the morning.

Frank Connors

FOREWORD

When Frank Connors started writing his column in the People Plus newspaper more than a decade ago, he promised "to deliver energy, imagination, humor, creativity and common sense." Well, I'd say he's delivered. By turns funny, informative, nostalgic, and often touching, the columns are a wonderful chronicle of growing up and living in the mid-coast, especially Bowdoinham and Brunswick.

Every column opens a flood of memories—the wrecks of the Hester and Luther Little, landmarks on the Wiscasset waterfront for so many years, picking beans for Harry Prout (which my now 40-year-old son Duncan did in the eighties), renovating an old Maine farmhouse, the loss to the fabric of the region when BNAS closed, and many more. What comes through is a sense of the small joys that we often overlook as well as the importance of connections to family and community.

I especially enjoyed the role that Frank's estimable wife Jane plays in the columns. She is just there, slightly outside the action--often skeptical and sometimes gently critical, but always offering her comments with affection and wifely tolerance. It's apparent that she's the common sense part of his original promise for the columns.

In a very real sense, this book is a valentine to Maine's mid-coast. Anybody lucky enough to have lived in the area will immediately recognize the places and many of the people--but it's more than just a local memoir. In a larger sense, the stories of families and kids growing up, of work and fun, of special places and even more special people, are universal and will strike familiar chords for just about any reader.

Our lives are so busy and sometimes confusing, the small details around us are often missed--lost in the rush of work, activities and the demands of each day. Fortunately, Frank has given us this book to slow things down, to narrow our focus for a few hours, to remind us how precious each day can be. My advice is to take it in small chunks, as it was written; savor the insights and anecdotes, and just enjoy the ride.

I sure did.

Angus King
Brunswick,
November, 2013

CONTENTS

Speaking Frankly

Pieces of me...

Sig didn't say he expected me to do a monthly column for his newspaper when he hired me, that bit of information came up later in one of those, "oh, I was going to tell you," or, "oops, I forgot to mention," discussions we had during my first few weeks of employment at the Center a decade ago.

When he pressed and I offered a little resistance, Sig said something like, "Just give it your best shot. If Rose Mary can do it, I'm sure you can come up with something as good as 'Denman's Deliberations'."

So the challenge was down. It was July, 2002, and the hot-button items at the 55-Plus Center were safely (and legally) buying discount drugs from Canada; should the bingo players be allowed to smoke in the main hall; and should residents of Topsham, Harpswell, and other surrounding towns pay a surcharge to attend trips sponsored by the Center. The center was having end-of-fiscal-year budgetary problems and had just replaced a full-time Outreach Coordinator and a half-time outreach worker with a part-time, in-experienced outreach coordinator: me!

My first and only "Frank's column," was published soon after. I'd rate that first column as shaky at best. It offered attempts at being autobiographical, philosophical, and funny. I promised to deliver energy, imagination, humor, creativity and common sense to my job, and there was a reference to my grandfather saying, "You want to move a mountain, you have to bend down and pick up that first rock."

I declared the Brunswick area was a very special place, and "the Center," is one of the reasons the area is so special. A decade of hindsight leaves me saying the column was unremarkable... too short, and pretty fractured. We ended up filling the page with an aerial picture I'd taken of the Center from the tower of the First Parish Church across the street (the tower was being restored) and I was promising a better effort next month.

August brought a "Speaking Frankly" column about building an addition at my in-laws home. I introduced in-laws Barbara and Norman Marriner to my written world, and we were off! Sig said something about not having the Center mentioned in the column and I said that was by design. "You know what you're doing," he said. I just nodded and made him believe that I did.

In the coming months there were pieces about cemeteries, stacking wood, and climbing Mount Katahdin. Others were about Sunday rides, Santa visits, privies, picking the perfect Christmas tree, the bottom of winter, boiling sap, and waiting impatiently for spring. Other pieces remembered John Cole and Robert P.T. Coffin. I took to making fun of myself, giving Jane a hard time, digging down into my personal knowledge to write about apples, eagles, skunks, and smelt fishing, about driving to the drive-in, walking to the brook, spending the winter in Florida. The first reference to Vietnam came in November of 2003, and in July 2004 came the piece about traveling to DC with Norman to open the World War II monument.

June 2007 was the only time that we skipped a month. Our Publisher and Editor Verdi Tripp had died, and we went into a bit of a spin, wondering if the People Plus News would survive. It did, we did. Daryl Madore, an editor at the Times Record, became our new secret weapon.

My personal favorites over the years were one about "chucking" woodchucks, and the piece about 92-year-old

Norman and a high school chum going clam digging. The toughest for me to write was the one that blended the birth of our first grandson with the death of my mother.

The decade of "Speaking Frankly" pieces that it has been my pleasure to share with you has mirrored huge changes to the life of my family and to the Center. The one constant is that the stories are genuine, and I never tire of wondering what to do next.

It is my hope we have another decade together, and that one day soon the pieces all come together.

Worth the investment

I've learned to accept that I could have died, perhaps even SHOULD have died, on Nov. 21, 1967.That day I was a fire team leader for the 173rd Airborne Brigade, attached to Alpha Company, in the Central Highlands of Vietnam. This was a tortuous, violent, hellish area of triple canopy jungle, just a few miles from the Cambodian border.

Back in the "world," folks were stocking up for their Thanksgivings. Me? I'd just logged my sixth-month "in-country," had just enjoyed a five-day R & R in Japan, and had been hospitalized, quite unexpectedly, with a high fever the second day after returning to Saigon.

The Rev. Charles Watters, 32, from New Jersey, was almost bald, he disliked wearing his steel pot. He wore glasses that were always dirty. "The airborne priest" we called him, tried to make this young Baptist understand that, "his God," was, "everyone's God" in that godless place.

My men in Alpha, in my absence, were assigned to "clear" a no-name jungle ridge called Hill 875, and had stumbled upon an entrenched battalion of North Vietnamese Regulars. They soon found themselves locked in a life/death struggle that would last four days. Alpha had made the first contact the first day, had sustained heavy casualties, had pulled back to evacuate wounded and, in a horrible twist of fate, was devoured in the blast of a 500-pound bomb. Friendly fire!

Bobbie Blye, 19, from Ohio, was blond-headed, blue eyed, not quite 6-feet tall. We would joke he was "too cute" to be a paratrooper. Mere months earlier, Bobbie had yanked me from a swirling stream, keeping me from drowning. "You owe me, Connors," was his favorite expression.

My luckless Alpha became one of the first American units identified in the American press as, "decimated" in hand-to-hand combat. Back in Brunswick, Times Record editor John Cole, who was a good friend, saw the UPI reports, recognized my unit name, assumed the worst and wrote a wonderful eulogy.

"Frank first became a friend when he filled in for a sister as a baby sitter," Cole wrote. *"One summer he helped us paint our house...he wrote a little for the old Brunswick Record...The official casualty count for the battle was 277 Americans killed, 946 wounded. We can only keep our fingers crossed, but we need to remember, those aren't just numbers dying on those hills, they are all someone's Frank."*

I recovered from my malaria in time to return to the boonies and help rebuild Alpha Company. I became a squad leader, then platoon sergeant, promoted not because of my military skills, but because luck seemed to keep me alive. I finished my time, came home, and like so many veterans often do, tried to make my way in what seemed an uncaring, unsympathetic and oftentimes cruel civilian world.

I have my family, my circle of friends in Bowdoinham, and my Jane, my wonderful Jane, to thank for bringing me from those days to these.

Over the years, John Cole and I would cross paths and often joke about the "one time," he should have checked his facts just a little better. He actually came to the Center one day to participate in a Library of Congress sponsored, Veteran's History Project. Cole joked about his short career in the Air Corps, as a belly gunner in a heavy bomber. "Used to ride to work backwards," he quipped, "imagine that." But he stopped short of taping his story that day, and to my knowledge, never wrote the details down. "You keep doing what you're doing here," he said of the Center. "You do good work. I used to think 55 Plus was just a place for old poops to play cards...but these veteran's stories, they are important stuff."

Important stuff? Most vets' get through life by ignoring, or at least trying to get past who they were, and what they did in the military. But now, I find I'm the old vet, and there's a new crop of kids coming home from other wars, and needing so much help.

I can only tell you, if you know one, hug him tight, and keep him right. These guys are worth the investment.

Ah, mayflowers!

My friend Peg won't share her Mayflower patch with me.

At 93, Peg glories in her ability to sneak off to the woods, to find her special place where she knows her Mayflowers are waiting. She tenderly picks just enough to fill that special little bud vase she keeps from year to year and then, I suspect, she offers a quick and grateful prayer about enjoying yet another new year.

I can imagine her standing on the edge of the patch, her toes almost touching the tender white petals, as she once again inhales that intoxicating nectar of spring. I also see her reveling in the independence that brings her back to this sacred, secret spot, year after year.

I have to imagine her doing this, for Peg steadfastly rejects any of my efforts to join her, or ever help her with this annual pilgrimage. Five, maybe six years ago, I first suggested to Peg that she might want me to walk with her to this place. My intentions were noble, the experience was humbling.

The answer was a firm and absolute, "NO!"

My offer really was based on a genuine concern for the possibility that Peg could fall, could become lost, or might simply value, or welcome some company on this annual expedition.

My presentation must have been flawed. Peg said if she needed help, she would ask for it, but she doubted she would be asking me. She described me as transparent, and said my motives were obvious. She hissed that I just wanted her patch of mayflowers. She said any proper Maine boy should have found his own mayflower patch long before he had reached my age! I wonder why she didn't just reach over and punch me in my tummy.

Peg is like so many of my older friends and neighbors: all so very independent, so spirited, and so resourceful. It occurred to me that it has never really been about mayflowers.

Peg relishes the idea that she knows how (and where) to find mayflowers, and I do not. This knowledge gives her value, and it gives her strength. Some seasons she will call me to tell me that on this specific date, she has been out and she has picked mayflowers. One year, there was a single mayflower, lovingly wrapped in a damp paper towel and placed on a corner of my desk.

No further comment was needed.

More than once Peg has called to ask if I knew the mayflowers were out yet. Always, she asks if I've found any mayflowers yet. Always, when I have to tell her not yet, that I'm still looking, I sense Peg's pleasure at my confession, and at my continuing failure.

Peg has seen her world shrink. When Peg walks, she walks with a cane, and her steps are close and guarded. She admits a nap in the afternoon is essential. She doesn't dare to drive anymore. I think her car was given to a granddaughter, perhaps with the provision that there be an annual pilgrimage to a mayflower patch. I hope so.

Two years ago, I know another friend delivered mayflowers to her (she was in the midst of a bad spell) but she took credit for the pick. She didn't want me to know that she was not able to go out and gather her own bunch.

And this year came the note.

Just a very few days ago, in an envelope with no return address, came a single piece of folded paper. A dried mayflower fell from the envelope when I opened it. A crude, hand-penciled map directed me to a known road, to a special, easily identified stand of pine trees, to a brook, and finally, to a shoulder of sunny woodland where the snow often clears first. I've passed this place a million times and apparently never looked at it close enough. There was no signature on the map, nothing to indicate directions, or what it was, or to show the name of the sender. None of that was necessary.

Tonight, on the drive home from work, I plan to pick a bunch of mayflowers for Peg.

Planning to plant?

Jane is what I consider a perpetual gardener, so when she announced in January, when the annual flood of seed catalogs started, that she "might not do a garden this season," I commenced to fret. Was she ill? Was it something I did? Was she just kidding??

This is a woman who spends hours of her winter - no, days of her winter - bundled in a heap on our living room couch, crumpled under a blanket not a few feet from our wood stove, plowing through pages and pictures in her seed catalogs.

She takes notes. She compares prices. She chats with friends about seed production. She figures planting dates. She decides when we'll have beans and zucchini next summer. She calls the kids. She makes more notes. She draws a garden plan. She rips whole pages from catalogs and files them away for future reference, and then yes, she takes even more notes.

This process has always been one of the crutches she uses to help her through the darkest days of winter, and to feed her need for rooting around in the soil.

Usually by now there is a pretty good stack of catalogs piled away for reference, and the bucket of garden tools usually has the first offering of seeds all ordered, on hand and ready to plant. But this year, catalog after catalog has been recycled. Also this year, the buzz among her friends is over other stuff, and so far, I have seen no garden plan on the drawing board. I'm starting to believe that this really could be the year!

When we were first married, we had this huge, half-acre garden in east Bowdoinham we called the "truck" farm. Friends thought we were obsessed. I was the proud owner of a bright red, Troy-Bilt rota-tiller that could whip that magnificent, river-bottom soil 12-inches deep and to the consistency of cottage cheese.

Weeds appeared on that corner at their peril.

We planted, we grew, we canned and we froze. When the kids arrived, they pretty much learned to crawl and to weed in the same summer. Now Miles is a master gardener, and Abbie and George are the ones grooming the half-acre garden. Somewhere along the line Jane took over the garden space with her dad at his house, we put a small kitchen garden where the barn used to be in Bowdoinham, and the plot "over East," has been put back to hay.

Jane's dad Norman still insists on "hoeing a row" at the age of 93, and we all have to remember (so he won't have to remind us) that he used to work for the Daggett Brothers for 20 cents per hour, back when it was possible to buy fresh-from-the-garden celery, carrots, and lettuce, home grown on Topsham heights.

Jane and her dad are worlds apart with their gardening techniques. He is a 5-10-10 fertilizing kind of guy (more IS always better) and Jane would rather use composted manures, with straw, old newspapers and daily care to control weeds.

When planting day comes I just make sure the plot is tilled and ready (if Joe Bryant hasn't already done it) and stay out of their way. Nothing is ever gained by me trying to inject MY vast knowledge of horticulture. Certainly, a long tradition of great gardens has been a tribute to both their crafts.

And now there is this season's conundrum. We know if Norman can walk this spring, he'll be ready and wanting to hoe, and I just can't imagine Jane without a garden to tend. What would she do with herself? We are between houses, spending too much time on the road, commuting when I know Jane would rather be in her old jeans, yanking weeds, picking bugs, and talking to blossoms.

Guess I'd better rota-till both spots this spring...if we ever get rid of this snow... and we'll just need to wait and see what happens.

Artwork by John Gable

Playing with marbles

You take the heel of your shoe and drill a hole in the fresh-thawed, water-infested earth. You and your buddies step off three or four paces, and the games begin.

I have always been partial to the sound (and feel) of marbles rattling around in my pocket. I suspect accumulating marbles was perhaps one of the first really materialistic urges I experienced as a wee lad. From a very early age, it was important to me to own more marbles than either of my brothers, and more than any of my friends.

I really did like the rattle and rolling.

I wouldn't cheat to accumulate marbles, and I promise I never stole any...unless you count the few my younger brother may have been careless enough to leave untended... but folks, the temptations were always there, and I have to admit there were some moments when I stretched the rules to acquire more marbles.

Glass-eyes, agates, croakers, cat-eyes, glassers, twirlers and clay drops or taws; I coveted them all. I stored them in mittens and filled a sock or two in a good season. I sometimes hid them in places so secret I'd forget where they were. I often slept with my stash under my pillow, only because I always doubted my brother's values more than I ever questioned my own.

We'd play for one-sies or two-sies; we'd play "off the wall," or "drop the bomb," or a dozen other games taught us by older classmates, or simply created by us as we went along. My personal favorite was "off the wall," with two or ten guys deftly tossing marbles toward an immovable object. Rule was that the marble had to hit the ground once and roll toward the goal without touching it! If your marble touched the wall, you were out of the game, you lost your marbles. Sorry! Closest marble to the wall without touching it took the whole line. Simple and brutal, jungle-like warfare; a perfect game for kids of every age.

Sometimes, we'd have to go find a girl we trusted enough to settle a tie. A fellow with a gentle toss could clean up dozens of marbles in just a few games of "Off the Wall." The secret of success was to deliver a high, arching toss, and have a pretty good eye. I got pretty good at it.

One spring I recall cutting a hole in the top of a Quaker Oats box, and challenging guys to drop marbles through that hole. Rule was to hold the marble higher than your belt. I made a bunch of marbles off that gig! I'd tell them they could keep all the marbles in the box if their marble went through, I'd keep their marbles if they missed. It sounded so easy, and I'd rattle

24

that box wickedly, making them think there was a hundred marbles in there and ripe for the taking. (In fact, I never had more than a dozen marbles in the box.)

And it was always about spring. Playing marbles as a boy was a genuine and official rite of spring. We'd drill the holes for games on the south side of school, and be playing weeks before the snow was gone from the north side.

As a married man and father, the scattered remains of my marble collection (not consumed by my kids) gravitated to a glass jar that we always stored on the sill of our dining room window. The way the sun played through those marvelous glass morsels never failed to warm my heart.

Anytime in the past decade or three, whenever I'd happen to see stray marbles, I'd pick them up, "save 'em" if you will, and they'd rattle around in my pocket till I passed that jar, and I'd drop them in.

It has never been unusual for me to turn a marble or two when I'm working outside. I'd find them in our garden, over where the old sandbox used to be or when I'm digging holes. Another prime spot was at the schoolyard, not far from our home.

I guess I should have missed that jar when it disappeared.

A year ago, while visiting our son and his new wife in their new home, I was startled to see that jar of marbles in THEIR south-facing window! There were several immediate and surly comments about grand theft-marbles- but secretly, I was delighted to discover he wanted that piece of my home, of my life, in his home!

I almost told him so, but resisted.

Last fall on a weekend trip to the Strawberry Banke

restoration in New Hampshire, Jane and I encountered a huge and colorful marble display in the museum store. I was shocked by the prices, but had to have at least enough to fill one pocket. Jane rolled her eyes but paid the bill, muttering something about boys who never seem to grow up. I told her we would put these "museum quality" marbles in our kids' stockings at Christmas, and she agreed. And we did.

Visiting Miles last month, we were offered back that original jar of marbles! He took it right off that window and had it right in his hand, ready for the trip back to Maine. He had assumed, (I'm betting with some coaching from his very savvy wife) that the gift of stocking marbles at Christmas was a hint that I really wanted him to return my original stash.

But they missed the point, folks. I love the idea that he has claimed those marbles and that he also treasures the way the sun floods through that jar. I love that he sees them as a piece of my heritage, and now of his.

I'll just start a new jar for my window.

Artwork by John Gable

Me and my canoe

More times than I want to remember, I've heard Jane tell folks she would have never taken that second date with me were it not for the promise of a canoe ride.

I'm guessing I should accept at least two points from this startling revelation: (1) our first date (it was blind, and an April Fool's Day party) apparently didn't set HER world afire; and (2) that canoe should be very, VERY near the top of the list of the material things which I value most from my life.

My canoe is a 16-foot Chestnut, built in Canada some 70-75 years ago. Cedar-planked, oak-ribbed, and sheathed with canvas, she is a real classic.

I bought this canoe from a friend for $150 shortly after my return from Vietnam. By the time of that first date, the canoe was no doubt a bigger part of my personality than I cared to admit. Some days I'd go out with that canoe and just drift and

27

dream; other days I'd just paddle as hard as I could and think of nothing.

But I will say this folks, the day I added Jane to the bow of that boat, it was obvious to all that progress was being made. Together we did Merrymeeting Bay, its sands, and all of its rivers. There were several blue water trips out of Stonington and off Popham, several more to Moosehead, to Flagstaff, to the Forks and the Harpswells. One early spring day, we hosted the minister who would marry us on a ride up the Abagadasset River, Bowdoinham) because he wanted to see "how an Indian might feel" cruising that river.

One day on the upper Saco River, we "hallooed" a fisherman on a bridge and asked him how far we were from Fryeburg. He laughed at our navigational skills and said, "about 25,000 miles, the way that boat is headed..." and he advised us to get out of the river, since we were headed for a section of rapids and falls. You'll have to know this was in the days before Delorme atlases. Seemed we were already below the town, not above it where I thought.

When the kids came along, we added seats, life jackets, turtle hunts and a hundred other adventures to that canoe. One of their favorite trips was the upper Cathance River, from Route 201 (Topsham) upstream toward Bradley Pond. There would be turtles galore and on a good day, the Bisson's cows would be astride the stream and we would coast right up to them. "Go under, go under..." the kids would yell, always pointing out the biggest bull...and those big cows would just look at us, watching and waiting.

So, wouldn't you think I'd have taken better care of that boat?

There were seasons when I should have painted or varnished her, and I didn't. There came a rip in the canvas one year, I should have sewn it, and didn't. And during those years we were tearing down the barn (the barn was the canoe's off-water home) she took a direct hit from a flying beam, costing her a rib and a couple planks. A little late, we took the wounded craft to Norman's and stuck her between the rafters of his garage, where for several years, she was out of sight and out of mind.

Well, not quite out of mind.

As is often the case these days, friends of our kids stepped up and offered solutions. John, a student at Mount Ararat with Miles and Abbie, now has a little boat repair business going. His quote was affordable, his outlook was optimistic. The old canoe came out of the rafters and went to his shop. I nearly cried in anticipation as she went down the driveway.

John called the other night to say his job is done and I'm to start mine. It seems I said I could paint and re-varnish the boat myself if he did the fancy work. I couldn't be happier, and will go to the brushes willingly.

One of the neat points to this story is coming to realize how many of my kids' friends are now young adults in our community and contributing to the fabric of our society, as we always wondered if they would, or even could.

Anyway, the stage is nearly set. For this anniversary, I think I'll surprise Jane with a canoe ride... maybe up the Abagadassett once again, like the Indians did.

Sharing my secret place

The water is still cold enough to pucker a fingernail, but do we care? I mean, Miles and I are in the first year of a spring tradition, dropping our grand Green Lady into the Cathance while there is still gray and decaying ice pack in the shady corners of the north shore, and we are psyched!

Well, I am anyway.

I suspect if I really dared to look my son directly in the eye, I might see some apprehension, some questioning and just a dash of disbelief. So I just won't look. The pine paddle that belonged to Jane's granddad offered that luscious, hollow echo as it clattered onto the cedar keel of our little craft. "We're ready," says I.

I have to accept some of Miles' misgivings I suppose, since we do have his son along. That was NOT an easy negotiation with either his mother or my Jane. At four, Jadon is a slender, spirited little guy who might weight 50 pounds, soaking wet. (But yes, WE had to promise to keep him "perfectly" dry this day)

Jadon is right into this latest adventure, wearing at least 45 pounds of clothes, an oversized hat and a life jacket that could circle his frame, maybe twice. His grin makes his ears wiggle in anticipation as he steps gamely over the rail and plumps down in the bottom of the boat. "Sit carefully," I advise, and those great, black eyes flash excitement, trust and approval.

Miles takes the bow end, with just a little reluctance. I know he's bigger than me, and stronger, and doesn't like paddling from the bow, but hey, the Green Lady is mine, at least for a few more years. I'm the Captain, I sit where I want, I take the stern. (It's really not about power, anyway, it is about me getting to watch the excitement in little Jadon's eyes, and frankly, Miles gets more of that than I do.)

Jadon is a game and willing customer, he holds the canoe rail so tightly with both hands, his little knuckles whiten. We pitch the craft into the narrow, gentle stream and push toward Bradley Pond. It is just exciting for me to think of him experiencing this trip for the first time, first of many, I hope. His dad, Aunt Abbie and I made this trip several times, and it was always my hope to do it more frequently. The Cathance River is just one of those underused, secret places of our area.

We all had to call on "Mr. Echo," as we paddled under the 201 bridge. It's too early for painted turtles, the snappers are still down-river, and the bulls from the Bisson farm are still in the barn, but the river still offers its surprises. Early on, the river has created a lake of its own over a corn field, we drift in it for a few minutes, poling our way when the paddles fail, adoring the sun as it washes our faces.

The first bend in the river scares up a pair of Canada geese. Trapped without a runway, the geese paddle feverishly to stay ahead of us, Jadon laughs as they honk and scream their complaints. Finally, they enter a stretch of straight river and get away, turning into the wind right over our heads. Jadon lifts a hand from the rail to wave his farewell.

We retrieve a beaver stick from the mud for Jadon to take to his mother, and we were delighted to catch a beaver just off shore as we rounded one of the many mud-banked corners. The beaver's slapping tail on the water lets us know he thinks HE owns this river! Miles slaps back with his paddle, just like I showed him, all those years ago. We talk about how they can stand the cold water, as we realize it may be just a little too early, that this run up the Cathance is a warm up for others this summer.

Miles reminded me of the year we entered the Kenduskeag River Canoe race, and we rolled over more than twice in the 40-ish degree water. We finished that race a few minutes behind Uncle Grant and Ty, and maybe an hour behind the winners, but we finished.

"We were younger then," I suggested, "and smarter now." Miles guided the canoe around a tree blown into the river, and reminded me there could be NO turn-overs today.

My Green Lady ground across a submerged limb just then, and I make a face for Jadon as I visualize a gouge across her perfect body. "First scratch is always the worst one," Miles says with a grin, but we decided to call it a day, and head home. Going back we find no more geese, we skirt the corn lake.

We say good bye to Mr. Echo and pull the lady from the water. Jadon is shivering as I turn the heater on in the truck but he looks at me and smiles, "can we go again tomorrow," he asks? "Real soon," says I, delighted to show another secret place to yet another generation.

Artwork by John Gable

Riding in wheelbarrows

Imagine my glee as I put my slightly skeptical, three-year old grandson in my brand new, shining red wooden wheelbarrow and asked him where he wanted to go. Bless his heart, he really did look at me and very seriously announced his first choice was "Bowdoinham!" (12 miles away, give or take a few feet). I looked right back to him, slightly shocked, and asked if down the driveway would do. He nodded yes, and we took off.

I suspect that until that moment, Jadon didn't even know what a wheelbarrow was. I'm sure he'd never been in one, at least not on MY side of the Piscataquis River. I ran, and I ran faster. I couldn't see his face since he faced forward, but the squeals that came from that boy told me he was loving it, even if his knuckles were white! I ran like I still had two good shoulders and two good knees. I ran till I was winded! (That took about 100 yards, or 40-odd seconds.)

Where the driveway enters the woods, I slowed to a more

33

leisurely pace and caught my breath. It was a cool, early spring evening, trees just budding, birds singing, the wheel making that unique grind as it rolled over the gravel. Jadon looked up at me, grinned and kicked the front board to go faster again. I told him he might end up hauling ME home.

I don't want you to consider me a hopeless romantic, but that was one of those moments when this old Vietnam vet was happy he got through the war.

Consider the humble wheelbarrow for just a moment. It's a simple wooden box on a frame, attached to one wheel. I'm no engineer, but I'll bet that the wheelbarrow is one of the oldest forms of transportation remaining virtually unchanged as we progress ever deeper into our crazy, high-tech world.

I used to haul our kids in the Bowdoinham parades in a wheelbarrow, till they got so old they wanted to do the route on their big wheels or bicycles. We used to sneak into the parade line, right behind the honor guard from the Navy base, and the guys got quite a great kick out of us.

My Grandfather used to haul me in his creaky old wheelbarrow. We'd go to the store, around the block, or across a field. There was a hill in town we called Back Hill, which plunged toward the Cathance River at a pretty alarming angle. He never shied away from the hill, but he never ran it either. He used to call "whoa, there" on the down trip, like he was driving a horse. What impressed me more, thinking back over 60-odd years, is that he CLIMBED that hill with me on board, and more often than not, we'd be sharing the wheelbarrow with some animal feed or a grain bag, or some fire wood.

Hank Welzel, an 80-plus-year-old People Plus member, "made" this wheelbarrow from scratch! He had an old wheel in his barn, one that he said was older than him. He made the frame and handles of oak, he crafted the steel parts on some sort of forge, and built the body of pine. It stands rigid, it's built stout. When I suggested the red color is a bit flashy for a working wheelbarrow, he said he picked it to match my truck.

Last fall as Jane and I were packing to leave Bowdoinham, she caught me placing the remains of another old, sub-sized wheelbarrow on my truck. One handle was broken, its sides were missing... it was a sorry representation of what it once had been. I found it in a dark loft of our barn when we bought the place in 1975. "What is that, "she asked. "A wheelbarrow, "I offered weakly, knowing I'd been caught. "That is NOT going to Brunswick," she decreed. "Well," said I, grasping at splinters, "I know this guy who can fix it, I wasn't going to take it to your dad's..." Jane rolled her eyes, muttering something under her breath as she walked away.

I did take that old frame to Hank, and he made that pint-sized wheelbarrow look better than new. I believe Jadon's (and MY) enthusiasm for that little barrow motivated Hank to build the bigger beauty.

We're now a two-wheelbarrow family, and I'm thinking even Jane likes that!

You gotta' love April!

You gotta' love April. I mean, can you honestly think of another month, ANY month that will offer so much variety, or change, or just plain ol' pizaz-z?

It starts, of course, with April Fools, or All Fools Day, and only gets better. I'm a guy who loves a good practical joke, and I do what I can do to orchestrate a good one any April Fool's Day. I consider it a right, I consider it a duty. Just ask Nancy March, or Jon Ouellette. I don't want to brag, but I'm one up on both of them. I do have this circle of friends, potential victims all, who are always watching for ways to reciprocate. It's a great way to inflict a little excitement in our lives, with no harm done, of course.

Want an example? We woke one morning to find a bushel of "horse dressing" dumped on our front steps. It was a Sunday, and my mother came by with a plate of home-made donuts, just as I was shoveling the last of it into a basket for delivery to our compost heap.

"What's that?" says she.

"Horse droppings," says me.

"How did it get on your front steps?" she asked me.

"I'm thinking a friend may have dumped it last night," I said smiling, "It's April Fool's Day, you know," I added. Mom walked on to the back door with the donuts, muttering something about me having weird friends.

Before the month was ended, I'd determined from whom the donation came, and I'd managed to have some of the same droppings, carefully filleted, draped with lettuce and seasoned with mustard, substituted for meatloaf in my buddy's noonday sandwich. His wife was my co-conspirator on that!

Of course, he never admitted to biting into it.

And I met my wife at an April Fool's Day party but folks, that was no joke! (at least not to me!)

Think about April's weather for a moment. Daylight Savings time ends, so we end the month with a net gain of nearly two hours of daylight in thirty days! Who can complain about that?

All the birds are back, from Robins, to Ospreys, to Finches, to Canada Geese. The geese have to be my favorites, soaring in their great V-formations, resting in the newly opened fields, gaggling in their sociable groups, and honking as they plan the next leg of their trip, moving even further north.

It is not unusual to have one last good snowstorm for the month. My grandfather used to call it "poor man's fertilizer," and say it was a good thing. I don't want to jinx us, but given that this has been an "old fashioned winter," could this be the year of the next April blizzard?

I want to promise you, before this month ends, snow WILL be a novelty. Those last granulated piles of snow left on the shady sides of the barn or on the north slopes in the woods are fun to hunt. I see it as a final triumph by me over winter. I take a son, a daughter, or friend and seek it out! Find that last secreted drift, kick off its top, inspect the stained layers and suck the moisture out of a handful. I promise you, you'll never get sick...

There are always days of the month that are simply sensational, so nice that you just have to get outside. Take a walk or clean the leaves, the sticks and trash from your lawn. I like to find a south facing corner and just SIT! The sun is warm again, life abounds and it becomes a moment to savor, Winter is done!

Oh, I do hate to fill my woodbox in April.

April is the month to take stock of my wood supply. All winter long, the burled wood, the wet wood, the odd pieces, they all have been getting tossed here and there as I go for the good stuff, and have dutifully lugged them to the woodbox. At some point in April Jane will tell me it's okay to skip the night's fire in the wood stove. THAT is a reason to celebrate!

April becomes the month to re-stack, re-stock, and yes, this year, start putting up next season's wood!

The rivers and lakes all have their ice out and then their high waters. Usually, if the weather gets wet there's a flood to visit. The kids and I often like to talk about walking Water Street in Brunswick, (or Augusta) or Gardiner, when the water is lapping in sheets along the pavement, and the rivers are telling the public works crews who is really in charge. The little brook that babbles behind our house has a week or two of genuine roaring, flexing against its banks like it wants to be a river.

April is a great time to turn the canoe over, chase the last pieces of ice out to the channel and then get reacquainted with the sandbars and ledges. Usually, only the sand has moved.

But the real joys of April are the new life.

Trees bud, flower, and break out. Lawns drain and seem to color overnight. There is a great rush, and a great flush, as the cold and the old is pushed aside, and new life takes command. It tells us all that life is good, life is exciting, life is again worth living.

There is life after winter and April is the exclamation point! Enjoy it and go pay your taxes.

Chuting the Androscoggin   by John Gable

Breaking into spring

One of the times mom really got mad with my brothers and me
was the day she discovered we'd been jumping ice cakes on the
river. It was a spring thing. We were young and a little stupid,
anxious for winter to end and for the river to open. We were
sick of the dull, white winter river, we were ready to fish, to
paddle and play.

We'd take long sticks for balance, clampers for traction, cookies
for the pocket and away we would go. Our Abagadasset River
was shallow and narrow, and if it weren't for the tide, there
would have been no current at all. Mostly, we'd just float, get
atop a big chunk of ice and pole it around. We'd bump one cake
against another, or race to cross to the opposite shore. None of
us ever fell in where the water was over our head. Usually,
when the cakes got tipping or rocking, it was us doing the

39

tipping on purpose.

Guess we're lucky she only caught us once.

Bruce, once my barber over in Richmond, used to take a lounge chair, a cooler of beer, a couple books, a reflector, a radio and literally "camp" on an ice floe as it meandered with the tide, up and down the Kennebec. If the sun stayed good, he'd do this for a day or two. It was always his plan to get his first tan of the season that way, (this is back before tanning beds) and it always worked, unless some shore dweller saw him, didn't know him, and reported his as a foundering fisherman, headed for the sea.

Wardens eventually got tired of the calls, and wrote him up at least once. He finally built a sheltered, south-facing deck off his house but always claimed the tanning was better on a chunk of ice.

At least three seasons, it was a privilege of mine to ride as a civilian aboard the Coast Guard ice breakers that opened the Kennebec in the spring. Thunder Bay was the name of one of those boats. I was a reporter for The Times Record back in those days, and I made ice-breaking one of my regular beats. The little ships ran in tandem, cracking and crunching. In case you didn't know it, a "breaker" is designed to take a running start, ride up atop the ice and crush it under its rounded and reinforced belly. If that sounds like a little less than a smooth ride upriver, you're right. In all those trips, I don't think I ever finished a cup of coffee without spilling part of it in my camera case.

The cutters would move quickly up river from Bath, encountering their first real ice after entering Merrymeeting Bay at the Chops. One vessel would turn immediately right, busting straight up the channel, while the other worked behind, pounding the thick, clear ice off the left, and then right sides. Remember, they like to work when the tide is running out.

Certainly, there's a current on the Kennebec, but with the tide as an ally, those boats could really clear ice.

The goal is flood control, clearing the river from the Chops to Gardiner, some 16-18 miles north. Much of the Kennebec is a broad, open river for that distance, but there's a little hook behind Swan Island, and a shallow spot at the Richmond Bridge. If the channel isn't opened before a significant spring rain, the river can and has flooded at both of these spots.

In 1936, sections of the new Richmond bridge were lifted off their piers and carried on the ice to the foot of Richmond's Main Street nearly a half-mile away.

In 1978, I found and photographed Maine's Gov. James Longley at that same bridge, as the two of us happened to visit one pre-dawn morning, just to see if the span stayed in place over night. I recall we both seemed pleased the bridge was safe; he was less than pleased to have me catch him and take his picture.

I offered small talk to his honor, suggesting an ice breaker would be a good thing to have right then, or perhaps we both might need a good straight stick, if the bridge failed and we needed to walk to shore on the ice. He looked away from me humorlessly, and motioned to the trooper standing on the Dresden end of the bridge. The cop walked briskly toward us.

Just like that, I figured the interview was over, and thanked him for his time. I headed to town for a cup of coffee, and a chance to say I'd met the governor. Ice was grinding at the steel-decked bridge but the structure held, and two days later, the cutters made it through and opened the channel. My brothers still make fun of me for almost getting arrested that morning, but my mother always told that story with just a little pride.

The season's first "Canadas"

I heard them first, their distinctive, throaty honking penetrated the foggy mists of our first pre-spring days. I stopped short on my step, excited and turned to look up and face their call head on.

The first "Canadas" of spring are always special. Those proud, black heads, banded with a pure white necklace, their massive, but grace-filled bodies tinted in black, and gray and brown, and all under-coated with a white as bold as any new December snow. That honk fills a promise, that first appearance is nothing short of uplifting. For me, it stirs a great feeling within.

This day there are only two flying close together. One is right on the tail of the other, strong wings working in perfect coordination. There was a casualness in their honk, perhaps a friendly conversation back and forth. I offered myself a guess: perhaps a mister goose and his lady, chatting together about their day.

They flew just over our treetops, not 50 yards above and away, but they paid me no mind. If they saw me there was no start of shock in their motion, no change to their direction. I could imagine hearing their great wings as they flew so effortless, so coordinated, so directed.

Geese and spring consume some of my earliest memories. As a kid, I'd walk into a flock of geese, hundreds of them, as they were massed and feeding in the agricultural fields of East Bowdoinham. There really were more of them then there are now. My brothers and I would just move easy on them, slowly, steadily sliding forward, picking out the guards of each flock, locking our vision on their dark, piercing eyes.

We'd move constantly at them until they lifted off in a great racket, a great flutter, flying easily to the next field, or out to shelter on Merrymeeting Bay. The game was always to walk slowly, to see how close we could be before they jumped off.

There was always a spring "camp out" or two, when we'd go with brothers or friends and spend the overnight on the shore of the bay, cooking mac & cheese (with hot dogs) on an open fire, but the real occasion was still the geese. We'd expect not to sleep, we'd know the constant din of a thousand honks, all night long, would be keeping us awake. We planned on it, we accepted it. We looked forward to it! We knew we could sleep after we walked home.

A goose, drifting slowly through water only recently opened by ice is a beautiful thing. Try to imagine this moment. It is very early in the morning, the dawn sun is still chasing shadows out of the woods. The only noise around is the honk, honk, honking of a multitude of unseen geese. You don't see them because the water where they drift is still covered with a delicate white mist. IF you are lucky, you catch sight of a head, then two, then twenty, as they paddle towards the shore. You have to be very careful not to move, geese are always very watchful.

If you have been attentive, if you choose not to breathe, you're rewarded by the site of the first pair, or eight, as they waddle from the gently lapping water. Right here, the drama turns to comedy. When geese walk they tend to look top-heavy, flat footed and funny. More than once my brothers and I have turned a flock to the air, just as they walked from the water. More than once they'd jump from our laughter.

I hope you've seen the movies about people adopting fledgling flocks of geese and encouraging them to migrate, or re-migrate. It is a tender story about dedicated naturalists willing to risk all sorts of trouble, just to put wild things back on a cycle.

The truth is, I'm told, that many geese today do fail to migrate (or choose not to) and therefore, over time, lose that ability all together. If my thousands of geese at Merrymeeting have turned to hundreds, I'm told it's because most of the balance of the flock chooses to stay in the south and lounge on the ever-green golf courses, or median strips along the interstate.

While I can't blame these great birds of spring, I feel poorer for not having the huge flocks to share with my kids, and with their kids. But I can content myself by seeing a pair of them. Knowing what they mean, these heralds of spring, will always be good enough for me.

Picking my way through summer

Ever wonder how many blueberries are in a quart??

Me too!

I'm sort of a berry connoisseur, you know. I start picking strawberries as early as I can in June, and I don't stop pursuing berries till the last "second crop" raspberry drops into my mouth, usually in mid-October. In between, mine is an ample and excitable, if fickle, love affair with strawberries, raspberries, blackberries, current berries, cherries, blueberries…you name it, I'll pick 'em, I'll eat 'em.

This year's strawberry season got off to a fast start. Visiting the kids in Newport, R.I., we got into our first pick-your–own operation just days after Memorial Day. I was unbelieving. There was a piece of me that didn't want to taste a Rhode Island berry, but there was this place called, "The Sweet Berry Farm," and Miles and Jadon just couldn't wait. We picked 4 quarts in as many minutes…at $4.00 a quart, thank you very much…then I sat back on my heels and ate another $3.00 worth.

Mark that off my list, first day of berry picking with my grandson!

The ladies in the strawberry fields at Bowdoinham just wouldn't know what to do without me. I tell them I'm a major contributor to their retirement plan, they tell me I shouldn't eat berries before I wash them.

Jane and I routinely pick 200-250 quarts of strawberries each year, and many years more than that. Some days I'm in the field at 7 a.m. after a fresh quart for our cereal, other days I show up with a five quart bowl, needing 25-30 quarts for something special. We always freeze 30-50 quarts, just to make it through the winter. I mean, four or five of Jane's very best fruit pies have strawberries as a base: strawberry-peach, strawberry rhubarb, strawberry-blueberry...you get the idea.

This is the year that we figured out that crushed strawberries, lightly sugared, will freeze just fine, store for months and taste fresh as the day they were picked when you thaw them out.

Raspberries come right on the heels of strawberries. Fact is in a good season, the two berries have a season overlap. I know life is worth living one more year, if we get a week in July when we have fresh, local strawberries and raspberries together in a bowl of Cheerios. Cheerios become optional. Yup, that happened again this year, and Linda's blackberries are right behind our raspberries!

Jane will tell you she picks almost twice as fast as I do, and I'll admit that is usually true. I will tell you I'm no slouch picking berries, I just EAT twice as many berries as she does. Who do you think enjoys picking more?

Oh, those ladies in Bowdoinham! At least one routinely threatens to weigh me as I go into the field, and again as I come out. She says she is only trying to protect her retirement.

Grampie and I spent many a day when I was a kid picking wild blueberries. Does anyone else remember the exceptional picking that used to be behind the Topsham Town Farm, off Foreside Road? Yes, the area is all houses now. We'd go in there early in the morning, trying to beat the August heat, and we intended to spend the whole day. Mom would pack us a lunch in one of our two-quart lard pails, and Grampie had this rule, we'd have to have one pail full before any food came out of the other.

That same Topsham ridge used to be a perfect place to watch the Blue Angels. We did most of the early BNAS air shows from over there. The pilots always came in low and slow on their approach to the runway, located just over the river. They were so low we could almost see the color of their eyes, and smell the kerosene from their jets. I used to come home with blueberry stains on my ears from trying to cover that delightful, exciting roar with the palm of my hands.

During the past decade or more, Jane and I have always ordered blueberries by the 20-pound flat from a grower down in Hope. Many years we'd order 200-250 pounds. I always look forward to that ride, mostly because of the return trip when I'd scoop berries off the top of the flat we'd picked up for my sister-in-law, and eat 'em as we drove up route 17. This year, that grower couldn't fill our order so we searched deeper down east, and Stan and Judy got to make that run. I have to wonder how many of MY berries THEY ate?

But here's the good news. Because we couldn't buy our berries all picked, Jane and I went off in search of wild patches again. I'd all but forgotten how pleasant that is. Two or three evenings, we wadded off into sun-drenched fields and picked berries together.

"Plunk, plunk, plunk," they'd go, dropping into that Tupperware bucket. We enjoyed the time, talking and laughing together, and the silence when there was nothing else to say. Jane once again proved she picks faster, and made fun of my blue-stained teeth. But next winter, when the wind howls down on our little home and Jane is baking another blueberry pie, we'll also be warmed by the memory of those walks on the blueberry barrens.

Oh, yes -17, 848 - that's how many blueberries in a standard quart! Doubt me? Go picking and count them yourself.

Making maple syrup

A forty to one ratio is always daunting, but with maple syrup I always consider the result worthy of the process. That first real spring day, ready or not, I always catch myself thinking about tapping a tree or two and making a new batch of maple syrup.

Making maple syrup is a ritual of spring that is pure New England. You just can't do it if you live in New York, or Florida, or Pennsylvania, or Transylvania. Well, you can't do it with the expectation of making real sweet, real amber, real MAINE maple syrup.

And the ritual is part of the story indeed.

Climbing through those declining, crystal snowdrifts, and looking up that gnarly, leafless old maple toward a faultless, promise-filled blue sky, always sets the mood. It confirms that another winter is done, that I beat it, and another spring, with all its expectations, promise, and excitement, is just around the corner.

Jane and I never tapped more than a tree or two, but I have some friends who were downright serious sugarers. My buddy Scott had his own Canaan, New Hampshire orchard complete with sugar house, and produced enough syrup to pay a piece of his board through Dartmouth College. Fifty years later, he will still tell you those crisp days in his mountain-side orchard were some of the sweetest in his life.

And David. My friend David had a sap route around Bowdoinham when I was growing up. He tapped a half a hundred maples around the village, collecting the sap in an old fire truck tank, and boiling it in a shack beside the Cathance River. I used to think of excuses to go visit him, just to stand downwind and inhale that sweet smelling steam. David's sap house burned one spring, destroying his evaporator, some buckets and a bunch of spirit I guess, because he never went back to it.

Aren't we all a little poorer when guys like these go out of these businesses?

John Burroughs, writing in 1881, called making maple syrup, "the most delightful of all rural occupations." How true that is. I have to believe that 150 years ago, when farmers all over this area produced syrup for their own consumption, or to barter a gallon or ten at the local store, must have considered the "sugaring off" process a holiday from their regular chores.

Jane and I boiled sap on the back of our kitchen woodstove for a dozen years, valuing the sweet smell and the moisture we added to our parched house, almost as much as the cupful or six of syrup we might typically produce in the average spring. Nope, we never worried about steaming off the wall paper. In a banner year, and not more than once or twice, we'd proudly point to a pint or two of syrup when April rolled around.

But it was never about quantity. Poured sparingly across a plate of pancakes, shared with the kids on a Sunday morning, that little dab of home brewed syrup really did taste better than all the quarts I've purchased at L.L. Bean's over the years.

I'm sure Scott and David both laughed at our puny efforts, but we cherished the process as a rite of spring, and as the welcome end of another hard winter season.

And folks, until you have taken a little homemade maple syrup, poured it hot onto a patch of fresh, white snow and then chewed on the sugar ice you produced with your own hands, in the company of your own kids, you just can't know what I'm talking about.

Now it's an occasion when I seek out a sap house in Bowdoin or Dresden or Farmington on Maine Maple Sugar Sunday and act like a tourist, climbing over snow banks to get a whiff of the evaporators, and settle for a tiny sample of maple sugar.

I'll be the first to admit that it has been too many years since I last took Grampie's rusty hand drill, and bored a tap into the south side of one of the ancient maples on our lawn. Last summer I caught Jane using one of my best sap buckets as a planter!

Something is missing from my spring when I have to say I didn't at least take the time to dip some ice cold sap from a bucket, separate the tiny black bugs and the bark from that nectar, and chug the whole thing down.

Maybe this will be the year, or maybe Jane's right, perhaps I am just a sap at heart.

That old door

A highlight of this spring in my family has been the construction of a small addition to the home of my in-laws. The first day of spring, we ripped off an old and rotting three-season porch and started work on a new story and a half addition. The construction is designed to make "Nan & Poppie," more comfortable and safer, and to present more options for their future and for ours.

Work is still progressing on the project as we approach mid-summer... and THE wedding... but this is not a commentary on missed deadlines, lost workdays, or missing contractors. This is a story of "the DOOR!"

Some thirty-plus years ago, I "rescued" an ancient, six-panel pine door from an abandoned house in Topsham. The old place was a dilapidated relic from my father-in-law's family, and the morning I first saw this door, I decided it had to be removed to be saved. The door had recently been kicked off its hinges by vandals. I took the door home and tucked it away in a corner of our barn, vowing to use it one day when I built a house, or something.

Last month I dusted that door off, took it to my in-laws, and suggested we install it as the door to a storage closet under the stairs. They seemed to like the idea very much.

This door suffered the day the vandals kicked it. There are some tooth marks on one corner, from some unknown, or well-known dog. The door was covered on both sides with some five or six layers of paint and it had a base layer of stain, or something, that absolutely defied removal. It has had a suffolk latch, a knob, and at least two pulls installed at various times during the two centuries it has existed. It has hung from

H-L hinges, a pair of strap hinges, and regular pin hinges. It's barely an inch thick, and measures only 29 by 74 inches.

I have accepted the restoration of this door as an obligation and a labor of love. I know the extra hours of tedious, dusty, dirty, meticulous work will be worth every minute. Just because.

The paint had to go away first. We're talking about layer after layer of that real, old-fashioned lead-based stuff. The dust makes my nose run, and coats my hands and hair with an awful, scary powder. Who knows what it does to my lungs. I scrape paint dry without the aid of those chemical strippers that come in the cans marked with the skull and crossed bones. Jane makes fun of me for that, but leaves me alone while I work. I use glass as a scraping aid, plus commercial paint scrapers and chisels, a pocket knife and an old spoon. The device has to be found to match the angle being scraped, or damage will be done to the soft and delicate pine.

I fashioned and glued two wooden plugs to repair holes in the surface of this old door, and crafted another patch with filler where the old jamb was booted. Then I decided to turn the door and leave the kick damage showing, from the inside. I'll call it a character wound that only another veteran can appreciate.

And I have to trim the door to square, even if it never was.

Like me, this old artifact has spread indelicately over the years. It measures 29 inches at its top and nearly 29 ½ at its base. Its new home in Brunswick, of course, is perfectly square. My neighbor Jon, a craftsman-carpenter, used a hand plane to help me with the final trimming, and we marveled together at the rich pumpkin color of the wood, and at the fact that this old door, perhaps older than our country, is held together with fewer than two dozen wooden pins.

I sand it gently, even reverently, and repaint it with reluctance. I take great satisfaction in the knowledge that because of my efforts, this fine old door, perhaps hung first as early as 1780, will once again see service.

Patched, sanded, repainted and again hinged, this door will hang in a secondary place, and will probably go unnoticed by most of the visitors to my in-law's home, but I know Norman and Barbara will be pleased. Maybe as they use this door they will recall their grandparents, their aunts, uncles and friends who used it, so very long ago.

And maybe, just maybe, the presence of this old door in its brand new setting will lead to discussions between my in-laws, and my children. I can only hope so. Isn't that one of the reasons we value old things??

Two gentle spirits

Judy.

Jadon.

Judy was one of my oldest and dearest friends, Jadon is my newest. As Jadon begins his tiny, precious life, Judy was ending hers.

Judy died last month, battered by kidney disease and a fragile heart. Her loss ended a courageous battle against three or four maladies of older age, any one of which could have taken her years ago, were it not for her iron will, and the knowledge that till now she had licked every challenge.

Judy was both a tough and tender lady. She had buried two husbands, and birthed seven children. She tolerated the awful heat and closeness of the bilge and frames of several Bath destroyers, because she believed that every tack, every weld she fixed, would bring her man and a hundred thousand like him home from the war she learned to despise.

Jadon, such a tiny bundle of manhood and just four months old, is the image of youth. I look into those deep, black eyes, and I see the potential for so much. Now I have to be comforted that this tiny but promise-filled spirit will always include pieces of Judy.

They touched you know. Judy placed that little man on her tired knees Christmas afternoon, and the connect was immediate. Tears cornered her eyes. She looked at my son, her grandson, and pronounced her newest GREAT-grandson was perfect, even beautiful. I could only agree, and add a tear or two of my own.

Judy was widowed at age 25, and left with five children to

either raise or give up. As with every other challenge in her life, however, "to give up," was not an option. Judy raised those five kids, remarried and added two more. She got them all through school, got them grown up, got them into families of their own.

If advice was asked of Judy, it was always offered frankly and sparingly. If it wasn't asked, it was seldom given. Judy was not one to intrude. She encouraged my curiosity and she always supported my decisions, good or bad.

Judy sent two of her sons to combat in Vietnam, never doubting it was their duty, or hers. But she never missed an opportunity to lecture on the wastefulness of war, or the usefulness of being gentle.

Judy is to blame for my love of Maine. She taught me to look at it, tree by tree, and to look at it as special. She made sure I knew Aroostook was more than potatoes, and the coast was more than lobsters. My days with her were marked by picnics in pastures, tours of old forts, beach walks, talks of Maine books and Maine stories. Last but never least, there was mile after mile of country drives, when nothing was ever said. Nothing need be said for the land and the company, spoke volumes.

As the memory of Judy fades, and I know it must, the memories and moments with Jadon will brighten. I know they will, and I treasure that prospect. I expect Jadon and I will run, play, laugh and learn a thousand lessons together. I can already see us sitting together, with me telling him stories of my childhood and of Judy. When that day comes, what will I remember first? What will I want to say? What will I want him to know?

He will need to be told to always be a steward of our earth, to treat his world and its people honestly. He will need to look for the sun in each day, and to place a value on the days with rain. He should approach life with humor and humility.

Judy would be pleased to see Jadon come on, just a little tough and a little tender. After all, that's the way she did life, and that's what I want to remember the longest.

Thanks, ma.

Doing Norman's flag

It was a year ago Saturday, when Joe and Norman brought that tear to my eye.

I had stepped in to say hi and, seeing the pole on the lawn was bare, I said something like, "Norman, can't believe we don't have the flag up yet, it'll be Memorial day before we know it!" I grabbed his flag, jogged over the lawn, raised it proudly and went back to where I'd left the guys chatting and listening to WJTO. There they were, Norman aged 95 and Joe aged 79, both standing at attention, each offering their pledge of allegiance. Norman, long since bent by pain, was teetering just inches from his walker, while Joe, whose speech had become sometimes fractured, was offering each word clearly, proudly, with no hesitation. I could think of nothing else to do, so I saluted right back at those two old veterans.

I could not have known that day, that both Norman and Joe would die in the year that followed.

I hope you see my motivation when I told Jane last weekend it was time to get the flag, "up" for the season.

There is a long list of things Jane and I want to do, and need to do, to get our "new" old home up to snuff. The flagpole was obviously higher on my list than on Jane's.

Jane was weeding a flower bed when I said the flag was going up and she kind of shrugged when I suggested the pole needed a new line. I asked if we didn't have a piece of line somewhere. She looked at me with that, "look" and suggested I was recalling what she intended to be her clothes line. I went back to the flagpole to decide if the old line would give us one more year.

Jane appeared beside me a few minutes later, new rope in

hand. It was neatly packaged at 250 feet long, I needed 50 feet, maybe 60. "We'll cut it once and it will be too short for both places," she predicted. I smiled. I stepped back and again estimated the height of the pole, she suggested we use the old line as a guide, and I said I didn't want to pull the old line because I would then have to drop the whole pole to restring it. I explained my process to her, cutting the new line to its appropriate length, taping the new line to the old line, pulling the new line through with the old line, tying the line off and being done in another five minutes.

It was Jane's turn to smile, she'd watched me attempting projects like this in the past. Jane handed me the electrical tape, I connected the two lines and pulled the tape tightly. Confidently, (hopefully) I yanked the line skyward. Half way to the top of our pole, the lines separated. I think there was a hint of a smile on Jane's face, just a touch of horror on mine. I tried to coax the line upwards, flipping the end I had left in my hand, but gravity resisted. Jane went back to her gardening, I was left to admit defeat.

I went to the barn, retrieved an old branch clipper that Norman had hanging on the top of a tool bench. I was attracted by its long, slender pole with its hooky thing on its end. My plan was to use the spring snip to trap the wayward line, pull it down and start over. I stretched the pole out as far as it would go, realized I needed just one foot more. I also realized Jane was watching this puny effort with just a certain amount of pleasure. I sat the pole down, went to her with my pride in my pocket and suggested if I extended the pole to its extreme and she worked the rope that it connected to, it "might" be just barely long enough. I extended the pole to its extreme and tickled the rope-end, now beating around in a pretty good breeze.

The two of us chased that rope's end six, maybe a dozen times. The wind played with us. it was obvious we were losing ground, an inch or two at a time. Once more, I was staring into the cold, mean eyes of defeat. Jane went back to her garden. Was she smiling again?

When I came back from the barn the next time it was with my 24-foot ladder in hand. I was serious about this.

Jane's face took on the horrified look, reminding me of my falling off that same ladder when it was leaned against our 36 foot Christmas tree, just a few months back. "No one died," I said. I put the ladder against the pole, extended it once, maybe twice. She reminded me that snow is more forgiving than the concrete pavers that surrounded the pole. "Maybe you want to lean against that pole," I suggested, wondering if the whole thing would pop from the ground when my weight was five or six feet into the air. "Maybe I don't want to be anywhere near the pole," she responded.

I climbed, the pole bent. Higher I went, over it went. I returned to the ground, wishing my arm was six inches longer, my body 20 pounds lighter.

"Hey," says I, "where is that little pick thing that Norman used to use to pick up stuff without bending over?" Jane was gone a minute and back in two, the device in her hand. It was obvious she wanted this exercise to be over, as well.

Up the ladder I went again, my whole world spinning as the line blew, the pole moved and the ladder slid. But I focused on that line, I clipped it with Norman's little clipper, I pulled it down and everything worked. I stepped down the ladder and got to the ground. Again, no one died! This time we taped the line more carefully, and this time the new line followed the old line to the top and then down. To my delight, when all the old line was at my feet and all the new line was on the pole, there was six feet of line left over!

We attached the clips to the new line, attached the flag to the clips and it was a real pleasure to shoot that flag to the top of the pole. Old glory blew proudly against the building breeze; seldom has it looked better in my eyes.

"Norman would be pleased," I offered as I carried the ladder up the hill. Jane was back at her weeding, but this time, smiling for all the right reasons.

My sergeant's taxes

I never get through tax day without thinking of Papa Lanzo.

Back in my paratrooper days in the 101st Airborne, my life was pretty much under the thumb of an NCO I'll call Fidel Lanzo. Sgt. Lanzo, or Papa Bear, or Pappie Lanzo was a golden glove champion boxer in the Caribbean, who might have stood five feet tall, (without his combat boots, which he was never without) He was wider than a cot at his chest, his shoulders were broader than his chest, and I never figured out where his shoulders stopped and his neck started.

When I met him in 1966 he was a decorated Korean War vet with a tour in Vietnam already behind him. He had ears like apricots, forearms that were bigger than my thighs, and a fist that looked like a bone-in ham whenever he put it near my nose.

Sgt. Lanzo was almost always nice to me (as nice went for him). From my first days at Fort Campbell, he always called me "Maine," or "college boy." Only once did I question the title, telling him I'd gone to college but hadn't graduated. He gave me one of his patented chest pats that always flipped me backwards at least three steps, then threw his head back and cawed that laugh saying, "a couple days of college would make you smarter than most of these guys," he offered a broad sweep of the barrack bunk room, his arm plowing that fist so close to my nose that I could smell him. "You read books," he added, "you smart!"

He tried to pat me again but I stayed out of his reach. "See," he laughed, "You smart college boy!"

I was pulling a lonesome radio watch one weekend when, two, maybe three hours after midnight, in walks Sgt. Lanzo!

"Just making sure things are right," he announced. We all assumed the man never slept. We'd heard stories of a wife but no one recalled ever seeing her.

Lanzo walked to my desk and sat on one corner. I was trapped. In two seconds I could tell I'd passed his inspection, because I was still in my chair. His bead-like eyes bounced over me, making sure my uniform was correct, that the radio was on frequency, that the volume was set at a correct level. I could see that he had checked that I had a side arm, and from where he was sitting, I just know he must have decided it was clean enough and loaded.

"What you reading?" he asked, pointing at an income tax guide someone had left on the desk. I'd picked it up once or twice, decided it was boring and had tossed it back to the desk. I shrugged, picked the guide up and flashed the cover at him.

"I work hard for my country," the sergeant announced, "I would die for my country," he added. I waited for him to pound his chest, he didn't. "Wouldn't you think I could catch a break with my income taxes?" I pouted, nodded my head to the affirmative. It seemed like a reasonable request. "Every year, I pay the government $800, sometimes a thousand dollars. You think that's right?" he asked. He jumped off my desk to emphasis the point. If I did think it was right, do you think I was going to tell him?

"How much do you pay in taxes?" he asked, I knew the rant was going to continue. I told him I was just a kid, and I had never filed. I think that confused him not a little.

"Hey, college boy," he came around the desk like he intended to wrestle me to the floor, "you think you might do my taxes, get me some money back?"

"Oh, man," thinks I, "I'm ambushed!" But after a second I was wondering how difficult it could be, then I made a quick, if bad, decision. "Sure," said I, "how much do you want back?"

"Pappie" gave me most of the next week off to do his taxes, he even let me skip morning march! His payroll was so basic it was unblemishable, so we came up with a bunch of imaginary expenses and deductions. I went to the post's post office and got a few special forms, and finally finished a return that impressed even me! What were the chances he'd ever get audited, I asked myself, the guy's practically a national hero!

We filed for a $1, 012 refund, and I worried my body would break because he hugged me so hard.

Four months later, I'm running a chopper unloading on a landing zone in Vietnam. Off with the ammo, c-rations, water and mail came a new guy I recognized from Lanzo's old outfit at Fort Campbell. "Hey, College Boy!" he yelled excitedly, recognizing me. We exchanged catch up for four, maybe five minutes and suddenly, he got all serious.

"Did you hear about Lanzo?" he asked. Without waiting for my answer, and with more joy than he should have had, he said, "the guy got audited, he wants you real bad! He ended up repaying the government his refund and maybe $6-800 in penalties and interest. They threatened to put him in jail! He almost got busted!! He's telling guys who are coming over here to find you and kill YOU!"

This story ends better than I could hope for. I never saw sergeant Lanzo again, so I was never put to death for the liberties I took with the IRS tax codes.

Best of all, my Jane still takes care of our taxes every season.

Settling mom's affairs

It was the next in a series of "family meetings" aimed at settling the affairs, and the effects, of my mother, who died March 6th. Darkening the door like an unwilling guest, I first noticed my older sister had been recently crying. Again. It was unsettling for us both, and not a good place to start. But where IS the good place?

I was 15 minutes late for this one, not from bad planning, but because I took the long road over, adding eight miles to the usual three-mile ride. I clearly was not looking forward to this encounter, and I wasn't the last of the family to arrive.

I have six brothers and sisters, aged 30 to 70. I accept that we are all processing this loss in our own ways, but there have been some surprises.

Sisters are supposed to be emotional, maybe one or two of mine aren't. My younger brother and I are both combat vets, should we be taking this death so hard?

But here we go again, sitting in a circle in Mom's family room. No one bothered to turn on extra lights. No one talked too much.

Mom is everywhere; Mom is gone.

My older sister took charge. At least that was predictable. And that was a blessing, certainly someone had to. She's a retired teacher, and very organized. That is a blessing, too. Mom was organized, at least in her own way, but the volume of stuff that accumulates over 50 years in a big, old house…well, don't you all know?

We're meeting to talk again about stuff -the books, the furniture, the clothing, the dishes, the cultch…the multitudes of things that were the collections of my mother's life. They were all around us, here for us to ponder, here for us to process.

By now we had all taken back the stuff that we had gifted to her, and she had never or seldom used. Two meetings before, we had all arrived with lists of Mom's possessions that we wanted, for whatever reason. I had asked for my Dad's casket flag, a toy truck, and an armload of books. Immediately there had been a contest. A sister had the truck on her list, a brother had the flag on his. My heart sank. It looked like the opening of an endless, draining process.

But my sister was good for the task. She offered a timeline for clearing the place one room at a time. She said there was an appraisal in process. She said there were legal obligations, as well as social obligations, to complete. We needed to stay focused. I reminded all I was the one who drove the big trucks the most, and I told my Brother I didn't want my father's flag leaving this state. Most in the room agreed with me, I put the flag and the truck under my arm.

This day my sister started with a fist full of papers and a little silver medal. "These are part of Uncle Frank's story," she said. She had my attention immediately because she was talking about my namesake, my mother's beloved brother Frank, who was killed in the opening days of WWII. For the first time in my 60 years, I saw documents and heard stories about his loss. There were answers to question Mom had always had but never had the courage to share. "You're going to want these, too," my sister said. There was a handful of old letters, written by me and postmarked from Fort Campbell, Kentucky, and Dak To, Vietnam.

I had always lived with a genuine awe of my Mother. She married my Dad just two weeks after the death of her brother, and less than a year before he was drafted and shipped overseas. She was widowed at 26 and left with five children to raise. Her life could seldom have been easy and her moments of joy most always hard for her to capture and enjoy. It's still hard to know that it's over.

I'm told it's a process.

We are trying and having good success at keeping the family on track and the emotions level. Controlling the feelings of seven people at a time like this is daunting, but so far we are doing it. We accept a common duty to our mother still. We know that her family was central to her life and we can't lessen that after, or because of her death.

Twice in the past couple of months I have set aside stuff to "show Mom." It was a little habit I'd developed in her last days when she seemed to enjoy my reading to her and sharing pictures of kids, of cats, and other things. I've been embarrassed each time and glad Jane didn't notice what I was up to, or at least, didn't make it a point.

As I leave her house with things that belonged to my Mother, I realize at the base of it, aren't we all just pieces of our Mother???

The magic of mom's house

Mom's house is one big ark of a place, three miles the other side of Bowdoinham village. Of course it was my home for many years, but in memory and spirit, it's still mostly mom's place, even with that bright red "For Sale" sign out front.

Several weeks ago, with our kids both in town, the Sunday morning coffee conversation turned to the sale. "Market's in the toilet," says I, "we'll be lucky if we're rid of it by fall."

But the words came with a lump.

We'd long ago checked with all the sisters and brothers. No one in the family needed the place, really even wanted the place, or could come up with a plan for the place. My brothers and I talked briefly about converting it to apartments, keeping the land, establishing a trust…doing this, doing that, but idea after idea was dismissed as a scheme that would probably only prolong and complicate the inevitable: letting the house go out of the family. And the wives were always there, reminding us of our own places, our own unfinished projects, and our own advancing ages.

This morning was one of those rare and delicious early spring days. Grass snapped like straw underfoot. Snow still lingered in the cracks of the field, limbs carried only hints of buds, and so far, no one had seen a black fly. We topped off our coffee cups, decided it was time for one more tour of the old house and one last walk to the river.

It's strange, wandering through an empty house that had long been at the core of my life. I identified marks on the walls, and pointed out projects I'd finished many years ago. Foot falls intruded in every room, and the smallest noise became a haunting echo, a stifling noise. It all looked so oddly large and horribly empty.

Books were my mother's treasure, and cooking was her trade. Now the shelves were empty and the cupboards all bare. It hit me hard and finally in her kitchen, mom really is gone from here. This can never be my family's home again.

My kids were asking questions, I just wanted to leave.

I gulped a great breath of relief when we stepped outside and started the single-file walk to the river. Here, really, was our old domain. Here, for years, my brothers and I had ruled the woods, fields and river. As we walked I recalled and retold some of the tales that had shaped our youth. Here, I pointed, was the place for wild strawberries in June. There, I guaranteed, would be fiddleheads by Mother's Day.

"Your uncle shot me out of that pine tree with a BB-gun," I told the kids, gesturing with a quivering finger. "How high?" Miles wanted to know, and I said, "right about here, center of mass," I laughed, patting my butt.

The Abagadasset is the muddy little tide-water river that ripples behind mom's place. Follow its curves, give it enough time, it will dump you into Merrymeeting Bay. The "Abby" was the destination for so many of our childhood adventures. We swam in it, skated it, fished it, canoed it. There I shot my first goose, learned to canoe, almost drowned. There I camped nearly a month when I returned from Vietnam.

We sat on the bank, adoring the warming sun and looking for rocks to plunk into the water. We found a rusty old boat my brothers and I had crafted from a halved oil barrel, some bolts and a couple of planks.

As we returned to the field, I felt renewed. Jadon finally abandoned my shoulders and ran on the field till he dropped. His dad picked him up, shook his head at me and said I was making the boy too tired. Miles tucked the little guy's face against his shoulder, and in minutes, he was sound asleep.

It occurred to me right then, as I admired the peace and love that enveloped my family that morning, that as much as things change, things will always stay the same. Here came yet another generation, once again overwhelmed by the magic of mom's place.

This old farm had done its job.

Fields of flames, sheets of smoke

Back when I was a boy, my brothers and I would watch in wonder from the tree line while firemen with great coats, boots and Indian tanks would jog through the dead brown grasses of a pasture or field until they had encircled it. "Touch 'er off," someone would yell, and in minutes two, maybe ten acres would be ablaze! Flames would roll skyward in great, unhindered sheets, and white smoke would billow into the light evening breeze. There would be snapping and crackling as the fire rushed past, and the sudden heat that tightened the skin on my cheeks made my skin flush. Firemen on the other side became ghostlike distorted figures as we watched them dance the line between the edge of the field and the surrounding woods.

There was always this one field burn, done right in the middle of town, that I anticipated with great excitement. It was a few hundred feet from the fire station, off Main Street, and surrounded on three sides by houses, a barn, and a church. I always marveled as the men mastered that field in minutes, never letting any of the property around catch fire.

John "Jack" Tourtelotte, a Bowdoinham fireman for 57 years and chief for the last 14, admits that he got his start in the local volunteer department as a "field burner." Retiring this spring, "leaving the job to younger hearts," he recalls field burns as something he will miss. "They were good training tools, and good opportunities to develop fire-fighting skills," he added.

They were more than that. The farmer who owned the field always donated $25-30 to the local axillary, and on a good April evening, if the air was clear and the grass dry, the crew could burn off four or five fields. That money became seed money for firefighting equipment for the department, and high school kids, those wanna-be firemen, got their first exposure to volunteering as a career.

For years, field burns in the spring would help farmers keep pastures and fields open. Bushes and brush in perimeter areas were kept in check by back burning. If you had a blueberry field, biannual burns were considered essential. There are many who suggest the burning process, "regenerates" a field, releasing nitrogen as the burn rolls over.

My Father-in-law, Norman, never burned his big field "out back," but he was always watching for a chance to burn one section right near the end of his house. He'd call the station and get a brush burning permit, and if the wind wasn't "too bad," he'd touch off that slope. He'd call it a "sideburn," and he assured everyone it was perfectly legal.

This area was loaded with a purple vetch all summer, but when the snow came off each April there was a treacherous mass of tinder dry vine, too big a temptation for him to ignore. Some years, he'd warn Barbara, (his wife) some years he wouldn't. Some years he'd ask for help, most years he wouldn't. There was one year that his mother-in-law was visiting, smelled smoke, and called the fire department. That almost got Norman in trouble, but Norman was a great talker. There were other years when Norman took Barbara's good kitchen broom, used it to sweep the perimeter sparks away from the house, and slipped it back into the kitchen when he was done. Most of those years he could NOT talk his way out of trouble.

Riding through the countryside today, many of these same old fields have a house or two on their front edges, and alders are creeping towards the woods behind. I catch myself wondering what happened to the farmers, and why someone isn't trying to keep those fields open with a nice spring burn.

Passing the flags

It has long been my privilege to place flags on veterans' graves for the Memorial Day observance for Bowdoinham. You may or may not know that I've "managed" what only I call, "a major metropolitan cemetery" (in Bowdoinham) for more than 30 years, and for at least a half dozen years have been that Town's cemetery sexton. A major component of each of these jobs is ceremonial flag placement in time for the Memorial day holiday.

I learned years ago, if a cemetery doesn't look good on Memorial day, you might just as well close for the season that weekend. For all those years, I've considered flags in the cemeteries as, "icing on the cake." I gave up mowing cemeteries long ago, leaving that job to the younger, the stronger, the dumber.

I have come to guard the flag job as my own. When I took it over some 20 years ago, the town was placing 40-50 flags a year; last year, I can say with real personal pride, we did more than 300 flags in a single year for the very first time! Back in the day, the flags landed in 4-6 of the town's larger cemeteries; last season we hit a new high of 26 cemeteries! Bowdoinham has a total of more than 60 cemeteries, so I hope you can appreciate the loftiness of our goals, see where we have been and where we are going.

Last year I started a list of vets, alphabetized and counted by cemetery, and yes, it is a paper list. What can I say, you have to walk before you run. The goal this year is to get a GPS reading for each of the cemeteries. The 10-year plan might be GPS numbers for each and every grave site.

I wonder, do I have 10 more years in me?

My kids helped me with flags, tagging along behind with a roll of 12, taking in the stories and the recollections as I moved from site, to site, to site. Fact is, I probably wore them out telling the same stories, year after year after year. "That's Joseph Green, did you know he sailed with John Paul Jones, and landed in a British prison?...that is T.T. Rideout, did you know he was wounded and died at Gettysburg?...and this one is "Snap" Prindall, did you know he helped select the casket of remains for the first tomb of the unknowns!?" And more recently, I'd point at a site and say, "he used to live down the street from us," or, "he and I were in school together."

Well, last year, my daughter came along for "the annual flag setting," after a "break" of more than several years, and she brought along her little guy Silas, who showed at least a passing interest in learning the trade. Several months before, it was Miles' son Jadon, helping me lift a Civil War Vet's stone out of the mud and resetting it vertically. Both these little guys show a keen interest in taking the trade to a new generation, if only I promise not to bore them with stories along the way. Both seem to be nurturing a passion for journeying around in the outdoors with their grandfather, seeing the deer and the birds, along with the gravestones. That is more than satisfying for me. If they come to know these veterans or not, these men, or women, worthy of remembering, I hope there will always be someone there to place the flags.

Last Christmas at Gurnet   Watercolor by John Doepp

Meeting an old friend

I bumped into an old friend at the Center last week, and it was such a pleasure to get reacquainted.

Robert Peter Tristram Coffin was feted by family and friends at the Center and I'm sure, if only in spirit, RPT was back in town for the party. I have always enjoyed reading Coffin, both his poetry and his prose. He had a unique feel, look and flair that will always make him special and different from all but a very few Maine writers.

I know now that my path and Coffin's must have crossed dozens of times in my youth, for he tramped around Brunswick and Bowdoinham, and Merrymeeting Bay with a poet's regularity and randomness, as I have. I'm certain that over time, we have each paused in some of the same places and done some of the same things. I have good friends and family who knew him. I know lots of people who have read his work, and a few others who still remember him.

Robert P.T. Coffin first came in focus for me when I had a chance encounter with one of my older home-town friends, a great lady named Polly Pratt. As a high school kid, I used to deliver home heating oil to her and hundreds of other places in the area, but her stop was always special. Polly always had something to say. One week there was a seemingly random comment about the Kennebec River, and the next week, she handed me a book and said, "you have to read this to understand..." It was Coffin's classic work, *"Kennebec, Cradle of Americans."* I took the book, got in my truck and drove off, but before the day was over, I was on the side of the road and reading. Perhaps I'd have finished that first read that first day, had I not received an anxious call from my dispatcher (another Polly), who was wondering where I was.

It is that sort of book.

My next complete read of that book came when I was a paratrooper in Vietnam. My mother had the good sense to keep me supplied with good cookies and good books while I was over there, "keeping you rooted," she called it.

Robert Coffin and Kenneth Roberts always topped my reading list. I remember Coffin's, "Cradle" book because it was a hardbound edition, and it took extra room in my pack. I was in a hospital the last time I read it, and it was like a window to home.

I gave it to a nurse from South Carolina when I left, and I've often wondered if she ever read it.

Shortly after Jane and I were married, we discovered RPT's grave site, in Cranberry Horn Hill Cemetery, right beside the Cundy's Harbor road. We've been back there dozens of times (that area is called "Coffin Country," you know,) and one birthday Jane did a colored rubbing of his slate gravestone, had it framed for me, and to this day, it hangs in our living room. I'm delighted when guests to our home ask if, the rubbing is of a family member's stone??!!" We do admit, "No," but I'm always secretly pleased by what I call, "a relation by association."

Over the years, I have read and re-read chapters from "Cradle" and other books to my own kids, and watched with delight when the stories by Coffin generate questions and ideas in the minds and imaginations of yet another generation.

When we lost Jane's gentle younger brother too many years ago, it was a Coffin poem titled, "Heavy Names," we offered as a reading at the memorial service.

Several times, I have used Coffin stories for history presentations at local schools, even local historical societies. More than one person has cautioned me about doing that, citing Coffin's reputation for spinning good yarns, sometimes at the expense of the complete and absolute truth, perhaps exaggerating points to make the story "run better." I always counter that by saying, "If I could make history as personal, as lively, and lovely as Mr. Coffin, I might be guilty of a little exaggeration myself!"

When the Center produced its "Christmas at Gurnet" print project last November, we were amazed to see the lines of Coffin friends, Coffin heirs, and Coffin relations who came in to order copies. Each seemed to have their own story, or two, about the poet, about his family, (or both) and the common thread, always, was love with a touch of humor.

What a legacy this poet has left for us.

Last month, when it was so cold I didn't want to do anything but sit beside the woodstove and read, I found myself with that "*Kennebec, Cradle of Americans*," back in my lap again. It is as good a read as ever, and this beloved man, this Robert Peter Tristram Coffin, is at the very heart of it.

High Noon, High Tide   by John Gable

A long and privileged line

Sig Knudsen often told me that dawn was the prettiest moment of any day, so the morning after his death found me standing at our kitchen window and waiting for the show. I shivered with anticipation. There was an aloneness that was all too familiar.

But this day would bring no disappointments. The horizon in front of me went from black to a streak of promise to a bright, exciting crimson in just minutes. The room, my world, magically filled with light and with newness and with promise. When that fantastic orange orb burst out of those pines and splashed over the bay with dazzling color, I just knew Sig was at it again and life was going to be okay.

The dawn thing started for us because I once told Sig that dawn for an infantryman in Vietnam was almost always a fear-filled moment, and we often used it for what we called a "mad minute." If we thought there were enemy troops in the area, we'd pick a tree in the shrouded jungle beyond us and "fire it up." More than once the tree would fire back. There was born my apprehension and suspicion of dawn and it lived with me from those days to this one. It became easier for me just to sleep through the moment.

The first time I told Sig the story of my mad minutes, tears welled in his eyes. He turned away quickly and stared for a full minute at the beautiful tower on First Parish Church. "Why do people do that to each other?" he asked me. We never came up with an answer.

So Sig became one of my confidants. "Time to get out of the jungle," he told me more than twice. He was such a giving and willing listener and he could take a complicated story, a memory that had crippled me in place, and chop it into silly, workable pieces. Those grand blue eyes could burn through you while he waited for an answer and when the two of us worked it out, chances are it was buried for good. I will miss that so much.

I don't for a moment think I was the only person Sig ever worked on and challenged to be better. I know I'm part of a long and privileged line.

And there begs another question for me. I have to believe that folks such as Sig – these rare, caring creatures of our world – ingest so much vile bile as they pilgrim their way through our nasty world, that the journey ultimately makes them sick and our disease takes them from us. If that sounds cold, or mean, I'll just apologize and ask you to prove me wrong. How else do we rationalize losing such a vibrant, vital person when they still have so much to give?

I don't want this to seem too bitter or negative, but when we lose good, productive people, or some around us are bothered and reduced by disease, can I help it if it makes me mad? Sig, in his quiet, calm way, would put his hand on a shoulder and tell us to take a breath and work through what's ailing us.

I'm trying to do that boss, taking a breath, working my way through another rough patch. The comfort this time, is knowing I have you as an example for the rest of my life, and knowing the long, privileged line has to close ranks again.

Sig, we'll see you on the other side. You are too soon gone, and the world is poorer for your passing.

A passion for privies

Some fail to understand my passion for privies.

When I lost my barn a few years back, one of the treasures that went away was my own personal "Pleasant Avenue," that little back-corner room, tucked away behind an old rough-board door, with its finely plastered and papered walls and its quaint, drafty from below "two holer."

I guess it all went public when I, late in the last century and a selectman for Bowdoinham, felt inspired when the town obtained a $5,000 Department of Conservation grant to build a privy at our refurbished town landing. After some pretty deep thinking, I decided Bowdoinham needed and deserved something better than those basic, shed-styled rest stations that dot the rest of Maine. So I proceeded with a plan to design a unique privy, one that looked more like a quaint railroad gate keeper's cottage than it did an outhouse. I guided that proposal through the halls of power in Augusta, and was delighted when the State of Maine told little old Bowdoinham to go ahead, just this once, and build a better privy.

The town put the plan to public bid, and when no one stepped up to complete this landmark project, my friend Jon, my son Miles, and I, decided to build it.

Jon knows how to build a privy. In fact, Jon could build a castle! Jon is a carpenter's craftsman. Saddling him with Miles and me did little to bring the project to rapid completion, but folks, when we were ready for the ceremonial toilet paper cutting that fall, the Times Record said old Bowdoinham was dedicating the "prettiest privy in Maine," and in due time, Downeast magazine echoed the opinion.

From that date to this, I pointed to that privy with particular pride. Many called that structure the enduring memory, if not the zenith, to my career as a Selectman. Following administrations have added electric lights, even a chrome water fountain to the up-wind side. Friends would visit, admire, and offer their congratulations for a privy well done, a privy quite extraordinary!

Some might even pause, go inside, and try it out. The ladies of the Town Landing Place restaurant offered me the ultimate compliment. They said they would send customers in search of my privy, and the customer sometimes would return, saying they never found it. Apparently, they had walked right past my privy, never even suspecting my pretty little building was their needed comfort station.

Yes, it was that pretty.

You might only imagine my sadness, my horror, on March 26th, when Jane came home from church and told me the privy, yes, MY privy, was GONE, burned flat to the ground! Could this actually be the first recorded act of terrorism in Bowdoinham?

It seems some unknown, cowardly and uncouth assailants, sometime during the Saturday overnight hours, splashed gas on my defenseless privy, lit it, and left it to flame up, burn flat and die. To add insult to the incident, the privy burned level to the ground without any sort of report! I'm told fire chief Tourtelotte, crossing the Cathance bridge early on Sunday morning, saw trails of smoke drifting from the site, checked it out, and was first to confirm the privy was gone.

I'm told an active investigation is continuing. I'm told the state Fire Marshal treats every case of arson as a very serious matter. But am I to believe the investigation into my ruined privy is attacked with the same zeal and professionalism as a gutted apartment building in Lewiston? How long before tracking this awful arson goes cold?

I'm told I shouldn't take it personally, but I feel the loss deeply. The cry of public support has been exceptional. A "pennies for our privy," jar at the town offices is collecting folding cash, not just change, and I hear there's an insurance check coming. I personally have received some 6-10 cards of sympathy, one with a hand drawn tombstone with a heartfelt, "RIP, Privy," message scrawled inside. But the neatest thing to come from all this is the "Ode to the Privy" poem that magically appeared all over town.

No, folks, I absolutely positively did NOT write that Ode! If the sitting selectmen are waiting for a sign (and it seems they always do), this has to be it. What a pretty piece of poetic perfection it is, a marvelous melody set to ink. I wish I DID write it! I won't reprint the ode here (copyright infringement rules, you know,) but if you make the trip up the Cathance, copies continue to appear in literary centers everywhere.

You really should make that trip.

Make note of that terrible, empty corner of the town landing, still marred with soot, spent waste, and random plumbing. See also that the town has installed one of those plastic, lime-blue, port-a-potties on the other corner. I hope you'll join me in the cry for a new privy, just like the other privy. It's such a little thing, really, but it means so much.

Ode to the Privy

Oh, what a dastardly deed is this
That took away our place to piss.

They who burnt our restroom to ashes

Should feel the pain of 40 lashes.

Along the shores of the Cathance River

See the sad lips all aquiver.

And in the grand ol' Town of Bowdoinham,

Some weaselly coward is on the lam.

To build this treasured work of art,

Took lots of work and lots of heart.

The Connors boys, both son and father,

Invested sweat and love and so much bother.

But sure as spring is slow in coming

There's bound to be some swell new plumbing.

Confess, confess o' scurry louse

Who dared to diss our noble house!

Barbara continues to teach

My mother-in-law left this life last month, following a brave struggle with kidney disease. Her passing leaves a huge hole in the group I call family, but the strength and faith that carried this lady to her very last days, through her very last days, will stand as the benchmark for all of us who remain.

Barbara taught Brunswick's second graders for nearly 25 years. She liked the little kids because they responded to her, and she knew it was genuine. She knew something about genuine, because that's the way she lived. She always said what she believed, no matter where the opinion led. If I did something stupid, I could count on Barbara to tell me so. If I did something right, you bet she was right there, too.

Her teaching career started in a one-room school in the Kennebec River town of Clinton, then later in West Bath. She told the stories of working for a few dollars a week, and of paying half of her salary to a "board," who was assigned her by the local school board. It was someone, she always acknowledged, who probably needed the money more than she. She told of walking miles to and from school, and I only half believed her, till that day we got in the car and clocked it. That became one of the times that compelled me to know another thing about Barbara. If she said it, I knew it was true.

But I'm here to tell you it was her last days, in so many ways, that impressed me the most about Barbara. She really did save her best for last.

Mind you, this woman decided it was time to go. The day she voluntarily decided it was time to stop kidney dialysis, a reverse clock started a count, and there was only one outcome available to her. She'd set that jaw, nod her grayed head, and say she knew. And she did. The doctors promised her 10-14 days; Barbara had the courage and connections to glean almost 30!   And we didn't waste those days, either. There were several gatherings with friends and family around, time to retell stories, time even for new information.

There were several family "discussions," but the decision was always hers. That wonderful social worker at the dialysis center was at the heart of so much, holding her hands, holding all our hands, looking steadily into her eyes to be sure she understood. Barbara left no doubts.

I know she and her husband of 63 years talked lots, too. Norman was more than a husband, he was her biggest fan, and her staunchest advocate. Norman always had that "we can lick this, Barb," attitude, and I think she started dialysis to get a few more months with Norman. But there was a day when she told him it was enough, and he respected that, as we all did, because it came from her.

And the hospice nurses...These ladies of grace are an incredible, unsung asset in our area. Would that I dare to print their names here. They had Barbara laughing when she was in pain, talking when she thought she's said it all. She looked forward to their coming. They won Norman over in a heartbeat. Their ability to come in, sit with her and make an end of life experience so tolerable goes so far past training that it is hard to believe. I just have to say they come from some wonderful, and very special place, a place ruled by love and the heart. God bless them.

And the cards have continued for weeks after her death. "Barbara was the best teacher I ever had…" Several wrote, "Barbara is the teacher I remember when I look back on my school years...Barbara was the reason I knew I had found the right Church...Barbara took me in …Barbara made me believe in myself again…Barbara, Barbara, Barbara…"

Barbara died quietly on the same weekend that protestors and police marched around the hospice center of Terri Schiavo in Florida. Even my simple mind drew some conclusions. This past Easter as Pope John struggled through his last days, it was heartening to watch him choose a quiet, calming end, surrounded by his people and his friends.

So these are sad times in our houses, but that sadness is tempered by the wonderful times that Barbara shared, and Barbara led. I'm a better person for knowing her, and a piece of my life will always compel me to live to her memory and standards. Thanks, Barbara.

Doing cemeteries

In my spare time, I do cemeteries.

In 1978, as Town Manager of Bowdoinham, I took on supervision of a local cemetery, "until we find someone to do it permanently." I've been doing it ever since. When I was Selectman in my hometown a few years ago, one of my goals was to "get help" for the 60-ish old cemeteries in our town. When I was a salesman working mid-coast Maine for several years, it was a good day when the sun came out and I could slip into a cemetery, sit on a granite stone and eat the lunch Jane had packed from home. When my kids were in high school, we negotiated a municipal cemetery mowing contract, and that money bought the kids their first real car.

Along the way I have dug graves, mowed lots, bashed fingers, placed veteran flags, fed flies, mucked out lost yards, righted and retrieved flattened stones, flirted with poison ivy, showed excited people where their great-great grand people were buried…and developed a lasting respect for the generations that came before me.

The life of a cemetery manager is most hectic in the spring. There are the winter deaths to be buried, leaves by the ton to be relocated, a limb or a dozen to be hauled away, and all has to be done with an eye towards Memorial Day and the start of summer. "If you don't look good by Memorial Day," I've been told by discriminating cemetery visitors, "you may as well stay home for the rest of the summer." I believe that.

Veteran flags have become a project of mine. I started putting them out in my town at least a dozen years ago. In those days, we used to place 40 or 50 little flags each season. It was a ritual with my kids for a few years, one I still rank as a privilege, not an obligation. Last year we placed more than 200 flags and the list still grows. I think last year we placed flags in 16 or 18 different cemeteries, and other volunteers did three or four more. The town's three largest cemeteries all have added individual flagpoles, donated by the local Legion post. This is a very small gesture a town can make to honor these veterans' service to country, and I'm glad to be a part of it.

My Bowdoinham is like so many other towns in New England, dotted by those small family cemeteries now a century or more in age. It's these yards that tug at my heart.

Some of these old cemeteries are now lost in the woods; others are located in back corners of neglected farms. We have one old cemetery that ended in the median strip of Interstate 95, but that's a story for another time. It seems like all these yards need attention. It would be easy to become frustrated by the amount of work that should be done, and the amount of work I can do. Each year, just before the black flies and the mosquitoes devour my enthusiasm, I try to clean out two or three.

Each year, with every visit, I'm re-impressed by the grace and love these old white monuments represent. It's hard to visit these yards, read the old names, such as Patience, Zebulon, Loyalist and Jewel, and not feel a connection to these people who once were. Each visit reminds me about life's frailty and, at the same moment, about the levels of love that once bonded people together.

If there is one cemetery related story to regret, I'd confess, it would take me back too many years ago, when I was a wild younger kid, visiting cemeteries with my grandparents in Aroostook County. Those visits found me wishing I was somewhere else, anywhere else. It was a rite of spring for several years and happened to coincide with the years I was learning to drive. The geraniums went into the trunk, and we'd head for "The County." I remember Grampie dismissing my mother's concerns about my lack of experience as a driver…"we'll crash or he'll learn," he'd say, and I did. I went for the adventure related to the drive, enduring what I knew to be obligatory visits to family cemeteries. I tried to be patient, but I know I wasn't patient enough.

Thirty years after my grandparents' deaths, I know the real value of those trips was the time I spent with them, listening as Sadie and Miles told those funny, sad, happy, human stories about all these ancestors I could never know. I didn't know it then, but those visits were building the bridge for me that would lead to a lifelong interest in old cemeteries, old stories, old folks.

Last summer, my sister called and asked how to get a load of loam from the town. I asked what she wanted it for; she encouraged me to come see. Her mother-in-law had recently died, and the family had decided to bury her in a small family cemetery not far from where she had lived, not far from where Ruthie lives, and near where her family is gathered. My sister and her family have adopted that cemetery, cleaned out the brush, fixed and cleaned the stones, filled the depressions. It's a first class cemetery now, a credit to the town and to the love and labor of my sister. More people should do that. Her cemetery now has a new lease on another century.

If there is a point to the commentary, it's this…there are thousands of these old yards in Maine, hundreds right here in our area. If you do nothing else with your summer, I'd encourage you to pull into one of these cemeteries, weed a plot, level a stone. You'll come away from your visit enlightened, and you'll be delighted by the people you meet.

Parading into summer

What I remember most about my first parades is the wheelbarrow.

The parades, of course, were down Bowdoinham's steep and winding Main Street. As parades go, these were a big deal in Bowdoinham, but light years away from being a Macy's thing. Certainly there were a couple of fire trucks, sure there was an honor guard from the navy base in Brunswick with flags and rifles. Win Dodge always loaned a couple shining new cars for the old vets to ride in, and there was a scout troop or two, a float from the Baptist church, some excited kids and some excitable horses. Probably the whole thing passed us by in five or six minutes, tops.

Back to the wheelbarrow.

That wheelbarrow was an ancient wooden, beaten thing with a springless metal wheel that sounded so cool when we rolled with it down the street. It would bounce us around with even the hint of a pebble under the tread, and we just knew that Grampie used to aim for the pebbles to make us squeal.

My grandfather would load two or four of us kids in that wheelbarrow, and haul us to a shady spot near the church where we could watch in wonder. Mom or someone came around with a jar of cookies and a soda or two, always arriving magically, just ahead of the marchers. Grampie always sat there with us, nodding or waving as the marchers passed. I think he knew everyone in town. It all proved that Memorial Day was here, and that summer was on.

I was a boy scout as a teenager, and marched in several parades myself. We waved our own little flags, our line of march usually following the veterans from the World wars.

We always tried to look serious, orderly and grim, just like them. We tried to hear their cadence, march to their step and stay in their shadows. Several of them had physical disabilities that certainly made the trek tough for them, but it was obvious to us they had seen tougher times.

We always marched to the river where some old navy guy tossed a wreath off the bridge, tears welling in his eyes as the thing drifted downstream.

My most embarrassing parade came on a practice field at Fort Campbell, Kentucky. I was the tall white boy in my company of paratroopers, so it became PFC Frank Connors' job to carry the unit's flag. "Guidon bearer," the sergeant major called me. That day was breezy, with the wind against me. Sarge called out the "unit le-f-t" command, I heard the call, drove the flag smartly skyward and took a snappy RIGHT-HAND turn!

I was off in the field and all by myself some 20 feet before I sensed the rest of the troops went the other way. "Guess that's why we practice," I suggested to my humorless NCO. I had orders for Vietnam in less than two months.

Back in Bowdoinham and now a young father, I took the wheelbarrow thing to the next level. It became a family event for me to haul my kids around the parade route in my newest and best-looking wheelbarrow, complete with pneumatic tire. In those days we renamed Pleasant Street to "Heartbreak Hill" in those days, it fell to us to wave at our neighbors, and to roll along flagless in the wake of the Marine Corps honor guard.

In more than one season, Miles and Abbie took to the road themselves, joining with several of their buddies to do the parade route on the big-wheeled tricycles. I never quite decided if they wanted to do their big wheels to be independent, or if they were just getting too old and embarrassed to have their friends see them riding in a wheelbarrow.

The most important parade of my life will almost certainly be the march that I and 10,000 of my buddies took down the streets of Washington D.C., in 1982. The Vietnam War Memorial was being dedicated and a parade had been scheduled. I was lucky enough to be in attendance, but sitting on a curb, content to watch as the parade passed me by.

But I was with the Palmer family that morning, and those Palmer boys have never let anything pass them by. They pulled me to my feet when the tiny contingent from Maine appeared, and we walked in the shadow of my state's flag, all the way to the shinning new memorial. The walking seemed to get easier with every step, and I still point to that weekend when folks ask me how I survived that war, when others have not.

Summer comes to Maine every May folks, pick your parade and march right into your season.

Holiday at Merrymeeing Park   by Ernest "Bev" Bevilacqua

Those Sunday rides

When I was a kid, Sunday meant going for rides. I always thought scouting around Maine in the family vehicle was more interesting, and more exciting, than church.

I remember rides in search of apples, or driving to pick up fish, or vegetables, or the latest piece of furniture, or a random part for my stepfather's little business. There were trips to leave sisters at camp, or brothers on camping trips. There were many rides to see shows, to visit friends, or family, or museums, or other places. There were many times we'd read about something in the Sunday paper, and then pile into the car to go find it. I even remember getting in the car, not knowing or caring where we were going, but enjoying every mile of it.

There were five of us kids when my mother married for the second time, and it wasn't long after that there were two more sisters, so "pile into the car" can be said in a very literal sense.

There was always a bunch of jockeying and politicking going on to get beside a window, to not get the back seat that faced backward, or to NOT sit by the brother (or sister) who was out of favor that particular minute, or day. There was always the subconscious plan to stay away from the brother (or sister) who tended to get car sick, or the sister who tended to be bossy.

In the earliest days of my mother's second marriage, our new father had only a pick-up truck for transportation. That was quickly remedied by the purchase of a car, but in the meantime we did our Sunday rides in the truck. Picture me and my siblings, all five of us, shoulder to shoulder and hanging on to the oak headboard of that old Ford. Now, that was a way to see Maine!

In the off-season we would snuggle down close to the cab and imagine all the heat that never leaked through. We would usually stand in the coldest of weather, just to alert the rest if there was some 'good stuff' coming up.

The cars, when they came, were a great parade of big old wagons. I remember a couple "woodies," even if the panels were only painted. These cars were steel on steel behemoths, even by today's SUV standards. There were no seat belts. There were no airbags. We sat four, even five to the seat. We never even considered we were insecure, and never seemed to experience anything more dangerous than a flat tire.

Most of those trips led to food. There were picnics at the shore, near a mountain, beside a lake…always at the side of a road. Maine used to maintain more roadside picnic areas back then, and it used to be easier to find businesses with public restrooms. My mother used to pack these incredible lunch baskets. Bread by the loaf, cold cuts from Blake's store, a bottomless jar of peanut butter and several jars of home-made jam. There was always some fruit, and that great, glass jar of cookies. Or two.

And you better believe we knew more than half the ice cream vendors in Maine on a first name basis.

If we stopped at a restaurant, and some Sundays we did, it was probably a small diner, not a fast food franchise…open turkey sandwiches, hamburgers or the like…and sure, I remember retrieving many large trays of hot dogs from Mike's Place in Brunswick. It never occurred to me back then, but what we must have looked like, nine of us walking into a restaurant and always getting a warm greeting from the waitresses. I don't ever remember a 'bad' incident.

There were games that counted cows and sheep, and arguments over reports of certain out-of-state license plates. There were moments in anticipation of billboards. Once in a while, when one of my brothers or sisters was unruly (never me), my mother would call for a TWO mile, or FIVE mile, time out. "No one speaks for five miles," she'd dictate flatly, and none of us would, not even a whisper. Not ever.

Lots of these Sunday rides would follow set routes. We would get excited about seeing that huge pasture filled with cows, or be watching in the springtime for young ponies, gangly calves or fluffy lambs. We would know the places to pull off and watch trains, or in Bath, Kittery or South Portland, we'd have special places to peek at ships. Bridges were special, and sometimes, we did them twice.

Lots of these rides would be aimless. My stepfather had a knack for seeing a fork in the road and driving down the side he'd never seen. He used to say that we were lucky to live in a place where you turn right to see the ocean, and left to get to a mountain. More than once we ended up turning round in a field, chuckling about being lost. He'd never admit to being lost, you know. He'd just say, in a few miles, he'd have a better idea where he was. And we did always get home in time to do homework, or to watch the Ed Sullivan Show.

I know these trips planted the seed that grew into my love of Maine.

Those endless, aimless rides bonded my family in many unique and wonderful ways. We're still tighter than the average family of nine, and I know a piece of that bond is/was the rides. The stories I tell my own children, and to the kids of my brothers and sisters, have become part of the family fabric.

Years later, I find myself driving into some little town east of Kittery and west of Lubec, wondering first where I am and then catching myself, spotting a MacDonald's on a corner and thinking that was the spot where…and I fill in the blank. I catch myself smiling. Suddenly I know where I am, even if Jane still thinks I'm lost.

Here's my point.

Gas might cost eight times what it did in 1950. Lots of the little brown roadside-rest areas are gone. There may be a Wal-Mart in the field where we used to picnic. God knows there are lots more cars on the road. Per capita, there are many more "no trespassing" signs than there ever used to be.

But, if you and your kids, or grandkids, 'pile in your car' next Sunday, pack a box of peanut butter or bologna sandwiches, chips, and cookies in the trunk, and just drive till you're hungry, it will be a day to cherish. I guarantee it. Maine awaits!

Raiding the cherry tree

This is a public confession, folks.

There is a marvelous and fruitful cherry tree in front of our little Center on Noble Street, and for several days last month, I'd stop, I'd contemplate, and I'd compete with the cardinals and the robins for a handful of delectable fruit.

This is plump, red, tart, juicy, wicked TART fruit, just like the ones we buy in the market, only better! Really! At various times, I shared a handful or two with the staffers here, and, as the days passed I'd catch myself wondering why, oh why, was no one picking and using those cherries?

Why?

Then came Jane's cousins, Robert & Beth, to town, and Frank Wicks' amazing show; "*Soldier Come Home!*" to the First Parish church. I think it was August 8th, you might remember the night as hot, wet, and muggy...it was a night in the long string of oppressive nights that seemed to consume our August this year.

We all went to the show, eager to experience those incredible, historic Civil War words in the confines of that incredible, historic church, and we were not disappointed. The air was electric in that building as the evening light waning through General Chamberlain's memorial window, those massive beams overhead disappearing into the gloom as the words poured out. There was sweat, and there were tears.

"*Soldier*" tells such a wonderful, powerful, human story. There is love, death, war, humor, and heartache. Love again. Death again. If you have not yet seen this program, get to the next one.

Now, however, back to the cherries.

The tepid air did not make us want to rush into the church. We lingered on the sidewalk till the rain started again, we lingered in the vestry till it started to fill...then I remembered the cherries. "Wait here," I commanded all, then I galloped across the street, darting through traffic, across the soaking grass, quickly picking a mounded handful of the luscious, tart fruit. I popped two or three in my mouth, and spit the pits in the middle of Maine Street, in the path of an approaching car from Massachusetts. I was back at the church in five minutes, triumphantly handing cherries to family and friends. I made converts of them all. As "Soldier" came up, Jane whispered, "I'll make the pie, if you pick and pit the cherries!"

I love that girl!

This is a great place to repeat that Jane's pies are legendary. We had an instant deal. I settled into "Soldier" and the Pringle family letters, but my mind was darting to cherry pie.

The show ended about 9 p.m., I know this because we were hoping to fit a Cote's ice cream into the evening as well. Cousin Beth does love her Cote's ice cream.

But you don't just jump up and run out after experiencing "Soldier Come Home!" at the First Parish Church! I mean, you have to give it a minute to settle in, There is some emotion you have to deal with, folks.

We stepped off into a gentle rain, several of us moving downhill toward the ice cream, others headed across the street toward the cherry tree. I was in the team going for the tree, and I love ice cream!

On the darkened lawn of the 55 Plus Center, we realized we had nothing in which to pick the cherries. I already had a handful, and dumped them into the hood of cousin Beth's raincoat. "Hey," she complained slightly, "I wanted to use that hood!" Soon too, we realized it was hard to see dark, red ripe cherries against a rain-soaked night-darkened sky. Hard, but certainly not impossible. Five of us picked and the hood filled fast.

Enter Vivian.

I'd already shaken water-soaked tree limbs on Jane and Beth, and had picked two, maybe three hands full when out of the night came the challenge, "Frank, is that you?" A lady on the sidewalk, her dog on a leash, her hands on her hips, obviously wanted to know what I and my cohorts thought we were doing there in the dark, ripping cherries off the Center's tree!

Busted!

I knew I was doing nothing wrong, but guilt still riddled my rain-soaked frame.

"Yes," I admitted to Vivian Kemp, member extraordinaire and center conscience. "See, these cherries will go to waste if no one picks them," I predicted weakly, then, I even offered her a half handful of cherries. She stood rigid and less than impressed. "Since it's you," she offered finally, "I guess I don't need to call the police."

I thanked her for reaching that conclusion.

I think I heard Jane and Beth giggling at my handling of the situation.

Vivian and I soon agreed that the cherries were better off in a Bowdoinham pie than in the belly of a bird, or wasting on the tree, and in time we all retired to Cote's for that ice cream. I was tempted to order the cherry vanilla. The cousins headed for Bailey Island, and Jane and I rolled home. I pitted maybe five pounds of cherries that night before bed, and the next morning, Jane made good on her promise of pie. In fact, she made TWO!

I consider myself a real judge of pie, but folks, I have to say those cherry pies were among the very best ever. EVER!

Maybe it was the gentle summer rain, maybe it was the dramatic reading in the wonderful old church, maybe it was the gaggle of childlike adults, jockeying around that tree, getting wet, throwing cherries, being the best of friends, relishing what was truly a hot, HOT summer night.

Maybe it was the hint of larceny, and yes, getting caught!

Whatever it was, the evening hinted of magic, and once in a while, there need to be more nights like this in all of our lives!

Ah, strawberries!

Given inches or ounces, I can think of nothing in this world more perfectly packed than a strawberry. These red, luscious rubies of packed sunlight, bursting with flavor and juice, just don't come soon enough and are gone before you know it, but while they are here, life is good. So very, very good!

I take them as a package. Picking them is right up there with eating them, smelling them is almost as sweet as tasting them. I'm thinking the first day of strawberry picking should at least be a local holiday.

When I was a kid probably 13 or 14 years old, I became a professional picker. Not real good, or not real fast, but that has to be where the passion began. A farmer named Lloyd, with berry fields maybe a mile up the road, hired me and my brother to help him get the morsels to market. This was my first experience with vertical marketing. Get there at dawn, pick as many berries as we could before nine a.m., and load them in the bed of his old Ford pickup so he could take them "around" and sell them. I think he paid us 20 cents a quart, and sold them at market for 75 cents.

It didn't hurt that Lloyd had two lovely daughters working in the fields, but in those days, I was still more interested in the berries.

Before we get into this discussion too deeply, how many people have had a bowl of WILD strawberries to eat? Those tender, tiny, tasty delights are something from a different world, they are so very good! Wild berries are always worth the hunt, and hunt you must. An open, rolling hay field is a good bet, and you should be out looking right now. Locating a mass of delicate yellow-white blossoms before the field fills with its higher Timothy and sweet grasses will give you a "leg up" to locating a patch when what is a terribly short season ripens off.

I remember wild strawberry picking with my grandmother Sadie Ruth. She was a tiny lady, but she could gallop through a field, skirt and apron billowing in the gentle breeze. She would roam from patch to patch till she had gathered a quart or two. Me, I'd still be picking my first pint. She seemed to have a sense where every patch was. She was one of those ordered people who hulled her berries in the field, and still picked so many more than me. She'd hold a tiny berry between her dainty, blood-red fingers and thumb, and drop it gently to the bucket. "Pick 'em and prepare 'em," she'd say, "never handle them more than you need."

My sister Marilyn used to love picking wild berries and disliked eating them! Who can imagine? It was the best of both worlds! She picked me many a saucer full in her younger days, but I'm guessing I upset her once (or perhaps twice) because it has been too many years since she last offered me berries.

Many, many of my Jane's famous fruit pies are based on strawberries. If there is a person in this world who can add value to strawberries, it would be Jane. Strawberry-rhubarb, strawberry-peach, strawberry-blueberry, are you getting the idea? Just a little tart, always sweet, always flavor-filled, and just crusty enough.

And there are the strawberry shortcakes! Real biscuits, just like the ones my mother used to make (and yes, Jane can!) take them fresh from the oven, split them open and daub them with butter. Berries mashed so hard they start to bleed, and sugar them lightly, just to make the flavor pop. I'm thinking it's the confusion of sweet against sour that makes a shortcake work. Pour the berries on till the biscuit starts to float, then leave it to soak. The bottom of that bread needs to get soggy! If you're after perfection, there has to be a little crispness in the top biscuit, but always keep pouring on the mashed berries. Top the whole thing with one bright berry, the largest one in your quart if your aim is to impress. Whipped cream is optional, even anticlimactic, but I still recommend it. We're talking the very essence of summer here, folks, go for it!

Prout's, Fenimore's, Rackley's or Popp's, you just have to get yourself to a "pick you own" operation during strawberry season. Maine right then is at its best. Days are long and song-bird filled. The sun is high and the temperature, day and night, is perfect.

Get on your knees, lift the leaves and pick more than you need. Make sure that Polly or Pat are looking away, then eat a few. Eat some more! I've had field owners threaten to weigh me in, weight me out...I eat that many! I've even been seen taking a pocket full of Cheerios into the field with me!

If there is a better way to spend a summer evening, I haven't discovered it yet, and I'm a great lover of summer evenings. Ruby red, beautiful juice-filled baubles-I think strawberries should become the national fruit.

Hang up the phone and drive!

It happened again at the DuPont concert last week, in the grand hall of Boothbay's beautiful botanical gardens. Engrossed the exceptional, mesmerizing music, majestic surrounding; the makings of a magical, marvelous moment...suddenly, a metallic, abrasive "dnn-n-n-n dnn-n-n-n-n, dnn-n-n-n-n," vibrating sound Interrupted us, destroying the moment.

The vision and thoughts once fixed solely upon the suddenly disconnected as everyone around joined me in the search for the cell phone. The guy was located two rows over, and he let it ring one more time while he checked to see who was calling, then he shut it off.

What do these people think?

DO they think?

Do they really believe they are so important that they have the right to cheapen the experience of everyone around them?

The same thing has happened at the music theater, at business meetings, at the movies. I bet you've watched in wonder at the supermarket while some schmuck calls his wife and asks if he should buy the two liter or one liter bottle of coke.

Last month, I was picking strawberries in a big, river-side field in Bowdoinham. It was early in the morning, birds were singing, there was a gentle succulent breeze lapping at the water.

In short, it was the sort of moment I wait for all winter. Between quart two and three, I become aware of this guy at the end of the rows, some 50 feet away and strutting back and forth. "Now," he kept asking, "can you hear me now?...NOW?

He'd move another 15 or 20 feet, "NOW?" he asked again. I heard him mutter something about the lack of cell towers, "out here in the woods."

Several rows away from me, a prettier than average strawberry picker kept glancing toward this rude cell guy. Perhaps I mistook her interest.

"Hey," says me to her; wearing my best, wider-than-average boyish grin, "wouldn't it be great if someone walked over there and chucked that fools phone into the Kennebec?

How's that for an early morning pick up line?

She smiled pleasantly enough, but busied herself picking berries. The rude guy played on another 10 minutes, trying and retrying the phone. He walked to the door on the porta-pottie, assuming (I guess) that the metal frame might give him better reception. I considered yelling for him to go inside and close the door for a try, but I picked another fist full of berries instead.

Finally, apparently at his wits end, he stormed back into the field, approached the pretty picker and demanded, "don't you have enough berries? I need to make some calls...I can't believe there's no reception down here. She smiled weakly at me as the two left the field together.

Another time, I was waiting in line at a gas station, two guys back from a guy who was just chattering away. I though he was talking with the cashier. Turns out, as he turned around, he had one of those ear-phone things, and both the cashier and I waited for him to finish his conversation before he paid for his gas. I just could not contain myself. As the guy walked away, I looked at the cashier, jerked my thumb after the guy and asked the lady if he wasn't the rudest customer she'd ever waited on. To my disbelief, she said, "no," and indicated those sort of things happen all the time!

I've been almost bumpered out of crosswalks by drivers talking on cell phones, and I've been threatened with head-on collisions by drivers more concerned with who they're talking with, than what's coming at them at 75 or 80 miles per hour!

There's a bumper sticker I see on Brunswick's Maine Street a lot, it simply offers this wisdom: "hang up the phone and drive!

Sure, Jane and I have a cell phone, we're not dinosaurs!(Jane isn't anyway) But our phone is off so much more that it's on. We have it mostly for trips and as a comfort against emergencies.

Sure, it is very useful as we're moving, confirming reservations, locations, that sort of thing. We call the kids when we're getting close to their homes. Jane usually carries it and it makes her feel more secure. I'm glad she j=has it with her when she's away.

Can't we make this stop?

One or two generations from now, will there be any public decency left? What about privacy? Where is Emily Post when we really need her?

I see people stopped beside the road, using their phones. I see folks getting away at meeting breaks, going outside and checking messages. (They may as well, they can't smoke) Both these practices seem to be reasonable, considerate, polite uses for a technology that is all too easy to abuse.

And civil! Doesn't it just come down to being civil toward each other?

Opening the WW II Memorial

My father-in-law and I shared a memorable Memorial Day last month traveling to Washington D.C. to add pieces of our souls with those dedicating the WWII monument. It was something else. Lots of flag waving, people patting and cheering. Lots of remembering lots of projecting. Incredible positive energy was everywhere. I think it was a moment for him. I know it was a moment for me. It did our hearts real good.

We bussed to Boston, and took the train from Boston to D.C., right into Union Station. I recommend that process. It was a long day (11 hours, counting the drive to Portland) but we could not have driven that distance in that time. Planes were just not an option and we certainly would never have arrived in the shape we were in, relaxed, well rested and ready for what was next, on anything but the train.

We have cousins in D.C.: Robert, Beth and Jen. Everyone should have cousins like this trio. They were our salvation, our secret weapons. They knew the streets of the Capital, they knew the subway, they had a car, they knew where to eat, they knew where NOT to go. They were always in charge of what was next.

They even had a wheelchair.

Norman is a Pacific theater sailor-type WWII veteran. South Pacific early, China and then Japan in the very first days AFTER the war ended. He owns and proudly wears a red-white and blue "rock-hard Republican" baseball cap. You question this man's patriotism at your peril. He's big and strong at 88, and looked at that wheelchair very suspiciously, then he sucked in his pride and sat down. Getting there was that important to him.

Saturday of the Dedication could not have been more perfect. Steady sun, 70 degrees, none of the humidity that Washington is famous for. We got the Metro downtown, a special shuttle on to the Mall, and took a place in a never ending line.

There were three primary sites for the festivities, each tried to contain some 50-75,000 people. Ours was a soccer field some 200 yards from the monument and not far from the reflecting pool. We bought $3 ice cream bars, drank bottled water donated by WalMart and waited. The program, when it came, was broadcast on a large movie screen maybe 50 yards away.

Speakers included President George W. Bush, Tom Hanks, Tom Brokaw and Senator Robert Dole, but the two I'll always recall were sitting right behind us. Members of the Purple Heart Society, one wounded in Europe, one in the Pacific Islands, they were strangers till the moment they happened to sit beside each other, brothers bonded by hellish events some sixty years previous. My ears drifted in and out of their conversation as they made friends, talked about marriages, about children and careers. It took them maybe ten minutes to focus on buddies who didn't come home, and from there, right there, the discussion never wavered. "It's all about them," one said.

It was Sunday morning when Norman and I rolled through the oval-shaped memorial. Crowds of the curious surrounded us, but we still visited every corner of what will certainly become one of the city's most visited sites. It sits astride the lower end of the reflecting pool, facing the Lincoln Memorial and across 17th Street from the Washington Monument. Each state and territory of the United States has its own granite tablet, all bound together by great bronze ropes. East and west are marked with towered tributes to Atlantic and Pacific theater veterans. Major battles are carved there in impressive stone.

But what takes your breath are the stars. 40,000 bronze stars line a vertical wall in a precise, military formation, one star for every 100 casualties absorbed by America's military during that "second" war of the world. One can only look in awe.

There was a private moment for me amidst all those people. I had pictures and a letter from my dad that I kissed once and placed on the State of Maine's stone in that grand semi-circle of precious stones. My father died of wounds received during the assault on Germany, so you see, part of the reason I went was to honor him. Norman just patted my shoulder.

We walked around the tidal basin, visited the FDR and the Jefferson memorials. After another brief stop for a $6 sandwich, we finished the afternoon with a tour of the Korean and Vietnam memorials. Robert and I pulled off a cell phone synchronized exit of the city. We gook a little breather, and got back to the MCI Center to watch a contemporary version of a USO Show.

There were dozens of moments that made the weekend priceless:

- We spotted a mother duck nesting amid the hard, battle weary images of the Korean Monument.

- We got to pick six quarts of strawberries one month early, thanks to Beth.

- Two or three times people we'll never know walked up to Norman, smiled at him and said, "Thanks."

- Chicata bugs were everywhere.

- We went into a really fancy restaurant and both ordered liver and onions just 'cause we could, and because Jane and Barbara weren't with us.

- 50,000 motorcycles in one place is too many.

- We stood in the hot sun for nearly ten minutes, motionless because a policeman told us, "the President's motorcade is in the area." We never saw him.

Finally I came away with a new appreciation for America's greatest generation. They were heroes then, and they're heroes now, God bless them. All we can hope to do really is stand up straight in their shadows.

Artwork by John Gable

In pursuit of Sebastian Rasle

I knew it was not going to be "just another camping trip."

My buddy Bob, a holdover from my paratrooper days, was coming to town and the weekend included a challenge. He was a French & Indian war re-enactor, a bit of an adventurer, and yes, he was still a little bit crazy! "Let's go find Father Rasle," he'd said.

In the army, Bob and I used to pass hours, sitting on tarmacs and chatting about Father Sebastian Rasle, a French Jesuit priest who ministered to Maine Indians back in the early

1700's. To hear Bob tell the stories, this Rasle was a pretty amazing character, and I became more than a little fascinated. Rasle, it turns out, produced the first (and only) dictionary for the Abenaki language. He had a huge influence on his woodland parish, teaching them sanitary practices and helping them grow and store crops. His shortcoming, as it turned out, was to tell his Native American subjects that an English scalp or two hanging in their wigwams was going to be good for their church.

Maine in those pre-colonial days must have been a very interesting place. English settlers had just started to occupy their tiny centers along the coast and the rivers, while the interior, or forested areas of Maine, were controlled by the French traders and their priests, who answered to Quebec. Indian raids in this area where we live were a pretty common, and very frightening practice. The 1720's seems like a pivotal decade; the English gaining strength, the Indians scoring a couple of key raids, the English deciding the Indians had to be punished and Rasle, the devil priest, had to be eliminated. By 1724, at least two English assaults on the Indian stronghold at Norridgewock proved unsuccessful. In August of that year, came yet another try.

Let's pick pieces of the story from my old Abbott's History of Maine: "On the 19th of August, 1724, a party of 208 men, accompanied by three Mohawk Indians, left Richmond Fort for an attack on Norridgwock...the party commenced at a rapid march through the woods to strike the foe by surprise. On the evening of the 21st they overtook the noted chief Bomaseen, with his wife and daughter. The chief and child were shot, the wife was taken captive. A little after noon on the 22nd, the soldiers came in sight of the village, (which they encircled)" Some of the troops set in ambush, others, "were marshaled for an impetuous charge."

The surprise was complete. Vastly outnumbered, the villagers, "endeavored only to save their aged men, their wives their children." Those not slaughtered in the first volleys of deadly fire escaped to the river, where many more drowned. The beloved priest, "father to his flock, died in a singular shower of bullets."

Fast forward to 1969.

The story goes that this tortured site, 240 years later, was haunted. It is, in fact, a community cemetery, with a crude granite marker on the spot where Rasle met his end. That is where Bob and I decided to camp. We figured if there IS a ghost of Father Rasle, it will be active on the date of his death, and at the place where he died. We wanted to roast hot dogs, bed down, and wait for the father to come.

We cooked, watched the sun drop, the mosquitoes rise. It was a beautiful, clear summer night. The moon glistened off the grave stones that surrounded us. Bob was certain that any minute, a slight, black-robed creature would glide into our midst and scare the bajebbies out of us. I kept telling him he needed to stop telling his stories, or nothing was going to happen. Erring on the side of caution, we lounged in bed rolls, not sleeping bags. Neither of us intended to be a hero this night.

Sometime just before midnight, there was a rustling off to our left, over our shoulder and nearer to the river. Bob poked me, I jabbed him back. Something was definitely there, and I shook free of my blanket. A minute passed, maybe two. Bob moved to whisper to me, I motioned him to keep quiet. We both fixed on the sounds, now only two granite stones away. Another breathless minute passed; a blackish head projected from the night around the nearest stone.

It was a skunk. Bob was on his feet, running desperately for the car. I paused just long enough to push the remains of our meal in the direction of the beast.

No priest here, or if there was, we weren't waiting to find out.

Popping over to Popham

Fort Popham is my fort, but I'm glad to share it with you. Just drive to the bitter, bouncing, tortured terminus of Maine route 209, that my friend Lila Percy always called her, "16 mile driveway," and you'll find it, a granite masterpiece to warriors of another age, a massive monolith that is perhaps our most tangible local memorial to that worst of American military adventures, the Civil War.

I have described Fort Popham as one of the grandfathers of government boondoggles. I mean, construction began in 1861, when Maine's powerful congressional delegation must have spearheaded the effort to arm and protect our Kennebec River from anticipated predators from the south. Now we all know of the significant shipping interests on the Kennebec back in those days, and we all know, "them Rebs," made a couple half-hearted, (if not half-witted) stabs at northern centers, and we all know that the Kennebec must have been on many a southern terrorist's table. As the political fortunes of our James Blaine waned, however, so must have the budgets for the fort at Phippsburg, as the "coastal defensive land battery," was never quite finished, and construction was halted in 1869.

If nothing else, the fort is certainly impressive. Fort Popham's 30-foot tall, crescent-shaped walls are formed from granite blocks maybe two feet tall, 4-6 feet long and perhaps three feet thick, all quarried from nearby Fox and Dix islands. I'm no mason, but I'm going to say they were carved to interlock, not to be mortared together. It must have been a sight to watch this construction, and an exceptional place to work.

But you need to go inside to fully appreciate the masonry of this place. Two stone parapets serve the several levels of this old fort, and the single pieced, pie-shaped steps that spiral

116

from one story to the next are maybe one inch short of magnificent. Each of the 30-odd gun emplacements are rimmed and capped with brick arches that any cathedral might envy. It's a credit to the craftsmen of those early days that exposure to weather for nearly 150 years has not made the whole thing crumble.

It's too bad they didn't leave a gun or two in the fort, just to remind us this is a structure of war, not a place of beauty. The fort was designed to accommodate 36 Rodman guns, firing a ball some nine inches across, and there was a side-fort battery planned, that shot an even larger ball. There is a smaller, parrot rifle of the style used in the fort, over in front of the neighboring Percy's General store, but if you really want to see an original Fort Popham cannon, you're going to have go upriver to Bath, or Bowdoinham, or Bowdoin, where several of the guns were purchased and used as war memorials.

You need to see this place from the water if you can. When I was younger, more than once I'd launch my canoe from where the Coast Guard used to ramp their boats behind the fort, then paddle through Atkins Bay till the current from the Kennebec snatched my bow and pointed me toward Seguin Light. All I had to do then was avoid the seals and watch out for BIW destroyers. If I was having a smart day, there was lunch and a mate along, and we'd make land on Popham Beach, somewhere between Fox or Pond Islands and finish the day in style. If you don't have that boat, get to the fort during low tide and walk the ledges in front of that massive wall. You'll come away impressed, I promise.

Jane and I went to fort Popham with Abbie, George and Silas a couple weeks ago, and it was a delight to introduce the place to another generation. Abbie found a four-leaf clover on the ancient parade ground, and little Silas peeked into 16 places before we had to decide he'd had enough. It was a beautiful summer afternoon, like we never get enough of in Maine, and a wonderful chance to mix a little history with a great family outing. Watch your afternoons and get out there soon, summer's too short to miss it.

"Ear, ear...rows or circles?"

Eating corn on the cob off the cob can be a very personal experience. There are those who simply devour ear after ear in reckless abandon, and there are some who try to be polite about the whole operation, eating row after neat row until the cob has been bared.

Emily Post, that queen of all fashionable etiquette, describes corn on the cob as a pleasant tasting, "but not a very easy to manage vegetable...eat it as neatly as you may," she advises. "Attack the corn on the cob with as little ferocity as possible..." she added.

There was a clambake down at Norman Marriner's recently, and four native Mainers sat at a table eating their corn on the cob opposite four "out of staters." The difference was deafening. While the out of staters each ate their kernels in a circular fashion, the Maine folk ate their kernels row by row. The observation led to a rather spirited discussion.

One Mainer called the circular eating, "a funny, foreign form of feasting...an obvious flaw in the sociability," in the education of the New Yorkers. Not to be outdone, one of the Empire staters suggested the row upon row, repetitive motion so sacred to the Maine folks showed a definite "lack of imagination and creativity...a rather stuffy, STARCHY, boring way to eat corn." Only a kind word from the ever gracious host prevented a corn to cob confrontation over the picnic table.

Norman Marriner has hosted clambakes since he's been old enough to dig a clam and husk an ear of ripe corn. He assured the Mainers, and the New Yorkers, that both could easily be right. "Eat it any way you want," said Marriner, "when you have good fresh corn, there's no such thing as a bad way, or a wrong way, to eat it."

I agree the world is full of compromisers, but I'm not sure I was ready for the lady I ate corn with just the other night. She cleaned both ends of her cob in a quick and impressive, no-nonsense attack, rounding that thing like a beaver on a birch. I could just stop, watch and marvel. With both ends cleaned, she settles right down and eats the rest of her corn in tidy and precise rows. Not a kernel could survive an assault such as that! Here folks, is a lady who appreciates food!

When Miles visited last, I had to remind him of the time we were on the road to Farmington, and stopped beside a cornfield not far from the Sandy River. The stuff seemed to run on for acres, and grew taller than us both. "Cow corn," I announced, then we took off down one of those uncountable rows, headed for the river and a chance to dunk our feet. It was immediately cooler, and we were enveloped by a sweet smell.

On the river's bank we sat and ate an ear of corn, raw, picked but a minute before. That day it mattered not if we ate in rows or circles, that corn was probably the sweetest, snappiest, juiciest corn either of us will ever eat.

At the end of the day, when Norman heard the story, he affirmed that corn "off the field" is always the sweetest and best. "unless the farmer catches, you," he added.

Emily Post offers a last word of caution. "The real thing to avoid is too much buttering all at once, and too greedy eating," she says. Then she does suggest eating in a row fashion – like the Mainers – but she suggests eating no more than two rows at a time.

I'm here to say there aren't too many Mainers with that kind of self-control.

Recalling the derelict schooners

I suspect I'll never cross the "long bridge" at Wiscasset without craning my head to the right and taking yet another expectant look for the **Hesper** and the **Luther Little**. It matters not that they're gone, or that I know they're gone. I always find myself pausing to acknowledge that they used to be, and always mentioning them to anyone who will listen.

Last weekend my grandson and I crossed that bridge and true to form, I started rattling to that little guy (three-and-a half-years old) about those old boats. Jane just rolls her eyes, looks at the rest of the harbor for a second and then reaches over to turn the radio up an octave. Grandson Jadon just smiled at me and took another fistful of Cheez-its.

For those of you less-versed, the **Hesper** and the **Luther Little** were two wide-bodied schooner hulks that used to adorn the waterfront at Wiscasset. Photographers photographed them, painters painted them, tourists loved them, and finally, the Town of Wiscasset removed them. I'm told somewhere on a ridge beside the Wiscasset landfill, there still remains a pile of oak wood waste that refuses to rot. Except for that heap, and for the memories of people like me, they are forever gone.

I'm told both schooners were built in Massachusetts in the early 1900's. In fact, the days of these four-masted, white-hulled beauties were already numbered when they first hit the water as shining new relics destined to end an era, rather that open one. They each crossed the Atlantic several times, were sold and sold again, eventually coming to Maine as part of a scheme to haul coal.

The financial crash of the '30s doomed them to the ledges of Sheepscot Bay. In the 60 years they lay wasting in the mud, people tried to salvage them, burn them, move them and pillage them. What a terrible fate for these crafts of beauty.

Unless you study local history, you have no reason to know that Maine was once home to thousands of these grand vessels. The "Downeasters" that dotted the world's oceans in the 1800's took Maine families to every port in the world, and brought those places home to our state. There was a time in our state's past when nearly any farm with access to deep water sprouted a shipyard, and sent a vessel or two off to sea and to fortune. In the embargo that led to the War of 1812, I'm told vessels that tied up unused in Sheepscot Bay stretched all the way from Wiscasset to Edgecomb Island. No need for a bridge in those days!

Of course, I have my own Wiscasset schooner story. It was spring of 1967, and I was home on leave, headed for Vietnam in less than a week. I headed for Alna and the Sheepscot River, but 8 a.m. found me still in Wiscasset, drinking a coffee and looking at the two schooners. I noticed a kid taking pictures and went over to chat.

The guy was on his first trip to Maine, hailing from Nebraska or some other awful place. He was mesmerized by the grand old boats. "Hey," says I, "I have a canoe on my car, want to go aboard?"

He looked dumbfounded by his good luck, and in minutes, we were tying off between the two hulks. "Easier to get aboard," says I. "Less likely to get caught and stopped," I said to myself.

I was in great shape in those days, slipped up the side of the hull on a dangling steel cable, and tossed a rope off to "Nebraska."

Never mind "Nebraska" I will never forget what it was like to walk on that broad deck. It was impressive, even in ruin. We dropped below decks, listening intently as things scurried around us in the dark. I pulled out a flashlight and we found a hull number "216630" carved in a bulkhead. "Nebraska" went through four rolls of film in 15 minutes, and wished he had more. He wondered aloud if it was okay to be aboard, and I assured him I knew people. Under my breath I muttered, "what will they do, send me to Vietnam?"

We spent several hours on those vessels, moving from Bow to stern, from one to the other. I admit, I tried to twist a loose piece of handrail to take back to Bowdoinham, but failed. My souvenir will always have to be my memories. "Nebraska" put a big brass spike in his pocket.

Jadon smiled back at me in the rearview mirror as we crossed the bridge and headed toward the harbor. I do hope he never tires of my stories and that soon, he'll be starring in a few of them himself.

Running for the woods

Camps, tents or tree houses. Snow caves, river rides, hikes and overnighters. I grew up a long way from Walton's Mountain, but I'm thankful my childhood was as connected to the outdoor natural world as it was to the bedrooms I shared with my two brothers.

My brothers and I grew up in the woods and fields, walking, exploring, fishing, hunting or just foolin' around. If I happened to be reading a book, maybe it was a Lew Dietz novel about guiding in Maine, and probably I'd take it outside to read under a tree. I doubt there was a tree within a mile of our place we hadn't climbed, camped under or personally visited.

We hit the local rivers on rafts, poling them on single logs, or used boats we'd craft from barrels or boards. We'd bait eels and things with hot dogs, net and trap alewives for my grandfather's garden, or just swim naked from shore to shore on a good, hot day.

My first true love was a canoe. When I landed that first job, it was weeding, cultivating and harvesting vegetables for Harry Prout in his market gardens. Maybe I was 13, but no sweatshop or child labor concerns ever came into play.

Those years provided an extension of all the fresh air I could hope for, with carrots, beans and lettuce aplenty to eat. The 50 cents an hour was just icing on the cake. I do have to add (maybe just admit), my world was largely unencumbered by television. The neighbors had a little black and white two years before my mother did. In those days programming extended eight, maybe ten hours. And I was probably five years from even knowing what a computer was! When I came home from 'Nam all those years ago, I spent a week or two in a tent on the shore of Bowdoinham's Abagadasset River, just sleeping, gulping food my mother dropped off, and trying to focus on what was next.

When I'd met Jane and KNEW what was next, we vacationed at Mohegan Island, on Mount Katahdin, or many other woodland trails. Jane and I were visiting a game sanctuary last year, and the rule of these visits is she walks the paths with me if I do the gift shop with her.

While looking through the book section for a new entry for my grandson's library, my eyes focused instead on a volume titled, "Last Child in the Woods," with a subtitle of, "Saving our Children from Nature-deficit Disorder." I looked at it, read through the credits and put it down. We shopped another 10 minutes, and I dragged Jane over to look.

We knew we were moving and we were giving away books, not buying them. But both of us were drawn to the threatening title. Author Richard Louv is a social worker at heart and loves to gather statistics and case histories. I want to praise him for that; this book is full of them. "In two generations, "he writes, "Americans have transformed themselves from a rural to an urban nation.

Most people of my grandparents' generation had an intuitive sense of agricultural basics, "such as which animals and plants thrive in one's own area, what local frost cycles are, how tides work, what it means to see, to smell, to enjoy our basic natural world. "Too few people in my generation, "he adds "and approximately NONE of our children's generation," have these same basic senses and skills. "This knowledge has largely vanished from our culture, "he finishes, "and we have largely convinced ourselves it wasn't important." You gotta' read the book.

A few weeks ago, visiting the kids in Massachusetts, it was my delight when my son suggested we all go walking, and my grandson hit that field at a dead run, kicking dandelion buds and rolling in the new spring grasses. It occurred to me that my son had inherited some of my weird ways of seeing our world, and he was already planting them in our grandson. I'm so thankful for that.

I want to believe if we really hope to change our world, we have to do it one child at a time.

Keep those mountains close

I'm guessing I was about nose high to a juniper bush when my grandfather took me on my first mountain climb. We'd piled into the back of his Chevy sedan, Grammie and a couple sisters and brothers in tow, and we were all off to make it a day. We did Route One through Brunswick, out past the Deep Cut where he always stopped to let us, "exercise." There was a promise of frozen custard, but only when we came back. Grampie was a sly one, telling us those cold, tasty treats would land like a ball in our bellies and make us sick or climb sluggishly.

All the while, I think he was counting on our being exhausted and asleep for the run back to Bowdoinham, and he could slide right past the custard stand and save himself a couple bucks.

Freeport was just another sleepy little town in those days, Bean's was a manufacturing plant with the little store up a long, creaking staircase. We went downtown just because we liked to climb on the cannon in the park off Bow Street, and salute the stone soldier. Grampie really knew how to show us kids a good time. The road out to Pownal in those days had a dirt section, and we kids always tried to get Grampie to drive faster than his 45 mile 'deliberate' speed. We wanted to see a dust trail in the road, we told him. Riding with him always led to side adventures, mysteries and little talks.

Bradley Mountain was just as tall in those days as it is today. My legs were shorter. I'm not even sure it was yet a state park, but Grampie knew the trail to the top. He was a master of the natural world. He knew how to track a deer through a gravel pit, what leaves to lift to find random bugs, and if he didn't know the given name for that bug, he'd invent one. He showed me how to watch for broken branches, the occasional scratch on a tree, the tiny hole in the ground where a squirrel or a skunk may have fed. He taught me that the white pine has five needles, the red pine three. He showed me how to walk carefully and quietly in the woods if I wanted or hoped to see animals, and he told me that almost never is it possible to "surprise" an animal in its environment.

Grammie and the girls were usually bored by our side walks. Always at the top of the mountain, blanket spread on that beautiful ledge, when we made it to the top, there would be sandwiches, homemade cookies, lots of water, Kool-Aid and juices. Alden and I would look for ants to feed. Grampie would show us where to peek through the trees to see the ocean, and on the good days, there would be a search for that mother of mountains, Mt. Washington.

The last mountain Grampie and I climbed was Mars Hill in Aroostook. It was in 1966 and just months before he died. He was a potato farmer from the county so much of his life, and that little mountain was close to his heart. We did most of Mars Hill in a car that day, but when we left the vehicle to crest the summit, there was a real pep to his walk from his tired body. There were tears in his eyes when he put his hand on my shoulder and said, "Boy, keep mountains close to your heart."

My list of mountains includes most of Maine's best. I do Katahdin every chance I can. Katahdin was a birthday present to me and my son on my 60th, and the mountain and I have a date for my 70th birthday. If the peak has a fire tower on it, I'm game. South Turner, Doubletop, Borestone, Bigelow, Tumbledown, they all bear my mark. Saddleback and Sugarloaf are the winter favorites, I can ride their chair to their summits.

As spring breaks and the ice melts off these barren Maine summits, I catch myself thinking about making another climb. I try to stifle worries about my knee and my back for just one more season, and a chance for THIS Grampie to put the kids in a car and go "do" a mountain. Wish me luck.

Artwork by John Gable

Climbing Mount Katahdin

My son and I don't get out enough.

Miles is married, lives in Rhode Island and doing very well, thank you, so when we see each other, six or twenty times a year, it's an occasion.

Last month's occasion was a trip to Mount Katahdin.

I brought him up to knowing wherever he goes, Maine is his home. He believes that, and on occasion, has even been known to sneak back into the state and visit friends or places <u>without</u> stopping to see the old folks. I'll get more accepting of that, in time.

Christmas last, he gave me a little water-colored image he'd drawn of Katahdin, told me we had a site reserved at Roaring Brook in early June, and an appointment to "do" that mountain's Knife Edge. Perhaps you know the place. I crossed the Knife Edge as a kid (it was sharper then, so was I) but he never has. He's climbed Katahdin several times, we've climbed it together a couple of times, but the Knife Edge has never seen us together. We were out to change that.

Let me stop right here and explain something.

Mount Katahdin is the THE mountain of Maine. I don't take real quick to people who've lived in Maine and haven't done THE Mountain. I see that omission as a character flaw. You don't have to climb it, not to the crusty, unforgettable top, but you do have to go there, see its grandeur, touch its granite, and feel its energy.

If you're from Maine, it's spiritual, and it's personal.

Once I took a van load of friends from the Highlands up there, and again it was an experience, but that's a story for another time. Back to Miles, to me and my little Ford pickup.

Its 190 miles from home to the south gate of Baxter Park. That's three hours if the troopers let us be and we had a good time, just talking.

We got to the Park right after lunch, went truck touring around for an hour or two, got the obligatory moose sightings over quick, and landed at Roaring Brook for the walk into Sandy Stream Pond, and environs by mid-afternoon. You should know any attempt on Katahdin requires a warm-up hike. Me being six years from my last Katahdin climb, closer to 60 than youth, and pretty soft in the limbs, I'll admit, I was very anxious to loosen up.

The Park Ranger said the Knife Edge was not yet open for the season, (snow and ice, you know), but there were 2-3 other trails to the summit. We were disappointed, but not upset.

There were no moose in the pond, so we decided to circle the ridge behind, and see what we'd scare up. That was a very good idea. A half-mile above the point, we heard a branch snap off trail, and we pointed. Sure enough, another moose. We watched it, moved towards it, and took some pictures. Then we walked on towards the North Basin. Two or three pictures of a moose's tail are enough.

Miles was walking point now; we hit a dip in the trail and saw another bull moose, some 50 feet away and coming right at us! The look on Miles' face was a priceless question mark, on the moose's face nothing but indifference. I signaled Miles to back off the trail, and neither of us spoke. That moose sauntered right up to us, four legs going four ways, it seemed. He took one look at us, and went past. He was so close, he even smelled like a moose.

We were loose now, I can tell you. We walked on a little further, found a cross trail and cut back towards Roaring Brook.

Here's the part of the story my Jane will always insist I tell. Right there, in the trackless wilderness of Maine, I had a near life-altering thought!

Oh Gosh. "I said (sort of). "Miles, I think I forgot my sleeping bag, my poncho liner, and our camp stove." I have no idea why I thought of that, right then, Miles just smiled that knowing, 'someday we have to go home' smile and shrugged. He's a great kid. He remembered right away that his mother had said, "Don't forget the stuff on the bedroom floor when you load the truck." He loves moments like that.

We spent the night at the Big Moose Inn, having spectacular plates of smoked salmon and roasted red potatoes for supper. I never once missed the sleeping bag. I think I recovered pretty well.

Next morning, we were showered and breakfasted by 8 am, and trucked back to Roaring Brook by 9. Everything looked perfect, in fact, the Ranger on duty said the Knife Edge had just been opened, and we could be among the first across. We were both very excited.

It's three miles from Roaring Brook to Chimney Pond, a site

marking the lower approaches to the mountain proper, and one of the very few prettiest spots on earth. You just have to stand there and see the pure water, feel the fresh airs, and look up at that soaring granite to know what I'm talking about. If you haven't, you can't.

Miles and I made the trip to Chimney Pond in about two hours, snacked a snack, and headed up the Dudley Trail, up that grand granite face.

Now, the Dudley trail rises nearly 2,000 feet in a mile. It breaks out of the trees real fast, turns immediately to boulders bigger than my truck, and the little trail blazes start signaling us to climb over the granite, since there is no logical way around.

There is a tradition, you know, that the Native American Penobscots would not ascend above Katahdin's tree line. Something about evil spirits, danger, and bad times. Don't know all the details, but it makes me believe once again that maybe Indians are SMARTER than we pale-faces. Anyway, we proceeded above the tree line, summit in sight.

That climb up Dudley Trail reminded me Miles is nearly 30 years younger than me, and probably in better shape. We reached Pamola Peak about 1:30, that Knife Edge looming dark and ominous ahead of us.

"Wow," Miles said.

"Ow," I groaned.

But those "evil spirits" of Katahdin intervened just then, just as they often do on Maine's marvelous mountain.

Clouds were closing on us from two directions, and the only team to get across the edge that day (coming from the other side) was hurrying to get off. We paused to take pictures maybe five minutes, we were covered by clouds, seeing lightning bolts and hearing thunder. When the rain started, it was frozen and wind driven. We looked back once, the Knife Edge was gone, shrouded in storm. We concentrated on the trail under us, still tripping on the wet rocks, ducking uselessly at every clap of thunder.

Miles looked back for me more and more often.

The sheltering tree line brought new problems, trapping rain on the trail and dripping it on us whenever we touched anything. When we got off the mountain about 4:30, I was whipped, dripped and done. Miles was a little better than that, but still somewhat west of perfect. We put on dry clothes, got in the truck and booked it for Bowdoinham, smiling and happy when we walked through the door, unexpected. Jane could have been lots tougher on me about the missed bedroll than she was.

We sat at the table and ate a late supper, pouring over the new stories to tell, excited as a couple of kids, more tired than a pair of old guys. The best thing, really, one week later, is there's still a trip over the Knife Edge to look forward to.

Petting skunks

I know enough about skunks to know they're more than just black and white. I know that people tend to fear them, perhaps because they misunderstand them, but hey, most of my skunk stories have ended pretty well.

My grandfather had this little story about skunks. Seems he and his Sadie were headed for church and a mother skunk with a litter of three or four (the number was one of the details that gets diluted over the years) crossed the road right in front of them.

Well, in Aroostook in those days, there was a 25 cent bounty on skunks and for Grampie, that family was a found dollar, and a dollar was a dollar. He grabbed up a big stick and took off after those skunks, getting one, then another, then another…then the mother. Well the mother was a problem. Story was that he rounded a tree and there she was, business end up, and ready for business. She blasted him before he had time to blink.

Grampie never made it to church that day. Grammie almost didn't go herself. Seems there was some drifting stench that made it back to her before she could move and she was some 100 yards away. Grampie always said she wasn't in a very Christian mood for the rest of that day, and a few days that followed.

Grampie always looked for lessons in life, and was always willing to share. His lesson about that day was simple. Get home, get out of the clothes quick as you can, touch only what you have to, (too bad if they happen to be the Sunday meeting clothes) bury them in the ground, a foot or so deep, and leave them there four – maybe five - days. He always said he felt bad about the whole experience, but it wasn't like the clothes were ruined. He said he dug those digs up, washed them in a nearby brook (getting the dirt out, the smell was gone) and he said at least once he wore those clothes to church. I suspect he was trying to prove a point rather than look too dapper. That was his four dollar suit. Grammie never confirmed going to church with him but I always believe everything Grampie told me.

Perhaps my favorite skunk story has my son, Miles, and I going to Bath to retrieve a skunk a friend had snared in a Have-a-Heart trap. We got into the story when the friend called with one frantic question…"what do I do NOW?" We drove to Bath, found the skunk had been in the trap several days. My city friend didn't know it was trapped. "It didn't spray," he said. "How was I to know?"

Miles and I knew. We shared intelligence in the ways of these black and white beasts. We nodded knowing smiles. The skunk was too big to elevate his tail. "Skunks don't like their own stink." That was a Grampie rule I had shared with my son. No danger here. We tossed a blanket over the cage in our car and headed for Bowdoinham. We had a date with the "Skunk Man." It was noon when we passed Cooks Corner and Miles and I almost never passed on a reason to visit the hamburger store. We drove to the little microphone. I ordered meals for us and added, "oh, do a pack of fries for the skunk in the back." The voice on the speaker shared none of our mirth. She let a dreadful minute pass, then tried to be professional herself. "Your meals will be $5.25," she said, "please drive forward."

We drove forward, and I have to say I've never had such service at a burger joint. Three faces packed that window, and all three faces disappeared when they saw the trap and assumed there probably was a skunk under the blanket. Miles was ready to show them. The manager stepped to the window, a bag of food in one hand, the microphone in the other. "Sir," he said, "do you really have a skunk in the car?" I nodded and Miles moved to show him off. The manager partially closed the service window and commanded us to drive away from his business immediately. "Is our food in that bag?" I asked him. He nodded and said if we drove to the front parking lot we could come in and pick our food up. I muttered something about that "defeated the function of a drive-up window." He gestured with his finger, telling us again to move away from his building. I said if I drove away, I had no intention of returning for our food. I really don't think that bothered him much.

"Look," I said, waving a $10 bill at the closed window, "give us the food and we'll be on our way." The manager seemed unwilling to compromise, so I smiled at him, put the car in park and repeated, "Just give us the food, we'll be…"

That service window flew open and the bag of food came at us at a surprising rate of speed. When I again offered the money the window was slammed in our faces. The manager stood there, pointing the way toward the open road. I had to assume the meal was free, so I restarted the car and drove off. We did, after all, have a date with the "Skunk Man."

Miles smiled at me. "Hope we got ketchup," he said.

Me and the Skunk Man, (Everett Winslow) were both in the 101st Airborne Division but in different wars. He had a local reputation as an animal rehabilitator and his specialty was skunks. He always said skunks were a lot like people. "Treat 'em right, they'll treat you right, too." I don't think I was ever at his house when I didn't see a skunk and he always said he's never been sprayed. "Bring her in," he said, "let's get a look at this beauty."

We went to a shed, sat the cage in the middle of the floor. Everett popped the top on a cat food can and placed it where the skunk could whiff it. "Bet she's hungry," he said. He predicted the skunk was more scared of us than we were of her. He said she would probably stay in the cage until dark, then come out to eat. He dropped down beside the cage, flipped the door lever, and mister, that skunk flew out of that cage like a thoroughbred race horse.

Even Everett was surprised.

Miles looked to me for guidance, but I offered none. Everett saved the day. "We all better leave," he said, "very quietly."

"Learn or crash"

I was barely 16 when my grandfather cornered mom and said "I want Frankie to drive us to Aroostook this spring." Both predictable and a little terse, mom's response was swift, "He's still a kid," she said, "he can't drive yet."

Usually, that would have been the end of the discussion, for mom's word was pretty much the law in our house. This time Grampie persisted however, he was passionate, he went for it.

"I think he's ready," he argued, "the boy will learn or we'll crash." My first trip to "The County" was on.

You need to remember that Interstate 95 didn't exist in 1963. There really was a stretch of road, up North in Maine, called the Hainesville Woods, and it really was still unpaved! The last streetlight in Bangor was maybe 150 miles from Houlton; and Mapleton, our goal, was probably 50 miles "straight up" the old Military Road from Houlton.

What 16-year-old wouldn't bite into an adventure like that?

Grampie always drove a Chevrolet and it was always black. If we got an early start, he promised, we could stop in Etna and have cookies with cousins. Grammie had a gallon jar filled with oatmeal raisin cookies, just in case, and I had a plan for those cookies, cousins or not.

For Grampie, an early start was five in the morning, for me, five in the morning was still the middle of the night. We hit the road at 4:58 a.m. "Use the headlights," Grampie cautioned, "we don't want to hit anything."

My grandmother sat regally astride the rear seat, flanked by a basket of food, several pillows, her personal thermos of tea, three canning jars of water, a blanket, and two books. She liked to perch at the very center of that wide, bench seat. Top speed was something like 50 miles per hour, I think we got that on a straight stretch of the cement road north and west of Augusta. Grammie was often on the very edge of her seat to check and recheck our speed, and more than once urged Grampie to urge me to slow down.

Roads were narrower back then, or so it seemed.

After the early terror left me, I came to enjoy meeting the pulp and potato trucks, even on the corners.

Grampie was always a man of quiet encouragement. Once, when the car drifted off the pavement on the passenger's side for just a short distance, he could have grabbed the wheel, or benched me and told me it was time for him to drive. He chose instead to pat my knee after I regained control and said, "there, we learned something just then, didn't we?" Grammie sat back on her seat and thumbed through a book for the next several miles.

My grandfather was the first great man I ever knew.

This trip was the first time I put eyes on Mount Katahdin. When I saw that broad, beautiful behemoth from across the valley at Medway, it was love at first sight. We stopped. We gawked. We had already passed the cousins, so the cookies belonged to Grampie and me. We each ate three, and drank from our canning jars as Grampie pointed at Monument Peak, the rock slide, and Pamola Peak. When we reloaded the car, I vowed under my breath to return one day, and that affair continues.

We did a picnic on a bank of the Penobscot River; Grammie pulled a fishing pole from the trunk, and I grabbed a quick nap. Grampie tried to convince me that even blackflies were God's little creatures. After a big fish rolled not 20 feet from where Grammie was drowning her worm, I knew what he said was true. Then I swatted another of God's creatures, Grammie flicked the remains of her worm into the river and we remounted the Chevy.

Who knows, or cares, how many spruce trees flank the road between Lincoln and Smyrna Mills? That was the tedious part of the trip. But while the miles ticked off, both grandparents droned stories of their past, and of my mother's earliest days on their potato farm.

I just had no idea.

At the end of the journey, pulling safely into Bert and Lizzie's driveway, even Grammie admitted I'd done a pretty good job. Grampie suggested I send a postcard to my mother and tell her I'd learned to drive.

My grandparents and I made several more trips to Aroostook County, you can only assume I became a pretty good driver. Along the way, there were other picnics, and many more stories. I do recommend the process, it taught me so much more than how to drive.

Pride-filled products from home

My mother detested spiders. Fact is she feared them so, the only time she'd go down cellar (she so worried about seeing one) was once each fall, each November, to "inventory" her winter canning. Ma grew up in rural Aroostock County on a depression-era potato farm. Hers was a situation where you'd care for yourself, or go without. A war widow before she was 30 and the mother of five kids, life wasn't that much easier for her when she came down state and landed in Bowdoinham.

Her secret weapon was always her canning. She canned vegetables, fruits, even chicken Meat. She dried stuff, stored stuff, preserved stuff and hoarded stuff. There was always a spare closet in our house with squash stored on newspapers, apples in bushels, pickles in tubs and potatoes in barrels, but the center of her universe was the canning in our cellar. There was an old wash table that held her fruits, jellies and jams, and there were rough board shelves, four feet deep, that hung off the floor joists above, where her veggies were stored.

Mom mostly used the old-style glass canning jars with wire fasteners and rubber seals. Thinking about it now, I bet she would have killed or traded any one of us kids for a freezer! She had a fancy pressure canner ("You stand right there and you watch that pressure needle") and she had two or three of those Sears-Roebuck water bath canners. When she canned, it was seven or nine jars to a batch, and she accumulated batches until she had 50 or more jars. I can hear her saying, "52 jars of beans is a lot of beans, but it's still only one jar per week..." It wasn't unusual for her to "put up" 150-200 quarts of tomatoes, or string beans (we could choose from yellow or green) and half that again in corn, or carrots, sometimes even peas.

Her other secret weapon, of course, was my grandfather

Miles, who came south from Aroostook with her, and was master of her garden. Most years it was an acre or more, and he tended it all day and protected it all night.

When the beans came on, most other stuff stopped. They were picked, washed and cut into 1¼" sections. They were packed tightly in jars, sealed and boiled. And boiled some more. Seems like most of the beans came off during the hot days of late August, and the canning went late into those hot nights. It was a good night when the just-canned jars needed to be pulled from the canner and covered with a towel to cool, because that would mean there was a breeze in the kitchen. It took as long as it took.

My brothers and I had the job of loading the cellar shelves. She wanted the jars seven deep, she wanted them lined up like soldiers, she wanted them pretty. "Be careful on those stairs," she'd say, "Don't drop those jars!" We used to complain that she cared more for her jars than for our necks. "Keep them close but don't let them touch," She'd say, and some years, just to keep them from the dust of the floors above, we'd open a newspaper across the top as her inventory accumulated.

Some of the garden stuff came from Phil across the street, and from neighbors up and down the road. It never hurt to have Harry Prout growing carrots, squash, turnip and other stuffs, "over east." All of us kids worked for him as we grew up, and there was always stuff carried home. If it came through the door, mom knew how to deal with it. Sometimes there were gathered fiddleheads in the spring (always put up in pints) usually there was someone in town who would give mom a deer's neck so she could have a batch or two of Minced meat.

Always in early November, there would be an inventory taken. Grampie always took us boys down cellar to be sure the jars were lined properly, and the cobwebs of summer were all

143

cleared away. It was then that those creaking stairs got attention, NOT when we boys were running up and down the months before.

Mom would count the front jars, multiply by seven and nod her head. All would decide right then if the summer had been good, and could assume the winter was going to be okay. Mom would focus only on those pretty, pride-filled jars, and scoot immediately back upstairs. Grampie would smile and tell us it was good she didn't see any spiders.

Gwen & Madeline, more than blueberries

Ker-plink, ker-plank, ker-plunk!

Once, maybe twice each year, I'd see Gwen and always she'd be blue almost to her elbows. For nearly two decades the trip to Gwen's in South Hope has been a prized mid-summer ritual. She is the brains, the berry sorter and the bookkeeper of a family blueberry farm on the side of a mountain just east of Union.

We'd travel there one late afternoon, fill our car with twenty pound flats of perfectly clean, meticulously sorted blueberries, intoxicating with their smell, delighting in their taste. The sixty-mile trip was always interrupted by sweeping great handfuls of berries, from the box to my mouth, and on a good year, there would be snacks at Moody's Diner, a swim in a mill pond, or a walk on the Wiscasset waterfront.

Madeline is different. She's a local girl and we're always passing with a wave on the road or sharing a "hallo" on the street. When I was just a pup, she lived up the street from us in Bowdoinham. Now approaching 80, this lady still rises early on these succulent summer days, drives her dated Dodge van to a secret place and wanders the power lines all morning picking blueberries the hard way, one at a time. About noon she comes down, gets a "discount" hot dog from a relative/vendor on the mall, then parks the van in the shade and sells her berries a pint at a time, first come, first served. I feel blessed when I find her and can barter for a basket.

Maybe you don't know the difference between hand-picked and raked berries. Do you know the difference between night and day? The blueberry rake is a heavy, medieval looking

145

device that could be used as an instrument of torture in the off-season. Six-inch long, spike-like fingers strip the tender fruits along with assorted leaves, green berries, spiders and sticks, and the harvester dumps them into a basket or flat. The berries are later winnowed to sort out the light stuff and "picked over" to free most of the good from much of the bad.

Gwen always invited us up to try our hand at raking, but I always assumed I was smarter than that.

The Brodies do rake their berries, but Gwen has always been their secret weapon. When Gwen and her crew are done with them and when Gwen's loving touch has been applied, that flat of Brodie berries assumes perfection. There are no stems, no green fruit, no leaves. Not ever! Berries are moved from a South Hope flat directly into one of Jane's magical fruit pies with no concern for any imperfection.

Madeline picks each single berry, one perfect blue orb at a time. By hand. She could tell you how many berries are in a quart because she fills quart baskets, one berry at a time.

Last month we received a postcard from the Brodie family. "We're sorry," it read, "Brodies Blueberries will not be available..." Jane and I almost cried. After twenty or more years we wouldn't see Gwen up to her elbows in her precious, wonderful berries. And yes, we wouldn't see her berries, either! Last week, I bought my first quart of berries for the season from Madeline. Perfect and priceless at $7 a quart, they were, but she's saying how hot it is picking, how her family worries about her out there all alone, and how some of her favorite "patches" are getting overgrown.

Then it occurs to me, and scares me not a little bit. This is more than just blueberries. These old friends and old ways that have always made my Maine so special are getting harder and harder to keep together. I honestly worry that my grandson won't get that ride to Union with me, and the next generations may not know the difference between a raked and hand-picked berry.

Can you tell me I'm wrong here?

Chucking woodchucks

"How much wood would a woodchuck chuck if a woodchuck could chuck wood?" is a pretty old, if senseless, question. A better question to ponder, perhaps, is IF a wood chuck could chuck wood, would it ever bother?

I want to suggest here there are very few creatures on our wonderful earth that are as useless and lazy as a woodchuck. I mean, if they weren't sort of on the right side of cute, cuddly and foolish looking, would they have any use at all?

The first pesty woodchucks we see each season are out on the Interstate. Zing go the cars, fat sit the woodchuck on some sun soaked slope. I consider it a blessing when the two paths intersect, and the woodchuck wishes it had stayed off the road. Sorry if that seems a bit un-Christian, but I don't like them and I just have no use for them.

When I first came home from the war, one of the first things I did to decompress was to spend a long week with an old Army buddy in Troy, N.Y. (I was desperate, I hadn't met Jane yet) He was a budding French & Indian war re-enactor and the proud owner of several ponderous muzzle-loading pieces. It was spring, it became our habit to 'celebrate' late into the evenings, and early the next morning, to rise and go "woodchucking" in the fields above St. George Lake.

I had left Vietnam with the expectation that my days of belly crawling through fields were over, but I need to confess that I got right back into it with Bob, We'd move like snakes from one mound to the next, actually relishing the smell of the dandelions and the fresh grasses as they crushed under our noses and chins.

We simply waited for some over-weight woody to emerge to

148

catch some rays, and, "BOOM, BOOM," our weapons would belch in almost perfect unison.

Maybe you have never fired a muzzle-loader from the prone position. Properly loaded, the thing might push you sideways an inch or three, but Bob never loaded one of those things properly in his life. "If it don't kick, it can't kill," Bob used to say, then he'd splash in a little extra black powder and tamp it down. If we fired six times a morning, we had a half-dozen bruises on our bodies by nightfall.

I need to tell you right now, we never bruised a woodchuck.

A muzzle-loader fires in a two-step process... flashing powder in a pan ignites powder in the barrel that explodes the charge, and there isn't a woodchuck alive that can't turn and get down a hole between those two steps. But we had fun. It was spring after all, and we were young.

But to this day, I want to believe we may have scared more than one woodchuck to death.

If a woodchuck sets up residence in one of my town's cemeteries, they become my problem, since I'm the town's sexton. Ever field a phone call from a lady who has just visited the grave of her grandfather, only to find a big pile of dirt with a hip bone tossed on top? Me too! I fixed that chucker with a cherry bomb.

You need to know, as you hunt these critters, that they always have one back door and probably two. If you really want to get rid of woodchucks, you have to close off their escape holes, then do what you gotta' do.

Woodchucks can also be serious menaces if you're trying to be a gardener. They have insatiable appetites, and can lay waste to an unprotected garden overnight. You just can't let one live in your neighborhood. Our little kitchen plot has suffered

149

more than once at the chops of a woodchuck, and, when given the latitude, I try to blame my daughter, Abbie. This girl is so tender-hearted sometimes I catch myself wondering where she came from. She'd forbid me to shoot a woodchuck if it was feeding off flowers on our front deck. I have to confess to shooting one or two when Abbie wasn't looking, and I'll just continue to hope she continues NOT to read my columns.

I've tried to use Have-a-heart traps with no success. And here's another thing about woodchucks… you never have only ONE, and they will not go away by themselves. So, call a friend, do NOT call Abbie, or go buy a muzzle-loader for yourself. If you don't get rid of them right now, you're in for a long, hot summer.

Islands and me

Monhegan.

Swan Island.

Whaleboat.

Mackworth.

Deer Isle.

Crotch, Eagle, Acadia, and Little Brick.

Maine is seldom better than it is in August, and August in Maine is seldom better than when you're spending a day "aboard" an island.

The Maine Book of Lists, claims there are 2,100 islands "off" Maine, and the Maine Island Trail Association guesses only, "more than that."

I can only hope you are fortunate enough to have a Maine Island or two in your past.

Swan Island, awash in the middle of the Kennebec River, was once the tiny Town of Perkins. It was one of the places I haunted as a child. My brothers and I played cowboys and Indians there, and we stalked wild game there, just for the fun of it, just to get close. I climbed too many massive pines, trying to claim errant eagle feathers. I've biked there with Jane, I've walked there with my kids...and I can't wait to show it to my grandkids.

When Jane and I married one October, it was Monhegan where we chose to honeymoon. We had this little cottage where surf lulled us to sleep, and woke us in the morning. Monhegan has crashing surf! There were many memorable, long walks on magnificent, scenic trails. Many long talks and playful conversation on rocks and ledges, bathed in sunlight. Monhegan is a magnificent and special place, WITHOUT a honeymoon!

And Mackworth. Any time you're in Portland and want to break the back of a hot city afternoon, seek out Mackworth. It's a short causeway, but almost a world away.

Whaleboat and Eagle could be sisters. One looks at the other off a point and shoulder of Harpswell. These are Jewels of Casco bay, both. Eagle is a state park, museum, and history lesson, while Whaleboat stays wild, vacant and unbuilt. Forever.

My brother and his wife have this boat that taxis us to each, and who could ever be foolish enough to tire of those rides? Whaleboat has been the site of dozens of family picnics, and Whaleboat was the first place I showed our kids how to dive and pluck starfishes off ledges. You are guaranteed to see Ospreys, and you're gonna' see Herons. If you want a "real" Maine coast day, devote a tide to a walk around Whaleboat.

Deer Isle and its little brother Crotch Island are text book examples of Maine. Ask Henry and ask Harriet. That startling and magnificent bridge that soars above the Reach lets you know you're in for a treat, even before you set foot on the island. I like to walk that bridge (carefully) inhale the brine air and gaze down at the crystal water. Jane thinks I'm strange, and wonders if it's because I was a paratrooper once. If the bridge shakes, it's okay.

Again, just ask Henry or Harriet.

There are vistas all over Deer that you'll never forget, but my private vista capital has to be little Crotch Island. Go ahead, look up Crotch Island in your DeLorme atlas, and it will appear like a pair of pants, drifting off-shore of Deer Isle's

Stonington. We first started visiting 35 years ago, when the old granite works looked like the crew had left for lunch and never returned. There is a sunset off Crotch Island that makes Key West pray for cloudy evenings! I've walked into the crotch of Crotch Island at low tide, and dug edible clams with my bare hands!

I've saved the biggest and the smallest islands for last. Acadia is Maine. As Maine islands go, it is a huge sprawling, spectacular place, and was the first National park east of the Mississippi. If you pick most any trail off the loop, even in August, chances are you'll still find a place to be alone. My favorite Acadia spot is called Connors Nubble, go find it!

And now, Brick Island. Brick is a spot of stone, pine and dirt near the center of Merrymeeting Bay. It was a base camp when I was a Boy Scout. Near there I learned to swim, to water ski, to cook out, sleep out, act out. Every boy needs a Brick Island. I'm always happy to share mine.

So here's your new summer assignment. Borrow a DeLorme's if you don't have one, pick out an island and go for it. Engineer a boat trip if there is no bridge, borrow a canoe if you don't own one. But get yourself to an island this month. Create some stories of your own. Summer is just too short to do otherwise. Your island awaits!

Abbie's getting married

Everyone told me it wouldn't be easy having my little girl get married, and turns out, everyone was right

But the day did come. The plans were all made, the food selected, the tent erected, the portable potties delivered...and there we were, Abbie and me, standing alone all nervous and sweating, between two closed door at the First Parish church

White dress, hair in a fancy do, my gorgeous little girl smiled that smile, gave me this hug and said, "thank you, Dad, for everything." Who assumes that old paratroopers can't cry? Just then the heavy wood doors bumped open and Susan, the wedding lady said, "we're ready here!" The music changed and we were off. I wondered what Abbie was thinking.

It was one of the longest walks of my life, and the biggest worry I had was that I might step on a corner of her dress and trip us both. Friends and family whispered, waved and flirted. Those massive, arching beams of our elegant old church were never more inviting, more inclusive, more impressive.

Approaching her George together, it fell to me simply to kiss Abbie carefully, to release her arm, then turn and walk away. That was pretty tough, too. Wish I'd thought to whisper a thank you in her ears as well!

Abbie and George rode to their reception in a Rolls Royce, I went in my little Ford Ranger, but the view we shared was perfection. Her grandfather's field, wearing its 30x90 white tent like a hat, Jane's gardens and flowers all abloom, and Norman's lawns, trimmed perfectly by pine and water, were never more beautiful.

Abbie, always more a romantic than me, first and often talked of being married in this place when she was a youngster, and here it was now, swirling all around us.

The reception became a tribute to this young love, and a celebration of family and friends. People were visiting and laughing with folks they hadn't seen in years, people were sitting with folks they had never met, and were laughing and talking. Abbie was embraced and engulfed by family and relations, college friends and childhood buddies. George's family proved as numerous and energetic as ours. As the afternoon progressed, as Henry's fantastic food, the drink and Tasha's cake blended, it became more and more obvious that we had more and more in common.

That old saw about taking a village to raise a child comes into play. I'm thinking now it takes a village to make a good marriage!

Jane and I have been married more than 35 years, and as I looked around that tent that day, I knew why, and I only knew half the folks in the tent. We've been supported, coached and coaxed along the way by so many wonderful people. Advice when we needed it, silence when we wanted it. Free labor, the loan of a truck, the loan of a tool, a casserole, or a blanket or a table or a hundred bucks, always perfectly timed, always offered with no conditions.

So my hope for Abbie and George, and all like them, is pretty simple. As they lock hands and hearts and embark on their lives together, I hope we all have the good sense to help them when we can, and give them room when we should.

The kids have been over for supper twice since the wedding. Plowing through piles of wedding pictures has become the new family business of late. One Sunday, we four went for a ride and landed at a country fair. Along the way, it's neat to look in my rearview mirror and see the affection between these two. It's encouraging and fun to hear their snippets of progress as they set up housekeeping together.

I'll continue to offer help when I can, and advice when I'm asked. I have to admit this George guy is a capable and wonderful partner for our daughter. Jane gives me that look when she thinks I need it, and yes, there are times when I need it.

After all, Abbie is still my little girl!

Hitchhiking home

I was returning from the People Plus picnic in July, my truck chucked full with grills and other party stuff. Driving through the Bowdoin Pines, I couldn't help noticing a young woman moving beside the road, limping enough to be obvious, and carrying a bicycle on one shoulder. The day was hot, she appeared obviously distressed. I snapped the truck to the side of the road, got out and offered her a ride.

This woman was bleeding from one knee, had a cherry red, overexerted face, but immediately appeared challenged, and frightened by me. Her first response to my offer of assistance was an absolute, and positive "no".

I'm a pretty big guy, but don't think of myself as threatening. The white hair helps on many occasions, but not this time. I told her she appeared in obvious pain. She said she wasn't. I told her she could add to her injury and discomfort by not accepting my help. She said she'd risk it. I told her she could ride in the back of my truck if she didn't want to ride with me. She repeated she didn't want a ride. I told her I had a daughter about her age, and if Abbie was in trouble on the road, I hope someone well intentioned, someone like me, would help her.

The poor kid didn't know what to do and started to cry. "Please let me help you," I repeated, and finally, after awkward seconds, she offered me her bike. I smiled, put the bike beside the grills and asked her to ride up front. We rode into town without another word, and when I let her off, there was a limp thank you, and a huge sigh of relief.

I only wanted to help this kid, and at times like that, I inject my own kids, and my own experiences, into a situation.

What bothers me most, I guess, is the fact that when I was her age, I was bounding into people's cars willingly, daily. Hitchhiking was a way of life when I was her age, what a shame it can't be today. I thought nothing about "thumbing" my way to Brunswick.

If I stayed after school for any reason, more often than not, my "late bus" was my sneakers. I "bummed" rides from college, I got home on leave by hitchhiking in uniform. A couple guys and I "thumbed" into Canada more than one weekend ... the quickest way off most stateside army posts was a ride on my thumb. There's a humbling, if funny story about a midnight hitchhike from Rockland...no traffic...when I ended up walking some 18-19 miles!

Once, as a van driver for The Highlands, we picked up this young man...wearing a suit and tie...who told us a story about oversleeping. We took him right to his job site, and finished our regular ride. Turned out he was a lawyer, and a wonderful kid, but I sure got in trouble with my supervisor when she heard that story.

Another time, I got off a bus in Portsmouth, N.H., because it was going for a 20 minute layover, and I told the driver I was sure I could get home faster. She credited my ticket in full, told me to stay on Route one and he'd pick me up if he saw me on the road. I was in uniform, and thumbing maybe ten minutes before a Maine State Trooper stopped, and called me to his window.

"Hey" he said. "It's illegal to hitchhike in uniform. Where were you going?" he asked. He gestured with his thumb for me to get in his cruiser. I didn't like the way he said, "were," but he was a veteran and took me right to my folks' door, in Bowdoinham, and we got there in record time..

I'm quick to admit, however, I never encouraged my kids to hitchhike. I remember the conversations, I remember being very firm about it. Jane and I did lots of extra driving, and waiting, so neither of our kids felt the pressure to "bum" rides. I don't regret our commitment, but again, I was saddened by that loss of freedom.

I checked with Brunswick Police officer Terry Goen to learn the current laws about hitchhiking. "It's still legal," he said, "BUT..."

The buts include you must stay off the pavement if you are hitchhiking. It may not be after dark. You may not hitchhike on any major divided highway, like the Interstate, or the turnpike. You may well be asked for identification if an officer sees you. That office most likely will NOT drive you home.

I'm not here to say that hitchhiking was a good thing. It served many of us well, in a very different time. Fact is today, I guess the whole idea of thumbing most anywhere scares me more than a little. As a kid of the 60's however, I've got to tell you that hitchhiking was more than a marginal means of travel.

Given what I paid for gasoline this morning, I might consider going back to hitchhiking anyway.

The questions is, will you give me a ride?

The magic of a woman's voice

All they asked Norman and I to do was to tend the cat. Before Abbie left for vacation, she had groomed this two-page list, telling us (her father and grandfather) in extended detail, how to feed her cat when he was hungry, how to cuddle her cat when he seemed lonesome, how to pamper him when he seemed bored, and, last but certainly not least, "tricks" to get him in at night, so the foxes, the boogie man, the mean spirits, and the cat burglars(!?) would not get a chance to kidnap, devour, or do anything unfriendly to her sweet little Dilbert.

I call him Dill, Mr. Dills or Dillie, depending on our moods, and he really is a fine cat.

For two days, all went well. Late in the evening of the second day, Norman called in just a bit of a panic. Dillie had missed mess call. He wasn't waiting on the porch as darkness approached. He had not responded to any of Norman's calls. He was not to be seen in any of the several places he was known to 'hang out.' Norman was worried, and wanted some advice.

I was casual about it. I noted it was a warm, clear evening, with almost a perfect moon overhead. "If I was cat," I said, chuckling at the possibilities, "I wouldn't be in a hurry to come inside either…leave the porch light on," I suggested, "check again when the Red Sox are finished. Probably he's off on an adventure, I know he'll be back."

I added I'd be down in the morning, and I was sure that by then Dillie would be home. (Of course, I wasn't sure, but it sounded good.) Mid-day of the third day, I landed on the scene and Dillie was still missing. Norman was becoming more anxious, and when Norman gets anxious, I get anxious.

This is a man of action. This is not a man who wants to disappoint his granddaughter. He was looking for things for us to do. I walked at least a half mile of tree line that morning, searching, calling, looking for tufts of fur or other signs of interest, or evil. Signs of anything. Still nothing.

I visited four of the neighbors, giving them a description, asking them to call if they saw, heard, or even suspected something. Still nothing. We called the animal shelter, but now it was late in the day, and a Friday. We got the recording, "Call us Monday if you still have a problem..." Right. I walked the driveway again, then the main road, and searched secluded ditches for at least another hour and a half. It was hot and dusty, but I didn't like to disappoint Abbie either.

Abbie checked in that evening, and Norman confessed that Dillie was among the missing. "I can't lie to my only granddaughter," he said. I smiled. I told him I thought I could. Abbie is famous for the way she worries about her pets, her everything. I was hoping we weren't spoiling her trip with some bad news.

The next day, cousin Linda came to visit with her two friends, Nyree and Jill. In seconds, they seemed to sense anxiety among the menfolk. Within minutes, we had spilled the whole sordid cat tale.

The girls seemed to handle our situation much too casually. As they walked off to check Norman's gardens, Nyree said they would "try a call" for the cat before they left.

Now, I consider myself to be a pretty enlightened male, but this woman's attitude pretty much put me off! I carefully reviewed ALL the things Norman and I had done for this cat, just in case she had missed something, and I invited her to walk the dusty, hot miles I'd walked. Then perhaps a little abruptly, I explained how I guessed that, "a woman's voice," could certainly add NOTHING to what we'd already done. She smiled, and I continued to steam.

Well, after the ladies did their garden tour and enjoyed their swim in the pool, they advised with a certain amount of pomp that it was time for THEIR cat search to begin. With the announcement, Nyree went to a nearby fence and called, "kittie, kittie, kittie," in only the sweetest of feminine tones. The look over her shoulder towards me was somewhat less than sweet.

Nothing happened. I was almost pleased. She called again, perhaps the tone was even a bit sweeter. For a moment, thought I, maybe if I were a cat, I might come to see what she wanted, then my real nature took over. Not a little out of character, I blurted out something like, "Ah HA, so much for the value of the feminine voice, so much..."

The sound was faint at first, but unmistakable. "MEOW." The way Nyree cupped her hand to her ear was first dramatic, and then demeaning. "M-E-E-OW!!" It was louder now, and closer. Moments later, Mr. Dills, my former friend, strolled from the woods and came directly toward Nyree. His tail was high, there was a definite swagger to his gait. It was like he'd been gone ten minutes. I felt betrayed. I knew I'd been betrayed! Aren't we guys supposed to stick together?

I went over and picked Dills up. He immediately started to purr. I held him tighter. There was a little piece of me that could have choked him. It was my intention to put him in the house, to lock the door and make him a house cat until Abbie came home. And it didn't hurt my feelings too much to get myself away from the ladies, before they...

"Oh Frank," it was Nyree, and that sweet little feminine voice was back. "Is there something you wanted to say to us about the way WE retrieve cats? Is there…"

Oh yes, I was sufficiently humbled. I mumbled something about the cat probably being hungry, and just kept on walking. Once again, I had learned to never underestimate that power of a lady's voice.

The question is, really, how could I have ever doubted, "the power," in the first place??

My favorite brook

My brook isn't really a fancy place, usually just a nondescript trickle of water that has babbled past my house since long before I lived there, in fact, since long before my house was there. But the brook is a very important place to me.

 You need to understand that at 58, I live across the street from the house where I lived as a kid, and, as a kid this brook was central to the stage I considered my world.

"The brook" was a place where my brothers and our friends played, fished, did battle, explored...and, as kids of today say, "hung out." It was a place where we were safe from our sisters, even safe from my mother (not that that was really a worry). It was a play world, an imagined world, and a better world, in addition to a real world.

The brook comes to my neighborhood through a huge culvert under Center Street. There is a series of three small pools, pretty impressive cropping of ledge and the brook tumbles over a waterfall of maybe ten feet. After another pool, it trickles through a bed of gravel and small rocks, opens to another pool, turns a corner and becomes a riverlet maybe 10-15 feet wide, and often two or three feet deep.

A half mile from my house, the brook gets tired of meandering behind the village cemetery, forms its most impressive pool ever, and tumbles through a series of rocky beds and a stone rimmed gorge to where it finally joins tide water at Sampson's Creek, then the Cathance River, Merrymeeting Bay, The Kennebec and finally that ocean.

Both shores of the brook harbor a wealth of vegetation, ranging from fiddleheads to poison ivy. Trees grow from towering willows to first growth oak to wild apples, and there are a dozen places where the brook is easily crossed over the back of a fallen tree.

I know now there are no bears, no elephants, no wildcats, but I will confirm the area hides deer, woodchuck, raccoons, lizards, skunks, and snakes in great numbers. Birds are everything from Eagles to chickadees. One of my favorite brook stories is about the heron which taught itself to land in the crown of a willow, then sail down to the brook like a glider, only to enjoy uninterrupted fishing for hours.

Mine is a third generation brook. My grandfather (and grandmother) and I used to fish trout and suckers in those waters, and though the sucker run is gone, Miles, Abbie and I spent more afternoons that I want to admit, casting for trout and settling for a chub or two. It was never about fishing for supper anyway, more about sitting in the sun, setting hooks, making plans and telling stories.

There is a little bluff where the brook turns, years ago we dug out a fire hole and when we camped, that was our base camp. We used to say it was just above the level where mosquitoes used to fly, but we all knew that was a joke.

Our little brook is right there in the middle of Bowdoinham village, but, because the land always drops to the brook area, and access is so remote, we could spend hours at the brook, within 100 yards of the town's school, town's church, or a dozen houses, and never have to admit we were within a mile of civilization.

We even used the area in winter. The brook would freeze, of course, and there were several places along Center Street where you could set a toboggan and slide right down to the water's edge.

A month ago, I walked the length of the brook for the first

time in more than two years. The kids are grown and away, so my own visits to the brook have become more scattered and less and less frequent.

Two things struck me after that last visit. First, I noticed how very common and ordinary the brook area is. There is absolutely nothing to set if off as a spectacular natural area, nothing to put it on a register of places, nothing to set it up as a necessity for the rest of the world to visit.

Second, I had to conclude the brook is special, only because of the time I spent there with my kids, my brothers, my grandparents, my friends.

I love the place because I can look at a pool and see my grandmother soaked to her knees and elbows, trying to school suckers to a shallow where I can trap them, or I can look at a tree bridge and remember the day when my son crossed there, almost tripped and fell in the water.

It's so important all of us have these places, either in our backyards or in our imaginations. Places where we can go to create memories, and quiet times with our families and friends. If you can't think of one to go visit, call me, we'll go for a walk along my brook.

Going to the drive-in

Don't we all remember those sweet summer evenings, getting into the car, going to the drive-in? I mean, windows were down and the breeze that washed your face from every side was so warm, so delicate, it only added to the excitement of the event.

And yes, going to the drive-in was an event.

The kids in our family totaled five to seven, depending on the year, and going to the drive-in was central to our summer survival-or to my mother's survival. If it was a summer weekend, and if it wasn't pouring rain, chances are pretty good we made it to the mobile movies. Where else could a car loaded with people find a show and hours of entertainment for a couple bucks?

There was the gallon-sized glass jar, full of chocolate chip cookies, there was a stack of cups, a jug of water or the favored jug of Kool-Aid. Sometimes too, we added a picnic basket with sandwiches, bananas or apples. There would always be blankets to share with my brothers (the sisters had to carry their own, and we all had our pillows that no one shared with anyone.

There was always a bit of jockeying, lobbying and politicking to score one of those cherished seats on the front. Mom always had the spot at the steering wheel, but there was always room for two on the bench seat beside her. The issue that always popped up was whether or not there was room for a third kid in front, and if so, who should it be? Near our birthdays we always tried to catch a break, but as luck would have it, ALL my brothers and sisters birthdays fall between July and October, all seven! Huh, what are the chances? We were not above bartering cookies for that cherished fourth seat, or playing tricks or making secret alliances that could better our chances.

I always knew which sister to sit behind and just where to breath or lean to pull her hair, in hopes that I might be moved forward. It was not uncommon, during "high season" to carry chairs from home and sit in front of the car to watch the show, but mom was always pretty nervous about that, and we could never count on the evening being mosquito free. It was a question of choices.

Brunswick had two drive-in theaters when I was growing up: the Bowdoin Drive-in located about where Wal-Mart is today, and the Brunswick Drive-in, out on old Route 1 about where Grant Road joins that road today. If that selection failed, there was also the Lisbon Drive-in at Lewiston (or was it the Lewiston Drive-in, at Lisbon?) Mom didn't like that Lisbon Drive-in much, used to say the crowd over there was a little rough.

We always tried to get to the Drive-in early. Mom liked a spot near the front, and on a line with the snack bar. We intended to use the swings, slides and ropes under the screen till it got dark, and even in those days, she didn't much like us being far from her sight. She always insisted we stick together, and we never knew when she would be checking.

Yes, we also had to be on a quick, straight line to the snack bar, because that was where the rest rooms were. The sisters always had to use the rest rooms, and they always wanted a brother to walk with them. That was okay, because we got to hang near the door and watch the people come and go for the snack bar food. The popcorn always smelled best, right there at the snack bar door.

Finally the headlights started to play on that huge white screen towering over us, and the horns started to blat all around. We'd join the herd of youngsters running back to our cars, skipping over the gentle mounds to where we all had parked, ever mindful of the cords that connected the cars to the sound. It was never good to hook a cord and pull at a stranger's window. Moments like that could end badly. There was always another last attempt to jockey for a better seat, then we'd all settle in for the cartoons, the coming attractions, and finally, the feature film. Most of the time, we did only the first feature, mom always saying we needed to get home and get our rest. It would be years before I realized there might be another reason.

Last summer, our daughter Abbie and I were talking about summer entertainment and we both realized that she, soon to be in her last year of college, had never been to a drive-in theater!

First I was surprised then I was perplexed, and went to work on a solution. Do you know the only Drive-ins left in Maine today are located in Bridgton, in Skowhegan, in South Portland and in Saco? Those huge flat screens that used to dot fields all over our state are all but gone, sacrificed to the televisions, the video games and the DVDs of the world. I made a personal pledge and said before another year went by, we should find a theater and get her to a drive-in. But it was too soon the last night of summer before Abbie went back to school. "Well dad," she said with a hint of sadness and disappointment, "I guess we don't get to a drive-in this year, either..."

I considered the challenge for just a moment. It was mid-afternoon and we were both deep into other projects. "Hey," said I confidently, "be ready in a hour!" I made a couple quick phone calls and soon we were on the road, speeding the 64 miles towards Skowhegan.

Abbie and I got there as the sun was washing off the screen and the cartoons and short subjects were starting. We tuned my truck radio to the movie, which turned out to be something just a little less than I really wanted to watch with my daughter, and yes, we skipped the second feature, too.

But guess what. We had a great evening together, talking about my brothers and sisters, talking about my past and her future. We shared sodas, a jumbo candy bar, and an over-priced bag of slightly stale popcorn. We borrowed a bottle of wind-x and a roll of paper towels from a complete stranger so we could wash my windshield, and we joked as little kids in pajamas passed us on their way to the rest rooms.

We realized that today, a hot dog costs more than a movie used to for a whole car of people, back when.

We drove home with the windows down, and noticed the moon for the first time in months. I realized that we were sharing one of those moments that both of us might smile about for the rest of our lives, and I realized that neither one of us do that often enough.

This summer, I hope we get to a drive-in movie again, and we'd love to see YOU there!

Topsham Fair   by John Gable

Going to Topsham Fair

Ah, "the Fair."

During one week of the year, every year since 1854, Topsham turns into a carnival, and what a time it is!

I think I first went to the fair with my grandfather. He was an Aroostook potato farmer turned vegetable gardener in Bowdoinham, and every year the best, the biggest and the brightest from his garden, "went to show," at the fair. Every year there would be a ribbon, or three, on his stuff in the Merrymeeting Grange exhibits, and more in the individual's show. He was always most proud when the ribbons came for his potatoes. Every year, headed to the fair in his car, there would be talk of fields he'd kept in Presque Isle.

I'm sure those ribbons brought him a form of validation. For me, the ribbons brought a pass through the gates. Exhibitors got in free, you see.

171

We just liked to hang out at the fair, my brothers and me. I think the fair is where I first became a people watcher. We'd tell our mother we were going to the library, or staying after school, and she'd let us get away with it. We almost never had money, so we'd sit on the fences, our backs to the racing trotter horses, and we'd chew grass and watch all the people walk by.

Everyone came to the fair, EVERYONE! There would be the oxen drivers who spit tobacco, and the "carnies" with the broad shoulders, bare chests, foul mouths and greasy hands. And the drunks. There was never any drinking in our house, so it was very entertaining to watch the guys drinking from bags as they stumbled past us on the great lighted way.

There were big guys in suspended pants; old people with canes; and farm kids who slept in the boxes with their cattle and their sheep. There were the slicks and the freaks, and the freak shows.

And yes, there were the "painted ladies."

"Don't you even look at them," my grandmother would say, she acted like they had some kind of disease. "No lady parades herself in public like that," she'd add. "NO lady!"

But I DID look at them, out of the corner of my eyes, around the corners of canvas tents, and from a stellar perch atop the giant Ferris wheels. "Yes SIR!" I'd watch them bump, I'd watch them grind, I'd listen to every word as their "barker" bragged about what they could do.

Through too many of my little boy years, I used to patch and scheme with my buddies to get a peek into that tent full of cheering, whistling men! I guess it's a flaw in my childhood, or a credit to my mother and grandmother, that I never did.

I was still pretty young when I got MY first blue ribbon at the

Topsham fair…for drawing a picture of something…the premium was perhaps 50 cents, but the ribbon was priceless.

I won several award at the fair for photography over the years, but my favorite ribbon was a plain white, third-place show. I was about 30 years-old, married, and our kids still very young. Rosie Greer (that football player who did needle point) was all the rage. Didn't they call him the "Refrigerator?"

Anyway, I hooked this bright yellow rug for Miles and Abbie's room, Raggedy Ann and Andy were the featured characters. That rug was a thing of uncommon beauty, not unlike those olden painted ladies, and I went proudly to the exhibition hall to enter it in the rug competition. The "unpainted lady" at the registration table refused to believe that I, "a big-handed man" (yes, she called me that) was capable of such fine work! She kept insinuating that my wife must have helped me. Or I had purchased the rug from an older lady. "A lot of that goes on, you know," she announced as she projected her beady little eyes through her bifocals.

No, I did not know!

To this day, I know I should have captured a blue ribbon for that rug, and that woman kept me out of the money. I think that old third place ribbon is rolled into that rug, and waiting for a grandchild to come play on it!

Speaking of money, I remember the year I saw a dollar bill blowing across the midway. I turned after it, snagged it, and had just started to think how I was going to spend it when this huge, meanest-looking Carnie grabbed my arm and said, "hey kid, that's mine." Of course it wasn't, and I chose to say so. "Give it to me," he sneered, "Never," I said. He pushed me, I hit the ground, the dollar was spent.

The fair used to be in October, you might remember, usually hitting Columbus Day on one side or the other. There were special trains and busses, and schools were closed for the week! Topsham used to be the last fair in Maine, and most years it was cold enough to raise goose bumps all over those painted ladies. More years than not, we'd have snow on the tents before the Carnies pulled them down.

Add me to the list of people who liked the late season fair. Now that I'm older, now that I'm over that fixation on the "ladies," I can see the real star of the fair was always agriculture: those great heaps of squash, of fresh pies, colorful canning jars, mammoth creatures, sleek horses and bright apples. Too bad we've moved away from that.

The fair is now 150 years old, and remains an exceptional tribute to volunteers, to the Maine way of life, and yes, to agriculture. It's worth a second look.

Lobster tales at the Marriner's

In a busy year Jane and I might cook 1,000 lobsters, some years even more. Wouldn't you think I could make them like Norman's?

When I entered the Marriner family some 40-plus years ago as an innocent (if willing) newbie, it didn't take me too long to realize some real "baggage" came along with my life's new station. Jane's folks had already owned their beautiful tidewater home for nearly 30 years, and Norman, back in those days, used to dig clams right in front of the place with nothing more than a shovel and a pail! There is an art I never mastered!

Norman was on the school board and Barbara was a teacher in those days, and it was very common for them to hold cookouts for staff, teachers, and friends from town. Jane's younger brother Gregg was a 'theater person' at Vickie's Brunswick Music Theater, and his list of, "friends from away who needed to eat a lobster" was obviously endless. I think Jane and I had been dating maybe a couple months before I was drafted (again?) to help out at my first bake with the Marriners.

Norman put me in charge of firewood, thinking, I suppose, there is no way I could mess it up.

You need to remember, I'm just a Bowdoinham boy. The tide water I knew flows fresh and not a little polluted through Merrymeeting Bay. Sturgeon, smelts and alewives may be common in that water, but a lobster dropped in that murky, brackish liquid would die before it hit the shallow bottom. Yes, there are clams in Merrymeeting Bay, but you eat them at your peril!

Why, I bet before I met Jane, I'd never touched a lobster!

So, for that first bake, eager to learn and more eager to please, I showed up with a trunk full of the best-cured firewood I could steal from my mother's barn. Beech burned hotter than oak, I knew. Maple split easy, burns quicker and makes an easy fire. Norman rolled his eyes, slammed the trunk and told me to take it all home. "Dry pine and spruce slab is all you need," he said. Lesson one was over. I decided I'd better just shut up and watch the master cook.

Norman built his fireplace of concrete blocks, (15) topping it with a four-square piece of ¼-inch plate steel. Under that he built a bed of snapping-dry spruce slab, pine boards and newspapers. "Needs to go from zero to 200 degrees in five minutes," he liked to say. "When spit bounces," was another expression of his. It means that the plate was hot enough for that bed of wet seaweed and fish.

A classic Marriner bake consists of 30-40 "bugs," (Norman's slang for lobster) and 25-30 pounds of soft-shell clams, garnished with two dozen hard boiled eggs, 25 hot dogs and some thirty ears of corn. He'd say the hot dogs and eggs were needed because cholesterol is naturally very low in lobster. He'd never admit he'd rather eat a hot dog rather than lobster.

"Tuck them in tight," Norman would say six times as he wrapped the whole meal in cotton sheets and painter's canvas. "Leave 'em alone, let 'em cook" he'd add, for those looking for a peek as the whole mess baked in its own juices.

Thirty minutes later, one of the prettiest sights you'll ever remember in Maine unfolded when Norman opens yet another bake. Lobsters now as red as the coals left smoldering under the steel plate, clams sweated white by the heat, corn as bright as the sun, eggs and hot dogs, "split open done."

Norman would put the whole thing together in a wheelbarrow and haul it off to a picnic table where it would be married perfectly with salads, pies and cakes crafted by Barbara and Jane, his "two girls."

Before the fourth of July, Jane and I will have hosted a half dozen bakes for family, for friends and for folks from away. Norman is gone now nearly two years, but I have to tell you, each time I throw bushels of 'bugs and clams" atop a blazing fire, I miss the old guy's broad shoulders and broader smile. And there's always a moment when I catch myself hoping this bake, and this life, is up to his standards.

Remembering John N. Cole

Add me to the list of people who will miss John Cole. Both personally and professionally, John was one of the standards I could use to gauge my own life.

When I was a teenager, John was a newcomer to Maine and renting a house on the shore of Merrymeeting Bay in East Bowdoinham, and not far from where I lived. He often hired me as a babysitter for his two kids, and when I went to high school and he edited the Brunswick Record, he hired me to "help" the hometown news correspondent, and to do some school sports reporting. He even conned me into writing a short-lived column about skiing in Maine. One summer, I helped him paint his house.

I recall a late night ride home with him after a stint with his kids. It was the night before deer hunting season was to open, and we had to stop on Pork Point Road to watch six deer bound through our headlights. They were making the last mile to safety on Swan Island, he guessed. Animals tend to be smarter than people, he announced. Think about a world where the animals have the guns, he suggested.

John wrote a letter of recommendation to the college I wanted to attend, and I suspect he worked quietly to help me get accepted. I know he cleverly articulated reasons why the school might overlook my casual attention to things academic in high school, and hinted there could be more substance found deeper within.

After being drafted, I made the decision to go into the Army, to become a paratrooper, to volunteer for duty in Vietnam. Once in Southeast Asia, I wrote him and offered to produce a column about the war, which he vigorously and continually opposed. His response was a three line letter telling me to bide my time, to get home and then write the story. "The Army has ways of dealing with guys like you," he cautioned, but then he took a collection of my letters sent home from the war zone, and crafted a poignant essay about those troubled days.

John once read an AP wire story and assumed I had just been killed in Vietnam. The eulogy of me he wrote was inspiring, to say the least. Many times after that, he used the item as an example of why it's always important for a reporter to check and recheck his facts. When I came home from Vietnam, John printed a number of features by me in his new weekly news magazine, the Maine Times. He also printed several Vietnam essays I wrote in those days, and he became a piece of the process that brought me through my Vietnam experience less tarnished. John also helped me make the decision that sent me to Washington DC for the dedication of the Vietnam memorial. That precious weekend, helped by him and a family of friends in DC, proved to be one of the pivotal times in my life.

John and I stayed in touch over the years, even served together once on a discussion group. He always wanted to know what I was doing when we met, asked about my family and wanted to know if there was any way he could help me. I always knew he was sincere, I never knew him when he was not.

Last fall, John showed up at the 55 Plus Center to talk about our fledgling Veterans' History Project. He smiled when he said it was his first visit to the Center, said he thought it was a place for "old fogies," to gather, and he was delighted we were going to get this "veterans' thing" going. He promised to help with the interviews any way that he could. "Those old guys have some good stories to tell," he promised.

John was a tail gunner in a WW II bomber unit. I'm sure there was a good story there, and probably two. The absence of John's story, and the lack of that wonderful gravelly voice, will make our veterans' collections just a little bit poorer.

The lack of John's voice will be felt by us all, for a very long time to come. John was one of those folks I'll always wish I had around but now that he's gone, I'll always be glad I had some time to learn from him.

Rites of September

The Golden Rod in our field is waist deep, already dripping with pollen and ever-changing tones of yellow, setting the stage for that eventual frost. The monarch butterflies are massing on the milkweed, making good on their goal to be on their way south before cold weather consumes them. The evenings are noticeably cooler, sooner...shadows are longer, and there is a new, more measurable moistness to the lawn each morning.

Nick and Zach are off to college, bus drivers have practiced their routes, and teachers are putting their finishing touches on all those classrooms with all those newly waxed floors. My brother Grant, NOT teaching after 42 straight seasons, is certainly suffering from some sort of withdrawal. He can't even talk about it, and I expect he's pacing the floor of his house, looking for something to do. I'm thinking the first day of school, I should play hookie for three hours, get him out somewhere and buy him a beer. What are little brothers for?

Our gardens were so-so, cucumbers by the bushel, string beans by the pound. But now Jane wants to eat the beans we planted for drying and shelling, "they look really good," says she, and our tomatoes were a disaster, defoliated first and bored by some unfound worm, or something. The row of sunflower plants is taller than I, and their blooms promise to dull the gloom of declining fall days.

The list of stuff I should have done is almost as long as the list of things completed, and now, Jane is wondering if we should have hired a kid or three to get more painting done. I remind her that we had NOT intended to do that south roof on the house this summer, and there is never a way to predict how many weekends we would be giving up to foul weather, to sitting on grandsons, entertaining friends from away, or cemetery business or clambakes. It seems like June was just a few weeks ago.

The freezer is full of blueberries and strawberries, and I'm making plans with Nate and Gabriella, ordering potatoes, beets and carrots to put away in the cellar, into what I still call Frank's Famous Food boxes. Even they were impressed with the simplicity of my system, and Miles was delighted to recall that an integral part of the process is to make a late season trip to the beach and collect the fine, salty sand. His father is no dummy. Time to show another generation how to put away food.

Jane is thinking that next season, maybe we should order more veggies from the kids, and grow less in the garden. We'll have a long winter to debate that idea.

But wait, all is never lost! September and October in Maine offers some of the most picture-perfect weather on earth. Mountains are waiting folks, Borestone, Katahdin, Doubletop or Roundtop, and the canoe and kayaks can be launched from a hundred local sites in a matter of minutes. We need to remember that winter is long, summer is short, and fall is the season that makes the difference for us all. Pick a day and enjoy it.

Sox fan in the Bronx

Yankee Stadium is not my favorite baseball park and I'm not even a fevered fan of baseball, but I can sense a good time and an historic moment when I hear of one. Certainly any chance I get to ride on a bus for 14 hours, you better believe I'm all over that!

It was my neighbor Jon's fault. He IS a Yankee fan, probably the last one living and well in Bowdoinham. Twice in the past decade, it has been my honor to nail a pair of red socks to the front gable of his house, which is just down the street from mine. I hope you get a sense of the feelings here.

In the dark of winter last, Jon decided it was important that he and his young family go to Yankee Stadium one last time before it is replaced by Steinbrenner's latest tribute to excess. Jon tends to do things right, and do things BIG when he does them, so he made some calls, tweaked some plans and before we knew it, there was to be a bus leaving Bowdoinham...destination, the Bronx. The pressure built to sign on.

My father-in-law, Norman, IS a professor of baseball. If he's forgotten it, there is no reason for me to know it, and I still believe he knew Yogi Berra personally. His heart is in Boston of course, but he was game, at least for a while, to visit the house of the Babe. The original plan was for the two of us to make the trip, but as the day drew nearer, he worried about his knees at age 92 and thought the long bus trip might be too much. He begged off. I even tried to trick him into going, but in the end, Norman knew best.

It was a little overcast that morning as coolers full of beer and seats full of kids assembled at Bowdoinham's town landing.

Fifty-four souls, one VIP tour bus…8a.m. The bus smelled fresh and new as we climbed aboard. Mothers checked lists like drill sergeants. Two drivers were on hand. I asked Jon about stewardesses, and he laughed. "They're on the Boston Bus," someone yelled. The bus climbed the long hill past our house, I-295 southbound was open, so we took it. We sang, "Take Me Out to the Ballgame," twice as we rumbled through Freeport. The kids aboard were watching a movie when we rolled past Hadlock Field. First break for food and other necessities came in Connecticut.

The Cross Bronx was everything it always is. I love to drive, but can't see myself piloting a bus amidst all those crazy, hurried, harried people. Twice we spotted the Empire State Building through the smog, and once we diverted a conversation about the missing towers of the World Trade Center. We knew we were close when we started down a street with elevated trains. We knew we were there when we saw "Yankee" this, or "Yankee" that on the bars and storefronts.

Yankee Stadium really is impressive. Yes, Jon, it really is. Sure, they all but strip search you at the main gate, more concerned about people sneaking in free water or food than they are about explosive devices .I did not have to surrender my bag of chocolate "gorp" but it took some pleading. I think I made the guy feel sorry for me. Maybe it was the Red Sox T-shirt I was wearing. The immediate and constant press of people stifles even a guy my size. And there is a real beer smell to the place. Maybe the stadium is getting old. Maybe it does need to be replaced.

We had seats in a nose-bleed tier slightly inside the left field line. We were right behind Johnny Damon the whole game, but decided he couldn't throw a ball to us if he had to. Several of the kids (and one of the mothers) tried to get his attention but he could barely hear us.

The Cincinnati Reds beat the Yankees 2-0 that night. It was a regulation game and we were back to the bus by 11 p.m. The night air in New York was fine, but again, the crush of people was tough. Did I mention we never lost even one kid? Seven more hours on a bus, several stops for coffee, the ride back to Maine was less than exciting. Bus seats should be bigger. A father, sitting right behind me with his two daughters was encouraging Jon to do the same thing next year, only make the destination a Sea Dogs game in Portland.

We got off the bus back in Bowdoinham about 5:45 a.m. I dragged myself up the hill, opened our kitchen door, tripped over a cat and relished the idea of "sleeping in" some three to four hours. Then I heard two little thumps on the floor. Jadon, our grandson, came 'round the corner, delighted that someone was up and ready to play. "Grampie," he said, and tossed me a baseball.

Maybe it's cultch, maybe just crap

I confess, I am a saver. I have piles and piles of stuff in places that would (and will) startle a squirrel.

I keep old pictures. I love old books. I have piles of old newspaper clippings. I keep boxes of old parts, jars of used nails. You want to borrow an old Down East magazine, I just might have it. I love (and keep) old hand tools. I collect pennies. I treasure a jar of marbles. On my living room desk I have a Blue Ribbon beer can I sent home to my mother from Vietnam in 1967. Forty years ago, it held unexposed film, sea shells and bamboo seeds, and now it collects miscellaneous pencils and pens. Mom saved it, so why shouldn't I?

I keep stuff because I know I will (or may) use it again one day. I keep stuff because it would be hard or impossible to replace, and yes, I keep stuff because I simply can't bear to throw it away.

I'll pick up two, maybe three brochures, whenever I pass one of those information stations at the supermarket, just because "I know" it's good to have a bus schedule for Maine and Massachusetts, information about a farm in Patten, or a museum in Bangor. Sometimes I pick them up because a picture or a color catches my eye. I mean, who can say when I'll need that stuff?

I don't think I'm compulsive. I think I'm thrifty.

One of the many things that makes my Jane SO special is the way she deals with this disease of mine. She lives among and has to look at these piles, which sometimes overlap and sometimes tumble into HER (usually tidy) work space. She'll point at a pile and tell me it's time to deal with it. She won't throw it away. She won't move it. She'll seldom even touch it.

She'll point at it and give me "the look" and she'll do that again, and again, until it's gone, or moved.

I can attribute some of these stashes of stuff to my interest in local history. Think about some other person cleaning out their house. They find a bag or box of old pictures or letters or clippings. They know to get it to Frank. "He'll know what to do with it...he'll get it to the records center, the meeting house, the historical society...he won't throw it away." Before you know it, it's gone from their house and into mine.

My work desk has bothered more than one boss. Paper can accumulate to two, even three, inches deep on the outside corners. But here's the thing, folks...I really can find stuff. Unless someone messes with my system, more often than not, I can grab a piece of paper by its smallest corner, give it a confident yank, and it "WILL" be the very piece I was looking for. Doesn't that upset a person who clears his/her desk every evening before heading home!

Unorganized piling? I choose to call it horizontal filing. But now I'm really up against it. Jane and I are planning to move, selling our house of 30-plus years. The piles are suddenly a BIG issue. Our realtor friend looked at them, smiled, and the words "unclutter" came from his lips. I think "crap" was muttered as an afterthought. He even made a jerking motion with his thumb, just for emphasis. Jane didn't need to be coached. I did. I saw Jane's lips twist into a hint of a smile. I sensed an "I told you so," coming. And the clock is ticking. The piles have to go before we can list...certainly before we can show. And this is the summer I want to be outside mowing lawns, doing gardens, chasing cats, sitting in chairs, taking naps. I do not want to sit at a table and sort through cultch.

I spent my last rainy Sunday morning going through two

boxes of stuff. I was motivated. Maybe these boxes weighed 50 pounds. I didn't count, but that means 2,000 to 3,000 pieces of paper. Some unknown force still compels me to look at every single one of them. A few things were filed away and many more were recycled. One was a missing piece I sat right down and offered a belated response. I am SO glad I didn't lose that! Most were thrown into the woodstove to await the next chilly evening. I emptied one, then two boxes. I felt tired, like I had done a day's work.

Jane came home from church and I proudly displayed those two empty boxes. I really expected a pat on the head. I almost worked up a sweat, I assured her. She rolled her eyes and pointed at another pile.

"That one next?" she asked.

Keeping Clutter off My Desk

I created a bit of a stir at the Center recently when I slipped in over the weekend and stripped some 50 pounds of loose and disheveled papers off the top of my desk.

People who came in Monday quickly noticed the polished, false-wood top of my desk for the first time and the rumors started to fly. "Frank has quit," some suggested kindly. "Frank has been fired," others suggested, not so kindly. "They moved Frank's office back to the rear of the building where no one can see his messy desk," at least one deeper thinker suggested.

It occurred to no one that I had voluntarily cleared my desk as a tribute, and as a simple gesture of good will and respect to Jim Pierce, still a friend and our departing interim executive director.

I suspect Jim's idea of a cluttered desk might be three or four papers, neatly stacked, certainly numbered and probably alphabetized.

It took maybe a week into Jim's administration for us to get into our first confrontation over my desk top. He alluded to wasted time, lost opportunities and he said appearances mattered. More than once, he threatened to come down with a garbage can and sweep my desk clean. But the weeks turned to months, and whenever Jim asked me for something that he considered hopelessly lost in that pile at my right hand, I was always able to retrieve it. At some point, (I think) he just decided to focus on other stuff.

Arthur G. Staples, an essayist on "common themes" and an old Bowdoinham mentor of mine, once wrote a piece on what he called "littered" desks. He called a man's desk a "hub of industry" and a place where no other man, or cleaning lady, should ever venture. He suggested the perfect location for a desk is in a corner and against a wall so "paper, relic and curios" might accumulate "without worry of collapse." Here is a man after my own heart and a new nemesis for Jim.

I once told Jim of a day in a former life, when I was out on a job and needed a name and phone number. I knew both were on my desk. I called my shop and asked an associate to go over to my desk and face the wall. "Of course I'll hold," I told the lady. (I didn't carry a cell phone either.) She got to my desk, moved my chair and over the open phone I heard her tell another person what I thought I was going to do. She said something like, "he thinks he know where a phone number might be in this awful mess."

They were enjoying a good laugh when I broke in. "look down to your right," I said, "and find a corner of a piece of orange paper." I ignored her attempts to apologize.

"I see the paper," she said. "Is that where the number is?"

"No," I answered. "Lift that piece of paper carefully so you don't disturb anything and the information I need is right under it on a lined piece of steno pad paper." I think I told her there was a coffee stain on the piece of paper.

It made me nervous when anyone else worked at my desk. It still does. She quietly gave me the phone number and when I came back to the shop she said she had a "new respect" for my filing systems. I don't think Jim ever got there.

Back to Mr. Staples for a minute: "I do not try to urge habits of untidiness," he wrote, "but I do say that whomsoever chooses to depend on a littered desk should be indulged in his idiosyncrasy. He should not be disturbed in his domain of dreams and peace. He should retain his prized pyramid of papers, books and clippings if they please him, and let one touch them at their peril." He concluded about his desk, "it loses nothing, it preserves much. It's all that can be created by me."

If Jim knows I have a box full of loose papers under my desk, he is gentleman enough not to acknowledge it, and you know, when I get a spare minute, I'm going through it, filing stuff, following up with stuff, throwing stuff, and yes, Jim, I DO throw more than I file. And there is a little piece of me that feels oddly satisfied at the end of each day.

Now my office desk has been pile-free for nearly a month, but no one should assume I've turned a corner. Now, my goal has to be to try to impress Stacy!

Hands-on teaching shapes future generations

"Ha," I laughed to Jane as I hung up the phone. "Grant has another whole new set of victims." Those Sunday evening phone calls have become numerous enough over the years to be almost predictable. "Here we go again," I chuckled.

The call was from a local dad, seeking inside information for a child just assigned to my brother, Grant's science class at Mt. Ararat Middle School. First day of school, Grant had offered cash awards for the first students to bring in Monarch or tomato caterpillars. Grant, then puts them in a terrarium, the students watch them as they spin cocoons, and finally become butterflies.

He has been known to band butterflies, if you can imagine. He calls this first show his Monarch show, and it's the first of a series of hands-on, mind-opening experiences where the kids end up dirty, wide-eyed and amazed by the study of the simple and wonderful natural world around them.

The parent wanted me to tell him where the best field was in Bowdoinham to catch these green and black Monarch worms and I did. The kid went to school the next day with 20 of these worms in his lunch box, and another school year was begun.

Grant is sort of a legend around SAD 75, and certainly in his own mind. A teacher locally for 38 years, he was there when they opened the high school and when they opened the middle school. (He was there when the opened Bowdoinham Community School as well, but in those days he was a student.)

He has been called the consummate science teacher. That he is a little irreverent to administration may be a family trait, that he is always on the side of his students is unquestioned. My son, Miles, had him back in the last century, came home and said, "Uncle Grant wants me to call him Mr. Connors."

"Is that a question?" says I. "If he was my teacher, I'd call him Mr. Connors, SIR!"

Over the years, Grant has produced videos that entice kids to wander in, and wonder at nature, and therein, is his genius. He can, and does precipitate in students a knowledge of and a curiosity for things natural, and that curiosity seems to deliver in such a convincing, if not shocking manner, that it stays with students for a lifetime.

Another secret is the spare freezer in the basement over to Grant's house. Grant is a collector of weird, natural stuff. For the longest time, there was a bear's head in that freezer, a tiny fawn, pieces of coyotes, and various other things, as "science samples" and he sprinkles them into his science presentations at school in such a way that he seldom has to worry about attendance in his classes. His is not a class to skip.

To this day, thanks to the fact that both Grant and I are a pair of white-haired Irishmen, and seem to bear several strong and similar characteristics, younger people often come up to me and say, "Hi, Mr. Connors." I know right then they must think I'm Grant because no one ever calls me "Mister" and Grant is the one with the reputation as he's often teaching the children of former students these days.

I have this undying respect for Grant. I went to college briefly to become a teacher, gave that up and landed in the Army. I hear his stories of the classroom and realize what a special place he and other dedicated teachers play in the raveling of society. It is safe to say a teacher, a good one, is often the person who makes or breaks a person and shapes the way so many people look at the rest of their whole life.

Congratulations on the start of yet another school year, Mr. Connors, SIR!

Apples, apples, apples!

Arlet.

Empire.

Prairie Spy.

Rome Beauty.

Arkansas Black.

Baldwin.

Duck's Bill.

Gold Rush.

Wealthy.

Russet.

Wolf River.

Cortland.

McIntosh.

This is not a quiz, not really, but I do wonder where in this list did you first think of "apples?"

Huh?

If you're from Maine, if you didn't grow up under a rock, you should have had a clue as early as "Empire." You certainly should have taken notice at "Baldwin," and by "Russett" and "Wolf River," the bud just had to be out of the bushel. Really, if you read "Cortland," even "McIntosh without guessing where this column was headed, well, God help you, 'cause I can't!

Apples are right up there with snowballs as a principal crop from our Pine Tree State.

And don't I love 'em!

I like to pick apples, eat apples, even hang out with apples. Apples remain one of the few basic food groups that I dare to cook!

Before I knew any better, I'd pick apples if for no other reason than to plug them at passing trucks, or slow moving sisters. During my stint at college, I supplemented my allowance, and elevated my sensitivities, as a picker at Berry Hill Orchards and a few other Franklin County farms. There are few images of those days that are any clearer in my mind than recollections of hitting an orchard early on a frosty Saturday morning, ladder over my shoulder, ready to face a day of picking, I worked at my own speed, took a break when I needed it, filling a pallet, then two, sometimes three on a good day, always wondering how those skinny, chain-smoking Indians, and Jamaicans, could still pick so much faster than me.

I guess I was too much in it for the experience, and they wanted their beer money.

I've fallen from trees, been pushed out of trees, had apple-laden limbs fall on top of me, and never broken a bone in my body. I love to stretch and capture the highest, sunniest, brightest apples, and will go to no end of trickery or deception to get them.

Welts and bruises the size of apples have appeared on my back, shoulders and head as grim testimony to battles I have won, lost or engaged in apple orchards.

It's good that an apple a day is the basic prescription from the best of Maine practitioners. They remain pretty cheap, always pretty good, always pretty effective. Right here I need to say that picking them should remain a piece of the prescription, folks. It is very good to eat them, but so much better still to get that ration of fresh air, sunshine and life as you pick them.

There are still a few pick-your-own operations in our area. Seek one out with your children, or grandchildren, and go get a bag, a bushel or a barrel. The act is more important than the quantity, any day.

And then there is cider.

I'm not talking about the pasteurized stuff you get at the supermarket, even though that stuff is better than most any soft drink. Find a place that still presses their own, or get to a carnival or fair where cider pressing is on a calendar as an event. It's worth the hunt. The flavor is unforgettable, one you'll treasure from one season to the next. A buddy of mine is the proud owner of an antique hand press. I'm enough of a purist to borrow that thing, find a couple old trees with wasting fruit and pick it clean, just for the quart or two of cider the old apples will offer.

REMEMBER, the best cider always comes from a blend of apple varieties off several trees, and the same formula holds for applesauce.

I have not a tiny reputation at the Center for the applesauce I produce. Peel the apples, slice regularly, add sugar, lemon juice and cinnamon to taste. Any dummy can do it, and this one does. Many a men's breakfast has been made memorable by this sweet nectar, honest.

So we've finally come full circle.

I'm not enough of a cook to have all the details, but apple chips in muffins, apples peeled for sauce, apples added to stuffing; Apple butter, cider, apple slices lathered in peanut butter… Get into the habit… apples, apples, apples!

The important thing is to get them, eat them, enjoy them. They are one of the things that make fall fun!

Chimney fire!

With not so much as a hint of pride, I have to admit I've endured more than my share of chimney fires.

Perhaps you've never lived through a chimney fire, never experienced that throaty, terrifying roar as it ripped through the very heart of your home. Perhaps you have never seen that brilliant orange plume of flame, blasting into the cold night air like a jet engine from the crown of your chimney, while you stand helplessly on your lawn as the fire spatters gobs of molten creosote onto your roof. Maybe the sirens, those flashing emergency lights, the ladders and the scampering, cursing firemen, ordering you to get out of their way, have never had to stop in front of your house.

Folks, if you haven't done it, you should try very hard to avoid it.

We live in a drafty old house and the woodstove in the living room pretty much makes the place habitable during the coldest months. For years, our stove of choice was a cast iron relic that generated creosote as a by-product of heat. The "airtight" design of our "parlor furnace" would allow us to run a continuous wood fire from November through March, but, since Jane and I both work, and since we both sleep, there are long strings of hours when the fire simmers untended with its damper closed tightly, and creosote was our reward. There were indeed some days when we wondered if we were making creosote faster than we were making heat.

The firemen never quite believed in my efforts to clean our chimney, though we do try faithfully, three or four times each season. The first real cleaning is always done in the fall, well before the first fire is needed.

At Thanksgiving, when the kids are home to help (and to encourage) we'd scrape it again. We'd pick a warmish day during the Christmas-New year's break for a third brushing, and a fourth, usually around Groundhog Day. Each time we swept, we cleared a gallon or three of that nasty, shiny black stuff from our clean-out door, and we'd blurt a prideful, "AH,HA," to anyone who would listen, "this will never start a chimney fire!" Most times, I'd show the nasty pail of "yuk" to Jane, who shared my enthusiasm for avoiding unscheduled visits by firemen.

I easily remember that first terrifying chimney fire like it was yesterday. Norman and I had been to Skowhegan, and when we rounded the corner on Center Street, we were confronted by that characteristic black pall over the house, and the dozens of flashing red lights that marked the trucks blocking our street. "OH NO," I said, "those lights are in front of our house!"

Another chimney fire we were on vacation, visiting our in-laws in Florida. We'd left a friend tending the cats and the fire and watching our house. Well, the fire got away from her that very first night, and she called us collect, in Clearwater. "HELP!" she cried, we shared her feeling of helplessness over the long distance, advised her to hang up and call out the fire department.

Funny, she never appeared interested in house sitting after that.

Most of our chimney fires occur because of human error. THIS human's error! We'd get home at night, the place would be pretty cold. There was supper to cook, the phone to check, cats to feed, kids looking to do something. Somewhere in there I'd open the damper, toss in some wood and let the fire get going. Sometimes I'd let it go too long!

On the lucky nights, I'd catch it, close it and watch closely as the heat and the tension eased. Crisis avoided.

On the unlucky nights, the temperature continued to rise, the stack would get cherry red and, "F-f-f-woom-m!" that chimney took off like a jet engine!

Pretty soon, Allen, Irvin and crew would arrive with their trucks.

We live in Bowdoinham village, with lots of neighbors around always ready to report anything I might be doing that was wrong, or stupid, always ready to call out the firemen after that first telltale hint of black smoke. Heck, Irvin lives maybe 200 yards away, in clear view of our place.

On chimney fire nights, I'd often catch myself wishing we lived farther out of town.

I admit to delaying, even resisting, some of my calls to the fire guys. I knew the chimney had to be pretty clean, and I had this neighbor, God bless you, Carmeline, who always told me a "little chimney fire," was not a bad thing. She said she'd let her fire go a little every morning, and that kept her chimney clean as a whistle. Yes, Carmeline lives away from the village on the back side of our hill. I liked to call it a "controlled burn." And a few times I got away with it.

But Jane never seemed to share my logic for controlled burns, and neither did the firefighters.

Now, I have to add a word here for the firemen. These guys all volunteer to climb around on my ice-shrouded roof, usually when it's dark, cold and storming. They run from their own warm houses in the middle of a frigid night, risking limb and life to keep me, to keep all of us safe. More often than not, these guys take off their boots before they come into my house to check the stove. They are gentlemen to my family and polite to me. They don't have to do what they do, but it is good that they do.

Several years ago, we bought a new stove. This thing is a marvel of steel and stone and engineering. It even has a window to see the flames. It has a catalytic combustor. This thing has the firemen thinking I've left town! I meet them in the store and they ask if I've stopped burning wood!

This will be my third year, chimney fire free (If I don't mess up) I'm wondering if that doesn't make me some sort of reformed wood burner/chimney fire specialist. I do feel good about this, but I have to tell you, somedays I miss seeing the firemen.

Going to Florida

Mom took us to Florida before Walt Disney made the Sunshine state famous. It was October, 1951, she packed us five kids into her two-door Chevrolet coupe and away we did go.

I have often wondered at the courage this trip must have demanded. I mean, I've jumped from planes, I've skied vast mountains, walked uncharted woods, and done other crazy stuff. But think about driving 1,600 miles, unassisted, with five kids under the age of ten?? Not me!

There was an older lady in town who started this whole idea. She had friends in Florida who had invited her south to pass the winter, but she didn't drive. Anyway, this nice lady, we'll call her "Aunt" Mae, offered my mother gas money and $100.00 if she would deliver her to Saint Cloud, Florida.

Mom's mother Sadie Ruth was dead-set against the idea and probably got downright rude to Mae, trying to scuttle the idea, but I know Grampie supported the plan in his effective, subtle way. Mom had been through so much. Only 29 years old, widowed by the war and left with five kids. Grampie would think a change of space would be a good idea and he quietly worked for it. He promised to tend the house, feed the chickens and mind the pets, removing the obstacles that made the idea seem silly. I bet he even slipped her some emergency money. "Don't tell my Ruth," he used to say as he quietly worked his magic.

I remember Mae brought more stuff than anyone expected – even a big hat box that she insisted on carrying. Luckily a neighbor had built us a roof rack complete with straps and big suction cups, and Grampie again worked his magic. That man could easily pack twenty pounds of stuff in a ten pound bag and still arrange it so the things you really needed were always on top.

By this time, even Grammie was being helpful and had packed fresh sugared donuts for us all. Mom had packed a couple gallon jars of cookies. There was a thermos of water and a big bag of apples, and a picnic basket in the back window that smelled really good, but we weren't allowed to touch it until we reached the Massachusetts line.

My brother and I weren't sure who Massachusetts was but we were looking forward to meeting him.

It was awfully early…still dark. Everything had been packed the night before and Grampie made sure the car was fueled. Gas was 26 cents per gallon. We all packed into the pillow-padded back seat…five kids wide. No reason for seatbelts here. The sun rose behind us as we drove through Freeport. Glenna and Grant stayed awake to keep Mom company… but Ruthie, Alden and me…we were asleep before we passed the baked bean plant in Portland.

At the Kittery Bridge we stopped in a park, found a restroom and chased seagulls till there were none in sight. Mom insisted, "run till you're too tired," she'd say, then "run some more." Mae waited in the car.

Mom drove, always. Mae sat in the front passenger's seat, always being more queen than aunt. None of us got lap time, not even the girls, not ever.

You have to remember there was no Interstate 95 system, so U.S. Route One was pretty much the road of choice. Route One went through the heart of darned near every city and town that was anyplace. It could not have been easy making time.

We reached New Jersey that first day, ate in a fancy Howard Johnson's, and then ran through another park while Mom catnapped. Then taking advantage of the "new and high speed" (55 MPH) Garden State Parkway, Mom drove all night while we slept, stacked against each other on that wide rear seat.

Morning found us in Washington, D.C. surrounded by those fine, white buildings. Mom napped again while we walked with Mae around the Washington Monument.

South of the Capitol, Aunt Mae opened that mysterious "hat" box and produced a trove of crayons, paper, books, metal soldiers, chocolates and mints. I saw her wink at my mother and tell her she had a wonderful family. Mom drove south. "Let's go find Richmond," she said. Grant and I chuckled. We knew Richmond was back there in Maine…what could Mom be thinking?

We made Georgia late that afternoon. Mae took a cabin and we six had another. Mom paid 50 cents more for the extra bed. We ate again in a restaurant and Mom went to sleep just before the sun went down. My brothers and I gave the sisters the slip, got out behind the cabins and went looking for alligators. Grampie had asked us to bring him back a Florida alligator. We found a snake and some great moss we took to bed with us. (the moss, not the snake.)

I remember the big yellow sun sign that announced we were in Florida. We all cheered and waved at people we passed. Mom stopped again for gas, pleased to see she could get five gallons for a dollar. We didn't like the guy pumping gas. He made faces right back at us. We told him we were from Maine and he asked us where Maine was. Mom told us to settle down and to watch where we were going. "Look," she said, "there's a herd of Brahma bulls."

Five faces pinned to the windows, we pounded down the remaining miles of road to Saint Cloud. Mom yawned and told us all to sign a post card to our grandparents. It was the beginning of our warmest winter.

VOTE!

It's such a simple exercise, really. You step in a booth and quickly, without uttering a word, you speak your mind.

Why would anyone hesitate, or not bother?

My first remembered act to support the vote was as a boy scout, probably in 1959-60.

John Kennedy was running against Richard Nixon for President, and my job, our troop's challenge, was to "get out the vote". We wanted to encourage everyone in Bowdoinham to vote. Our goal, as simple idealistic kids, was to see that everyone in town got to the polls. We offered rides (our parents were to drive), we offered reminder calls, we went door to door, and we put up posters. I remember the posters as representations of the Liberty Bell. I remember we received Certificates of Merits from the Town Clerk that year. She told us we made a difference, that because of our efforts, more than one half of the town's registered voters came to the polls and voted.

I was still a simple, idealistic kid, in the fall of 1967, when I wrote a letter to my town clerk, asking to register for my first vote. I'd just turned 21; I was a paratrooper in Vietnam. The process had a whole new meaning for me. My goal then was to vote against Lyndon Johnson, (this was in the days before his, "I will not seek nor will I accept your nomination" speech) and to vote for almost any peace candidate. I guess I was being selfish. The clerk sent me the forms and my first ballot was an absentee ballot. I have to believe that it got to town in time to be counted.

What sticks in my mind about that first vote are two things. When I got the ballot, I carried it for two days, and slept with it for two nights, in an effort to keep it dry and presentable. When I finally put it on a helicopter, it was slightly wet, slightly muddy. I have often wondered if the ballot counters ever noticed. The other point is rather humorous. When the clerk sent me the registration forms, she sent only the Republican enrollment card. The GOP was always her party affiliation, and she saw no reason not to help make it mine.

I've been a registered Republican, an Independent and a Democrat. I don't want you to think of me as casual or unfaithful, disconnected or uncommitted. Rather, put me down as one of those folks that Maine is noted for, changeable, unpredictable...old fashioned...willing to follow the man (or woman) who serves us the best.

I've been a municipal town manager, an elected Selectman, and a town committee person many times over, but the job from which I take the most pride, and staying power, is poll warden and/or ballot counter.

Bowdoinham tends to be traditional. It is about evenly split, Republican vs. Democrat. There are also more than your average Independents, and Greens, for a town with just under 2,000 registered voters. We do hand-marked ballots that are checked and counted, then rechecked and recounted. We're a light year away from (or behind) hanging chads, and other electronic ballot wizardry. And that's a good thing.

Election is a 14-18 hour marathon for wardens, and that's a good thing, too. We hang our flags and sharpen the pencils before the polls open at 8 a.m., chat and glad-hand voters for 12 hours, consume coffee and cookies at the fire auxiliary concession, and then lock the door, dump the ballots and count. And count again.

There is talk this year about an electronic, or mechanical

counter. Ballots will be marked in the old way, counted in a new process and by a machine. I'll believe that when I see it. The Clerk wonders if the Town's ready for such a radical change. So do I.

Come November, we're all going to be pretty badly burned out by debates, political ads, personal discussion, and all those posters along the road. More than once, we'll all have wished the process could just get over.

But the process is not over, not until you make that trip to the booth. You have to believe that your vote will count, it is important, and is necessary, that this country will not function without it. It is that important.

See you at the polls.

Thanksgiving is my favorite

THANKSGIVING is my most favorite holiday, and, I have to admit right up front, it's more about food, family and friends than it is about giving thanks.

First comes the food, led by turkey and all the trimmings. To me, trimmings means mashed potatoes (or baked in an off year) white and dark-meat turkey, brown gravy, turnip, squash, peas, cranberry sauce, breads and salads...more stuff than will commonly (or possibly), fit on the basic plate. And dessert! In my house, dessert has always been PIE...pumpkin and squash for sure, minced meat or chocolate of course, plus any one (or four) of a dozen fruit combinations that Jane may feel like doing.

We usually have 12-15 people at out Thanksgiving table. The in-laws, our kids, some of my family, a few of our friends. We always serve in the dining room...candles, cloth napkins, water glasses… all the good stuff comes out. Most of the food ends up on a side board or table, just because the serving table is so full.

Actually, there is often an attached table added to the extra leaf of the big table, and even then, sometimes we forget a space. Sometimes too, we're not really sure who was invited, and who plans to show up, not until the last minute.

There will be a fire snapping in the fireplace, another going in the living room stove. People and cats fight for the very best places on the couch or the softer chairs. The television is on low, first for the parades, then for the football. My father-in-law loves that football. Conversation steers away from politics, so no one has to get defensive (or offensive).

Most frequently, the best conversation begins with "remember the year." or "remember when," and someone launches a story about something that happened ten years ago, or fifteen, or when they were young.

There was the year our friend Jack showed up in his Volkswagen year our friend Orie, "field dressed and plucked" a turkey, right there in our front yard. There is always discussion about the first year that Henry and Marty celebrated Thanksgiving in Maine, and the first year Henry remembers bringing "green stuff" to our table. (Green stuff is a unique Jell-O, cheese, and nut concoction of questionable food value.)

If I'm prompted even a little, I'll tell about the Thanksgiving dinner I had in Vietnam, 1967, and Norman will tell about a shipboard feast or two.

There is talk about who's sick and who is not, who's in school, who's married, and who is getting a divorce. Sometimes there's talk of cutting the Christmas tree, and usually there's talk about who got their deer. (I don't hunt any more, but it's nice to act interested.) Maybe there's a letter (or e-mail) from the cousins in New York, Washington DC, or Florida. Sometimes, we'll phone someone, and find out how they're doing. Verizon has to eat, too.

A few of us will walk down to the brook, around the "block" (as that's defined in Bowdoinham) or down the street to visit neighbors. We finish the day as the 'turkey drug' kicks in, crashing on the couches, talking quietly one-on-one, or reading something in a quiet corner.

I usually close the festivities with my most favorite quote of the day: "I wonder what's for supper."

I just love history!

My girl Abbie and I were driving along the Kennebec River last weekend on our way to Augusta. We were enjoying the ride, relishing the company, chatting intermittently about things that mattered and things that didn't.

We'd driven a mile or two in semi-silence when we rounded a corner and a stretch of river opened in front of us. Excited, I pushed my finger general towards her face and pointed, saying, "See? Right down that bank is where Benedict Arnold and his army picked up their bateaus and started their march on Quebec, they would have changed history if..." She looked at me casually, interrupted and said, "Huh, Who?? Should I know who it is you're talking about?"

History has always been a passion of mine. I like to read it, study it, think it, love it… just enjoy it. A dear old friend of mine once called me a "throw back" to an earlier age. She said I belonged in the 18th Century, and called mine an old soul. I considered her observation a genuine compliment.

Abbie is smart, quick, articulate and capable. She's finishing her master's program at the university next spring. Having admitted all that, I don't understand for a second how she missed Benedict Arnold.

"You like history, dad, I don't," she offered a quick summary in what must have been one of her best, if shortest, analysis in her new social worker life. We drove another mile or two, me suffering mild shock, she offering that sweet little smile of hers that never failed to make her old dad melt.

Then she offered some clarification. "You know," she started, "I remember liking just one of my history classes in school. Mostly it was boring old stuff…bunches of dates, lists of wars,

211

people and treaties. I just never got interested.

Driving the next several miles in her spotless little Mazda, I told her how a buddy of mine and I talked of re-walking the whole Arnold trail when we were her age. We actually did more miles than I can believe, now that my knees are going bad. Just for good measure, I threw in some of my best anecdotes of Father Sebastian Rasle, and of the assault on Norridgewock. I dropped Robert Coffin and Kenneth Roberts' name liberally, hoping to impress. As I babbled, I can tell you I could almost smell the campfires from Arnold's army.

I guessed she might prefer to listen to the radio. Then came that smile again, and Abbie offered a shrug of apology. "You do make it sound pretty interesting," she said, "but I just don't see myself ever walking to Quebec they have roads, you know…"

Abbie and I soon found something else to chat about, but I wrote myself a mental note. I knew I had a new life's goal. Somehow, I had to help her see the fun, the joy, the reward and the life in the study of my state and this nation's history!

When my kids were kids, we were regular readers of Robert PT Coffin and Laura Ingalls Wilder. We even tried some of the Elijah Kellogg tales, when I could find them. Reading was often how I managed to put them to sleep. Now I wondered, was I misguided?

Our family has made several trips to the headwaters of the Kennebec, we've found some old Indian petroglyphs, and once Miles retrieved an ancient musket ball among the pebbles of the riverbank. We've spent many a weekend, peeking around many an old place. Could they have been entertaining ME?

I know the dangers of trying to inflict my values and my

interests onto my kids. On anyone!

But this is a New Year's resolution, folks. I'm going to dust off some of those old books, laugh and talk with Abbie and Miles about the old time, and maybe, just maybe, help them see the stories in a new and better light.

What do I have to lose?

Perfectly piled wood

There's a great ol' saw that says firewood is the perfect fuel, that it "heats" you three or four times during the cycle of its preparation…let's see, let's count. Once when you cut it, once when you haul it, again when you stack it, again when you 'fit' it to stove length, again when you re-stack it outside, again when you move it inside, and yes, finally, again when you carry it to the wood box. Yup, that's easily three or four times.

My mother is a great stacker of wood. In fact, I believe she has elevated her stacking to an art form. Her season's supply of wood stands at the front of her house like little monuments to perfection. I kid her about it, but only because it is one of the reasons I respect her, and because I know the process is important to her.

Five piles per year, a half-cord per pile, each stack standing straighter than my five brothers and sisters stood as we waited for the school bus, all those years ago. Each pile is stacked apart from the other in such a way to get maximum sun and maximum air, as she lets the wood cure outside and naturally. She re-stacks it in her garage, just before the fall rains start. Somehow, she always knows what that date will be too.

My mother grew up in Aroostook County, where winter was a serious thing. There, wood was always stacked near the house just so you could find it after the snows started. There was a wood shed on her place, out from the kitchen, out past the summer kitchen, down the enclosed shed, just beyond the outhouse… who doesn't recall THAT long, cold walk… but at least it was out of the blowing snow and frigid air.

My grandfather used to keep his wood a season or even two ahead, all the time. He would drop it and stack it, "stick length" in the woodlot, and let it "air dry" for a season. He is the same guy who used to say that next season's fire wood should be fitted and stacked before Easter Sunday. There were two reasons for that, he'd add: (1) the wood has a full summer to cure before use, and (2) it was a chore to prudently finish in early spring, before the hundred other things came along that used to occupy a farmer's mind, and his back. Grampie also knew the risks of wood burning; i.e., chimney fires. In Mapleton 75 years ago, these were serious problems indeed.

I consider myself a recreational user of firewood. A gas heater in the kitchen and an oil furnace in my basement have made my living room woodstove, "something warm to back up to," or "comfort heat." Abbie used to keep her shoulder warm all winter in the shadow of our parlor heater.

I have toppled trees in the woods and hauled raw wood to my yard. I have cut and carried eight-foot logs and four-foot bolts. I've had "log length" delivered, and cut it myself. Now that I consider myself a little older and wiser, my wood is dumped in the backyard, cut and split to a proper and uniform length. I suspect Grampie would be appalled at the price, and upset that I still let Easter come and go without a serious effort to put my wood away. I admit that. But the one thing I still insist on is the stacking. I like to watch that pile as it grows, and I like to be sure it goes up straight, and true.

Each piece of wood has its place, and sometimes, to get it right, I need to replace it. I always stack bark up, to best shed water. I don't have the old woodshed, so sometimes I get pretty fastidious about the way my pile is covered. I know a cold, January day can take a wheelbarrow full of wood, and I know my dining room woodbox will hold a wheelbarrow load of wood. I have been known to count the wheelbarrow trips as I stack.

This season's wood has been stacked, fitted and covered now for a month. I know this August heat won't last, and soon, the trips to the woodbox will begin again. That's okay, now that I accept that one of my connections to my mother, and my grandfather, is that woodpile.

Pork Pointers   by John Gable

Pigs and me

Pigs and me, we go back a long, long way.

When I was just a piglet myself (by today's standards,) the

family had this "pet" pig we called Josephine. She was one fine sow. But she was in the barn for pork. I knew it, my sisters and brothers knew it, Grampie knew it...I think even Josephine knew it.

Josephine was born in Topsham, the old pig farm at (or near) the Town Farm on Foreside Road. When we made our infrequent trips "to town," we almost always went down Foreside Road to see the pigs, and on a good day, to stop and feed them. There was an extended family of pigs right there beside the road, where we could toss apples, old bread or whatever we had, and they always seems appreciative. Josephine was the prettiest in the litter, so mom marched all five of us kids into the farmer's kitchen, struck her best deal, and we packed her into the car for the trip to Bowdoinham.

Josephine flourished under our pampering. We pulled grass for her, carried food scraps from the table, and waste food from Curtis' store. My oldest sister was caught reading comic books to her more than once.

Grampie was probably the first one to worry about the future of Josephine. We had cats for pets in our house, no room really to add a pig to the list. Since mom was often worrying, sometimes wondering, where future meals were coming from, she knew there was no room in our house for a pet porker. Summer wore on, and the situation only grew worse. Josephine was "escaping" from her pen, (where it was smelly and muddy) and wandering around the yard with us kids. It didn't take us too long to realize she love having her tummy rubbed...She never tried to run off, why should she?

When school came for my older sisters and brother that fall, Josephine more than once, walked the path behind Dudley's and followed them off to classes. The Raymond sisters (teachers) were NOT impressed. I think it fell to my grandfather more than once to retrieve Josie from the playground.

Mom would swear there was no connection, but that was the one fall/winter in our lives that she pulled up stakes, left Bowdoinham and drove to Florida for the winter. Josephine stayed behind with neighbors and suffered the ultimate fate of an animal destined to join the food chain.

We did NOT receive any pork chops in the mail. Mom still says pigs are a lot of work, and not worth the effort.

One of my lasting images as a paratrooper in Vietnam was the day this Infantry Sergeant called in a helicopter rescue mission to evacuate a big sow pig and five piglets from a village. They were shipped safely back to a refugee center, much to the dismay of the chopper crew. I like to think Josephine had a hand in that.

When Jane and I set up housekeeping in Bowdoinham some 25 years later, pigs were back in the picture. We were restoring an old farm, and pigs in a pen remain an effective and environmentally friendly way to reclaim the land. Each year for four or five years, we raised five pigs. One pig was food for our table, one was for my in-laws. One was raised for my brother's family, one for a chef in a Brunswick restaurant, who gave us "tons" of food wastes, and the last one, raised to market, provided cash from its sale to pay for the grain of the rest.

We cleared the best part of an acre over the years and it still is a beautiful lawn.

But Jane would remind me of the days we spilled 10-15 gallons of "slop" in the back of our truck, or when she ruined clothes ripping them on nails in the crude pens I'd build, or of the complaints of neighbors when the pigs "busted out," or the wind changed, and those piggy smells blew into their windows.

Delivery day for the pigs was always special. Friends and family gathered to round them up, put them in wooden boxes, and take them to "market" in Durham or Gardiner.

Pigs are smarter than the average animal (and some people) and I believe they can talk with each other. The first one always went in her box easiest, and, as the oinks turned to squeaks and squeals, it often became next to impossible to round all five up. Breakouts were common; disasters never unheard of.

Our love for liver and onions came from those days. In our circle of friends we found it was very common for one in a marriage to "love" pig liver, and for the spouse to dislike it. Every fall, we'd do a liver and onion party, liver was cooked outside, on the grill, and those who wanted to eat it did. Pork and beans were always available for the dissenters.

The other day, my Miles asked why we still didn't raise pigs. Jane immediately became defensive. He has become a master gardener, and I think an early lesson of his came with converting the pig pen to a garden. We talked very briefly about opening a new business, Pigs to Go, we'd call it. The plan was to buy a few hundred feet of electric fence, graze pigs for people, for a fee, and move them around all summer. In the fall we could take them in, or create another liver party.

Jane thinks the business plan needs a little work.

I was a hunter once

I started my days in the woods of Maine with a Daisy air rifle. I paid for that weapon selling Grit newspapers and Cloverine salve. I learned to love that gun, as hunters so often do, and that gun, in turn, gave me the first taste for the kill. That little B-B gun and I terrorized chickadees, chipmunks and occasionally passing motorists. Once, I shot my older brother in the rump!

My next gun was a hand-me-down 22 caliber rifle. With it, I learned I belonged in the woods. I would take that gun and camp among the spruce and fir, feeling one day like a pioneer, another day like a commando, and the next day like the great white hunter on an African safari. With that rifle, I became caught up in the mystique of gun handling.

I would go out in search of deer, bear and rabbits with that little 22, and I would return with a squirrel and woodchuck, a soda can, or nothing. Usually, nothing. Once, I shot the head off a bird from about 50 yards. That achievement won me lots of status on the bus ride to school, where we boys took great pride in telling, and retelling, the tales of our hunting exploits.

I came of age with that little 22, but I knew I was a man the day my big brother loaned me his 30-06. I knew I had arrived. That rifle was a heavy stocked, scope-mounted rifle, my first real weapon. It really was too heavy to lug in the brush around Bowdoinham, but I never really noticed, I relished the labor. That gun aroused feelings in me that must be common to all hunters, that feeling for the wild, a feeling of man against anything. A feeling of real power.

My next gun was an M-60 machine gun in a place called Dak To, Vietnam. Those feelings were still there, perhaps a bit

221

more acute, and certainly a little more brutal. For those first few short weeks, it was just another hunt, me on the trail of new game. All of that changes, however, when the game shoots back. The hunt takes on a different perspective when the game has guns, too. Suddenly, one of my friends had been hit. Suddenly, the hunt wasn't fun anymore.

Home in Bowdoinham after my year in the war, friends and I tried to pick up where we all had left off. We drove to Moosehead for a fall hunt, looking for deer, alert for bear. There, in the big woods once more, the adrenalin started to flow.

It was wet that day in the woods. Wet and quiet. A buddy and I were walking up a ridge, perhaps a quarter mile apart. My friend got cold and worked his way towards me. I was carrying the coffee. He snapped some brush as he approached, but didn't speak. I was startled, turned quickly and nearly shot my best friend.

The hunt just wasn't fun anymore.

The next fall found me on the shores of Merrymeeting Bay, duck hunting with a 12- gauge shotgun and the gentle young woman who became my wife. We had no boat, so we walked the shore, expecting to surprise birds in the browning, tide-washed grasses.

But the first duck we jumped had already been there. It was already crippled, bleeding and dragging a broken wing through the mud. Here again was the hunted, trying desperately to save itself from the hunter.

Jane took my shotgun, and I took off after that little duck, slipping, splashing, and sliding in the mud, making what must have been a ridiculous spectacle of myself if there were other hunters watching from the shore. We caught that duck, carried it home and did all we could do to make it comfortable. That night, the duck we'd name Bruce, died quietly in the little straw nest we fashioned together for it.

I haven't carried a gun since that October day.

I still love going out in the woods and now suspect those walks are what I liked most about hunting anyway. I enjoy the animals of the woods even more now, and have shared that love with our son and daughter. Walking in Baxter State park last weekend, enveloped by falling leaves, crystal water and first growth pine, it was easy to replicate the rush of so many other, earlier walks, and never miss the touch of the rifle.

I would never offer a judgment for or against other people who hunt. Were it not for some very real and personal experiences, I suspect I would still be out with them, beating the brush in pursuit of wild game. Since hunting season opening day, however, I've had several occasions to ride the back roads so often frequented by hunters. I can only look and the cars, sometimes parked bumper to bumper on these side roads and wonder…hasn't some of the fun gone from their hunt too?

One sweet mess of clams

It was a crystal day in October and Jerry wanted to go dig some clams. It had been a while so Jerry, age 94, called his high school chum Norman, age 93, and asked him about going. Norman thought for a minute, maybe two, and told Jerry to drive over. He had nothing better planned, he said, as the Red Sox weren't playing 'til after dark.

When I first met Norman, he could dig a "mess" of clams easy and still have plenty of tide left. He used to dig clams with a spade, claimed it was easier on his back. I can still see him tossing a shovel full of muck like it was a spoonful of potato, then plucking a clam or four from the splattered mud with all the deftness of a surgeon. But folks, that was 40 years ago.

Norman lives by the shore, and jokes that he intends to die there. Jerry arrived, the two debated for a minute and then Jerry decided he would dig with a traditional clam rake, or hoe, and leave the shovel in the barn. They had to make some concession to old age. He looked at the field between them and the shore as daunting, but Norman said not to fear, he had a golf cart. They piled in together and headed for the shore. The tide was still going out, there was plenty of time.

Norman was torn, but admitted to his chum that he didn't think he was capable of making the precipitous plunge from field's edge to flats. He admitted to his 94-year-old friend that "maybe" he was the one in better shape. Good decision, Norman, someone might be needed topside to go for help.

Jerry told Norman not to hover, to go about his day and return in an hour or so. He would be just fine, IF he got down over the bank. Norman walked with Jerry a short way, showed him where the poison ivy was, and cautioned him about slipping on the leaves or mud below. "Clams aren't worth a broken neck," Norman quipped.

Jerry went on and was soon down the path. Norman turned to return to his cart and lost his balance. He hit the ground like a shovel of muck and grunted.

Norman will admit he doesn't have the body strength to recover from a flat out position unless he has someone, or something, to grab for leverage. Jerry was gone down the bank, and pride would not allow Norman to call him back. He considered his options, remembered he had his Life-Line call button on, then rolled to his belly and crawled toward the cart. "The lifeline is for emergencies," he muttered to himself.

Norman made it to the cart, drove the field, got home and patched a scratch with a Band-Aid. He took a few nervous looks toward the shore, but Jerry was nowhere to be seen. By the time he'd retrieved his morning paper, it was time to go looking for Jerry. Back to the cart he went.

At the shore, Norman moved the cart as close to the rude path as he could. There was a second when it occurred to him there were some details missing from his recovery plan, then he heard Jerry crashing up the trail. "That was good," he thought.

Soon his friend was in sight, slogging up the trail, clutching a plastic bag of clams like he had a bag filled with gold. But Jerry didn't look quite like Norman remembered him. Covered with mud across both legs, his torso and one arm, Jerry was a mess. There was more mud in his hair, and splash spots on his face.

"How was the digging?" Norman asked. "Seen better," Jerry observed.   These two old friends raked some of the mud off Jerry's clothes, climbed onto the cart and took deep, relaxing breaths. Jerry held up the bag with his six prized clams. The two drove over the field in silence, remembering earlier days, I suspect, and pleased by their accomplishments of this day. They hosed off more muck from Jerry when they got to the house, cleaned the cart and decided perhaps they shouldn't tell too many people about their day.

"Don't want anyone thinking we're crazy," Norman said. Jerry left the clams with Norman to cook. I suspect he was worried about going home and explaining to his daughter where, or how, he got them. There was a slap on the shoulder as the two said so long, and Jerry headed down the drive.

It didn't take too long for the story to get out, of course, and now the tale of "the old guys" going clamming is fast becoming a piece of the folklore that is Jane's father. Naturally, the first thought is of the danger Norman and his friend exposed themselves to that day, but we should not linger there long. The real story here is that two old friends thought up an adventure, did it, got away clean and can laugh about it.

I think old age is supposed to have some days like that.

A season for wreaths

Grampie tipped his head forward, looked over his glasses at me and said sternly, "BOY," (he used to call me that when he needed my undivided attention) "you just decided what YOU are getting your grandmother for Christmas," then he all but threw the scissors back at me. I could not have been more wounded if the scissors had struck me.

I'd been hoodwinked and I knew it. My brother and I had spent the morning "picking" boughs in the woods, and he had purposefully handed me Grammie's scissors to use. Grant had his pocket knife; mom didn't want me carrying one. "Use the scissors," he'd encouraged me, and I did, all day long, snipping limb after limb, watching as the pitch and dirt accumulated on those spotless blades. I should have known better, and Grampie, with that one look, agreed.

Picking boughs was a December tradition in our house. It was one of those chores we boys always enjoyed, partly because it led to another fun project, the making of holiday wreaths. As kids, it was our job to help Grampie make wreaths for our front and back doors, for his front door, and for the huge door on the front of his barn. Happily, the task started with us going off to the woods, a bag of cookies in tow, and a couple of old bed sheets to fill with accumulated boughs. If the snow was deep, we'd head straight for the railroad tracks. If it wasn't so deep, we'd be down there soon enough. We knew that the best balsam fir, 10-15 feet tall, rimmed the railroad right-of-way, and we knew Grampie would only accept balsam boughs. Besides, walking the tracks was the quick way to get into the woods.

We knew to cut only "five-fingered boughs" about the size of Grampie's hand, and if the morning was crisp and fresh enough those boughs would just snap off in our hands, (or one quick snip of the scissors,) A morning of "good picking" was usually enough to fill a couple sheets, and a couple trips to the woods would usually be enough to fill the barn floor with a fragrant heap of boughs sufficient for a half-dozen wreaths. In a good year there would be enough for a "market wreath" or two, wreaths that we kids would hustle round the neighborhood, trying to raise five or six dollars to fatten our holiday shopping budgets.

Grampie was a master wreath maker. He'd scoop up four, maybe five of those boughs, slap them together with a quick twist and then lash them against the wire frame. "slide 'em up tight," he'd say 28 times in an afternoon, "you don't want anything to sag or fall apart on you." His wreaths would never sag or fall apart on us, that was the guarantee, and he could finish two while Grant and I were thinking about doing our first.

He would start the wreaths as soon as he got home from work, and we were always ready to help him on a moment's notice. Our feet could still be cold from slogging round in the woods, but we soon forgot that problem when he landed on the barn floor between us, telling us the same stories that seemed to change every year.

Grammie would often lavish us with hot chocolate, more cookies or other treats, but Grampie always made it clear that wreath making was man's work, and the stories we were hearing just might not be suited to a lady. This particular day I had another reason for my grandmother not to hang around. Wouldn't you know it, Grampie noticed when I slipped those pitch-stained scissors under my coat.

Work on the wreaths was always finished too fast. The last one built was the huge one for the barn doors, we always twisted wire around a barrel to make the frame and we always worked together to get it built. Grampie always twisted a few pine boughs into that one, saying it is high enough and out of the way so that it would pass anyone's inspection. "This one we do mostly for the cow and horse," he'd say with a wink.

At the end of the day we'd all rub our hands with kerosene to work off the pitch, rinsing them in a pail of cold water and Lava soap before we could go in the house for the final clean-up. Grampie said finally, "let's have a look at those scissors, maybe we can save 'em." He washed off most of the pitch, ran his hand over their blade and decreed, "we can get the pitch but I don't think we can save the edge." He wondered aloud if I had tried to cut rocks with them. I could feel my brother's smile on the back of my neck. Grampie reached into his pocket, pulled out a dollar bill and said, "this will help you out, but I think you better crack open your bank, get to Woolworth's and treat your grandmother to some new shears for Christmas. I'll try to convince her she lost this pair."

BEE-ing patient

My bees didn't make it.

Last April, with all the flair and expectations of a rookie who knew no better, I announced to the world I was becoming a beekeeper. My motives were so pure and unflawed. A hive in the yard would bring us better vegetables, brighter flowers, happier gardens. Everyone knows bees lead to a better world, and in the fall there would be the honey. "Really," I asked, "how hard could it be?"

My Grandfather Miles was a beekeeper. His early days as an Aroostook potato farmer mandated that he keep bees, and there were hives in the "warm corner" of each of his expansive potato fields. When he moved to Bowdoinham, some of the hives came with him. As a youngster, I remember watching him as he tended his swarms, on his knees, no special cover except a knitted cap. He would calmly hum some unknown tune, bees crawling all over him. "Bee's won't sting you unless you threaten them," he'd say, blowing a little smoke into a hive. "We have to protect the little creatures."

So it was a turn of a family wheel when my master gardener son Miles and I went to a weekend class on beekeeping last spring at Wiscasset's Morris Farm. It was a glowing event. A room filled with hope-filled novices and a sprinkling of bee-savvy veterans chatting back and forth, led by a lady named Christine who has known bees on a first name basis for years. There were movies, static displays, hives on exhibit. We took hives apart and reassembled them. We talked about diseases, maladies, and problems. The BEE-wilderment was gone, we were ready to go.

When we called two places to order bees, we were told most folks order in the winter, and were placed on a waiting list. Time ticked on, we worried, we wondered and waited, and finally, the call came. A friend and master keeper in Bowdoinham had an extra swarm of

Italian bees, fresh from Georgia, "They have been in my truck for three days," he said, "you need to come get them now." Another friend offered me a spare hive, my spirits soared and Wayne came the next day and helped me install my one personal swarm. Wayne is a longtime supplier of honey to our family, he came dressed like a spaceman to transfer our bees, open the queen box and get us going.

"You'll have to feed them till the blossoms come," Wayne reminded me, and for the next two weeks, we brewed a sugar and water tea, delighting that the swarm was drinking a couple cups a day.

Dandelions couldn't come soon enough, but when they did, our bees were all over them. I hated to mow, and worried that I was decimating my own herd, but all seemed well. Norman took to sitting and watching the bees come and go, and Jadon and I spent several afternoons, following bees from a bloom to their hive. I even took Silas for a visit or two, much to the chagrin of my Abbie.

It was late fall when we started to question the health of our bees. There seemed to be few and fewer bees in a season when there should have been lots of activity. I worried, I fretted, I finally admitted defeat. By October, we had no bees in our hive at all.

In these cold days of January, I'm laying a new plan for another year. We are ordering a new swarm and prepping for a new season. We're talking about taking another beekeeper's class, and we've made new contacts in what appears to be a very robust bee keeper's support group.

I know Grampie would be pleased.

Trinkets and treasures for the tree

I bet Martha Stewart would consider one of my Christmas trees an abomination. I often have stuff dangling off our tree that even members of my family have sometimes questioned, but that's just fine with me. I think a tree needs to speak for its family, and our trees have been known to speak loudly.

Lights go on first, of course. For the past several years, our tree has been tastefully illuminated with multitudes of tiny white bulbs, and I attribute that change to my Jane's fine taste and influence. But there were years when the bulbs would be large and multi-colored, even garish if you will, and each year we do have 12 or a dozen smallish, real candles, the kind that burn real flames mind you, put on just for looks. I keep suggesting we light them and watch them, but so far, more sane and stronger minds have prevailed

Then there was the year that my kids were into bunny droppings. I was always one to encourage creativity with our youngsters, so we did go to our bunny hutch, we did pick only the very best and roundest and firmest droppings, and we did make this sweet little chain, maybe three or four feet in length, that we did hang on our tree that year. Of course, there were also little baubles made of 4-6 little round poopies, scattered all over the tree. Miles even wanted to lacquer them, but I told him it was unnecessary, this was not a decoration we'd need to preserve and reuse. I'm thinking we dipped some of them in red, white and green paints, however, just to guarantee that unique, holiday flair.

Tree chains, braids, baubles and ropes are a common theme for our trees. They can be two feet long, stretching from one limb to another, or they can be 10-12 feet long. We have made tree chains of popcorn, of dried apples and cranberries. We've had chains of acorns, chestnuts and cranberries. We've made chains of pine cones, sea shells and paper angels, chains of Cheerios, Hershey kisses and dried fruits.

My son Miles has his birthday two days after Christmas, so we often had a party for him in the weeks before the big day, trying to avoid his complaints of being cheated. When he was maybe 10 or 12, the goal of the annual party was to create an ornament for the kids to take home and hang on their trees. Keep it clean, Jane warned. I had pre-cut some blanks from soft pine, and the plan was to make replicas of antique sleds, complete with runners. All the kids needed to do was assemble and paint, I said. Well, one hour into the project, the kids were borrowing my pocket knife and trim saw, and were deep into the custom sled competition of the season. The good news is we lost no fingers that day, and there are still trees in Bowdoinham graced with these sweet, little-boy sleds.

Tucked back near the stock of the tree, in shadows where only the most inquisitive might look, you might find a funky little ornament made from a twisted can cover. Here is my tribute to my own sad Christmas at war, 1967, when the guys and I tried to slip some sanity into our lives by decorating a pine tree someone hijacked via helicopter from a plantation outside of Saigon. We'd decorated that tree with spent rifle casings, stars we fashioned from c-ration can covers, even a couple pin rings from hand grenades.

Christmas is a time to remember the good and the bad.

Of course, there is always the tree itself. I have to admit I'm kind of a Charlie Brown tree guy. I could never suggest decorating a birch tree in our holiday living room, mind you, but I think most of these fancy, perfectly manicured farmed trees are just too far off the mark. Maybe it's a passive aggressive reaction on my part. I grew up in a family where we always harvested wild trees, usually from a neighbor's land. My sisters always had to make the final decision, and the annual search led to mindless meandering through miles of toe numbing, trackless snow, and carrying a tree for hours after the sisters had left it in our care and went home to warm their feet.

So my point, I guess, is to continue to do what makes you and yours happy. Make your tree a part of you and lavish it on your family and friends. That IS what the holidays are about.

Show up, dress up, it's SANTA!

There are some who suggest I lack the temperament, if not the physique, to be a good Santa. To them I say Humbug! HUMBUG!

You want to super-size YOUR Christmas spirit, just dress up like Santa and walk onto a train loaded with kids. Padding will make anyone appear roly-poly, and I swear, if you put on the suit, something magic happens.

I blame my mother for getting me into the business. She used to volunteer for Literacy Volunteers and at a meeting one night, there was fundraising talk of establishing a local Christmas train ride for kids. She dropped my name and said I had a red suit. The rest, as they say, is history. When the Literacy folks opened their Candy Cane Train, I said, "sure, I'd try it one time," and I was hooked. This year I think will be my fifth year.

All I have to do is show up, dress up and act up. What could be more natural? Hundreds of volunteers, from barber-shoppers to readers, give these little kids a ride they will never forget. There are cookies and goodies galore. High school cheerleaders dress like elves and offer exhibitions, sometimes in the snow of Wiscasset.

The Maine Eastern Railroad winds across the Kennebec from Bath, over the Sheepscot, and through the woods to Wiscasset and returns. Kids are treated like the treasures they are, being read to, sung to, pampered and promised. Every kids should have this experience once in their childhood. The two-hour round trip can be life changing.

Santa visits each of the four rail cars at least once on the trip. He hears every wish and hugs every child. He runs up and down the narrow, boot-filled aisles. He tucks notes under his belt. He pauses to be photographed. He 'Ho-ho-ho's," until he is hoarse.

Several stories stand out over the years. My favorite is the little kid who used to live down the street from me in Bowdoinham. He was a common visitor to our house, and his visits usually ended by Jane, or me, giving him a Tootsie Roll for his trip home. Well one year, this little kid and his grandma appeared on my train. I sat in Grammy's lap (she's a good friend, too) and asked his name and where he was from. His eyes filled with wonder as he said Eli, weakly, and added, Bowdoinham. I touched his nose and said, "Bowdoinham isn't that in Maine?" He was delighted that Santa might remember where he lived. "Eli," I added, "Eli, aren't you the guy with the two mean sisters who likes Tootsie Rolls?" You could have pushed that kid over with a candy cane, and before the train clicked down the track another hundred yards we had converted another child to the magic of Christmas.

I think I enjoy the day more than the kids. Every 10th kid or so looks at me like he is looking into the very eyes of old Saint Nick himself. And when that happens, my day is complete. If it happens with 50 kids, or 100, you just know the kind of day I'm having. Mothers and grandmothers pat my hand and thank me and Literacy Volunteers for a job well done.

Everyone is off to a merry Christmas. When my shift is over, and I spin in on my heel and wish all a very Merry Christmas, I only wish all my friends from People Plus could join in the salute.

Going black at Christmas

There's always a little piece of me that goes black each Christmas. Give me the good times, the gifts, the family and friends, the lights and food, the music and merriment (and I do love every one of those moments) but I don't ever get through this holiday of holidays without my private periods of pensiveness, even sadness ... and you know what, I've decided that's all right.

If I live to be older than Norman, I'll never forget that men's breakfast at the Center when, during a quiet moment, I asked the guys to recall a "sad," rather than a merry Christmas.

There was an awkward silence, then my good friend Jack Longworth cleared his throat and started an incredible, heart-wrenching monologue about his night as a 19-year old kid, when he had survived what would become known as the Battle of the Bulge. Jack talked of frozen feet, fractured nerves, primal fears. He never raised his voice, but told of being scared and shivering in a forest in France, hoping for dawn, fearing all the while he'd never get to see another Christmas, even another dawn, or get to make that prayed-for trip back home. When he finished with an almost gentle, "thank you" for listening, Jack's smile was weak, if genuine.

"I can tell you every Christmas since has been better than that," he concluded.

I had my Christmas at war, and there are thousands of brave American men, and women, in Iraq and Afghanistan today enduring that same lonely, terrifying ordeal. If you know one of these young warriors, or have a friend who can give you a name, take 10 minutes to sit down and send them a card with a couple pictures from home, and offer some kind words. You will never know the glow such a moment, such a simple gift, will bring to a very, very dark place.

But you need not go to a war zone to encounter holiday blackness.

Analyze your own neighborhood, your own town for the darkened houses of the elderly, the lonely, the hungry, the desperate. Not far down any street, you can find people who feel abandoned, neglected or hopeless. ANY street. There are folks with families who have just lost jobs, or elderly who have lost their families, their friends, their motivation. And remember, the lights and expectations of a holiday season always kicks that lost, abandoned feeling a notch or two higher in us all.

You can make a difference by offering a small donation to any of a dozen local funds that distribute food, gifts, even fuel, to the needy, or you can take a more direct approach. You can pick a family and drop off food, or select a young family member and be sure that one child gets a few extra gifts. Ask an older, shut-in neighbor if he or she would like to ride to Portland, or Freeport, and see the holiday lights. While you're in that house, check it for heat and basic cleanliness.

One way to be certain your Christmas season is most joyous is to be sure the season is shared.

The day is what we make it

From 2,000 feet, looking out the cargo door of our chopper, Hill 990 was no different from the hills surrounding it, until I noticed the impact flashes of the artillery rounds. On my right and on my left, new faces made this assault very different and not a little more frightening. I'd been in Vietnam for seven long months, and this one was like starting over with new guys all around, and this time, I'm in charge!

The helicopter made a plunging dive for the hill, side guns and rockets blazing. Acid smoke blew through the open cabin. Closing on that burning, tortured ridge line, we leveled for a moment and the crew chief yelled "GO!" Six, maybe ten feet above the rim we tumbled out, and in another second that was filled with hurricane winds and burning embers, the chopper was gone.

Firing blindly at nothing, we dug hot dust from our eyes and stumbled to the shelter of some wrecked trees. "Hold your fire," I yelled, trying to track my new team. I grabbed at a pack that had a man attached, leaped over one, then another downed tree, gathered my guys together and pushed to the extreme edge of the ridge, some 50 feet away. Behind us and down the ridge, more choppers were dumping more troops.

In less time than it takes to remember, a couple hundred men were dropped on that hilltop. We swept to the limits of the crest, linked right and left with other teams. We posted security, everyone else stripped to the waist and started to dig in. It was hot, terrible work, but the goal was to be prepared in minutes for a counterattack, or for enemy mortars, if they came.

Slicks came in, loaded with chainsaws, bars, c-4 explosive and sandbags. In less than two hours, the once lush tropical hill was stripped of vegetation, and lead teams were popping smoke grenades to bring in the artillery unit and their cannons.

We all took ten minutes and feasted on a can of cold C's.

"Christmas is four days away," observed Jesse, from Ohio. Maybe he was 19, probably not. Three weeks ago he was back in the Buckeye state watching TV with his mother. His voice dropped. "Guess this won't be much of a holiday, " he added.

An NCO in an Army unit often feels like a babysitter, I know that now. "Look," Said I, not knowing what to say, "the day is what we make it."

Vietnam-era forward assault bases usually had two positions for the line troops charged with defense and support. There were the slit trenches, where on-duty men half laid and half sat, watching constantly for what happened next; and there was a covered bunker, where off-duty troopers tried to eat, sleep, maintain their gear and play cards. Our trenches were set, we put a team on the bunker.

Six or a dozen men routinely move in and out of one of these reinforced holes in the ground. If you're being mortared, they are the safest place to be, otherwise, no. They stink, they're dark, they're wet. The good ones have pallets for flooring, most did not.

The log ceilings were always too low to allow anyone to stand.

"Hey," someone said, "let's make us a Christmas bunker." With four days to the holiday, and expectations of a truce, we all decided it would be a good idea.

We cut the floor a foot deeper, and into the sidewall we cut a fire pit. We reinforced the sidewalls with steel plates from a pallet, we fashioned a chimney out of two warped mortar tubes. We had our fireplace, we agreed no one would hang stockings on its mantel until they were completely and freshly washed. On the downwind side of the bunker, someone tunneled a hole for a window to give us extra light and ventilation. We stole common wire and pirated power from a command bunker generator.

When Bobbie went into the valley for water, he came back with a tree that looked absolutely nothing like a Maine spruce. We decided it was perfect. We decorated it with spent M-16 casings, and ornaments crafted for C-ration lids. Doc gave us gauze bandages to wrap the tree, and someone made little paper cones, ripped from a Playboy magazine, so our tree could have three angels!

Each dusk, I and several of the guys had tiny comfort fires, and sang Christmas songs until the word filtered around for us to quiet down. Men who never wrote home went into our fancy bunker, used our lights and sent holiday greetings home. The Protestant Chaplain, who almost never came to our forward bases, did come, spent two nights and led us in prayers.

A re-supply chopper came in blaring carols on its loudspeakers. By December 24th everyone's spirits were lifted, ever so slightly.

On Christmas Eve, during the holiday truce of 1967, my squad's radio crackled and we received orders to set up a listening post and reinforcing ambush in the valley below our firebase. We crept through the wire an hour before sunset, leaving our Christmas bunker to guys from Bravo Company. Troopers sang "Silent Night" as we slipped into the darkening jungle. Eight of us spent that Christmas Eve in the jungle on our bellies and butts, listening, watching and waiting for the enemy.

I heard Jesse sobbing in the night and kicked him to be silent.

For the past 40 years, and because of that night, it has been a Christmas duty of mine to try and make someone's Christmas just a little better, and, if I happen to get caught in a singing of "Silent Night," I just cough my way through the words and try to keep a dry eye.

Two yearlings

It's the eve of Jadon's first birthday already. The red eye of the digital clock mocks me flashing 3:46 a.m.! It disgusts me to be awake but I am, so I move ever so cautiously, trying not to wake Jane and not to disturb fat Maggie, the cat who sprawls on the other corner of our bed.

But move I do. I twist to get my feet out, and then flat to the cold floor. I leave the room dark and make my way downstairs. I sit on the couch, bathed and suddenly captivated by the stark, white light of the full moon.

Our Jadon was born on the full of the moon. No one sees as I smile at the recollection.

How quickly this year has passed. New friends are made, old friends are gone, but suddenly, so suddenly, this vital, incredible young life, this grandson, has become the focus of so many things we do.

Outside on the dark, bleached lawn, a movement catches my eye.

Head down, shoulders arced toward me, there is a small deer under our bird feeders. I have been throwing stale bread around our bird feeder again and he must be in it. I twist on the couch for a better look. I'm surprised that this young animal appears alone.

I creep through the dark, soundless house, make it to the shed door where I can slip unseen onto the back lawn, not 50 feet from the feeders and the little deer's flank. I mean him no harm, you understand. I would offer him extra stale bread if I had it, but I have this sudden desire to approach him, to test my skill against his.

I wished I had stopped for slippers and I know I should have taken a coat, but I still proceed in the shadow of the house, moving toward this young deer. And then, there's something else. As the cold starts to drench me and I realize I should go back to the house, I smile at my situation.

My mind moves back to little Jadon. This boy, who is so young he has no idea that a deer is anything more than a stuffed toy, will love this story one day…his Grampie, barefoot, and half-dressed, stalking a deer in his back yard. There were many moments years ago when my son (Jadon's Dad) and I would do things like this, and now, there will be opportunities like this for the next generation.

The very idea excites me.

But, back to this little deer. His head is still down, still nibbling at whatever was left on my lawn. I stop beside the last tree that offers cover, squat and look the area over very carefully. Where is this little guy's mother? I wonder, is she gone from us…lost to the November hunt? I wait for a snort or call from the woods behind us, but none comes. Could this little yearling be all alone?

Our little grandson has become the center of so much. He spends no time alone. The kids still check in the middle of the night to be sure he breathes. He is so dependent on so many for so much. We all hover ever so carefully as this child makes his first guarded crawl, his first step, his first steps. We wonder about his first word.

We hope, we plan, we dream.

The yearling deer is startled by something. There is a flash of white as the moon reflects in his round dark eyes, and another flash as his tail makes its own swipe toward the moon. He turns as he leaps, and with three quick bounds, he is gone.

Their paths are so different and so much the same. Much relates to planning, but so much more relates to chance. Can we really do more than hope for the best for them both?

God speed little ones.

Santas I have known

I became a Santa's helper quite by accident.

There are some who might suggest I have a flair for the dramatic or for the comic. Others might hint that I perhaps enjoy scaring little kids, but thirty years ago if you'd suggested to me I would spend December weekends wearing a tight, sweat-inducing bright red suit, a stringy white beard and a cone-shaped hat, I probably would have looked at you in disbelief.

Since 1980 however, I've had enough hours "suited up" at The Highlands, at local churches and fairs, Wal-Mart, the Pejepscot Historical Society and others (last year there was a four-hour stint on the Candy Cane Train for Literacy Volunteers) so that today, I can almost claim professional Santa status. I do it because it is unscripted fun, it's rewarding, and it puts a real twang in my own Christmas spirit.

There is a neighbor family down the street, several kids under the age of ten and a mother, very sweet and energetic. She was visiting our house several years ago complaining that the kids were making her crazy with their demands. There was a hint that one or two might not make it to the holiday in one piece if things didn't get better. I was suiting up for an evening party and suggested she go home, give the kids that Santa lecture, you know…"he sees all, he knows all, if you're not good little boys and girls, then…"

Thirty minutes later I crept to the kid's kitchen window where I could see all were eating supper. I put my bearded face to their glass, tapped twice with my white-gloved finger, pointing at one kid, then another. I spoke not one word.

Seeing Santa at that window brought an immediate and

positive result. Next day they were doing chores, opening doors, being nice to the point of surreal. Every year since I've returned to that window, and these kids, nearly teenagers now, still harbor just a glimmer of belief.

I also recall the night I was driving to Topsham for an evening gig, and all Santa-suited up. I crested a hill on a one-way street and was confronted by a street filled with Christmas carolers – 20 or 30 strong – and at least half of them were kids! I couldn't back up. I couldn't speed up. There I was, Santa Claus trapped in a blue Chevy Caprice. Both hands on the wheel, I decided all I could do was try to drive through the group unnoticed. Now there was a plan doomed for failure. I inched the car toward the group and was making headway when some little kid screamed, "SANTA, SANTA!...that's SANTA driving that car!"

Kids crushed on my car like teenagers at a Beatles concert. I locked the brakes and put the thing in park. Trapped! I knew there was a real danger I could hit someone in this swirling throng of Christmas revelers. I sat there motionless for seconds that seemed like hours. White, excited faces were pasted to every window of my car. I sprang from the car, having no idea what would happen next. I planted my feet and held my ground. "MY reindeer," I shouted, "I can't find my REINDEER! It will be Christmas in a week, and I can't find my Reindeer!!"

The crowd went hush. You could hear a snowball drop. There was a bunch of milling going on, and few of the kids would even consider eye contact with me. It was one of the smallest in the bunch who finally broke the stalemate.

He slipped through the crowd, locked his arms around my leg and looked up with more love than most kids can muster. "I'll help you find them" he volunteered. The "ohs" and "ahs" from that crowd were all but unanimous. I felt like the genuine Father Christmas when I patted that tiny head, promised to come get him if I needed him, and watched as the crowd magically parted to allow me to continue my search.

So this season, if you see a Santa look-a-like ringing a bell outside Grand City, drop some coin in the pot. It won't be me, I promise, but chances are it's someone working to bring a happier holiday to someone else. It's worth the coin. Isn't that what the season is all about?

Doing degree days

When I was a kid, my stepfather had a small fuel-oil delivery business in Bowdoinham. We had a couple 3,000 gallon fuel trucks, kerosene routes in two or three towns, a dirty old guy who worked on oil burners, and furnace oil that sold for 16-18 cents per gallon!

Oh, how ol' "Hink" loved January and February. He'd go to his office window every morning, (the business office was attached to our house) he'd rub his hand together and say, "this is gonna' be another 45-degree day!" and then he'd smile.

If you didn't know how he was thinking you might just dismiss the comment as a strange or novel way for him to look at his day. But we boys knew how he was thinking, and we all knew what was coming next. He'd look out that window, read his trusted thermometers, make a couple quick notations on a scrap of paper, do some quick math, sit at his desk and haul out "the book."

"The book" was his Degree Day Record. I think he kept it for years, I maintained it for two or more. I can only wish we had it now, each daily high temperature and each daily low temperature, entered right there in black and white. Add a little note about wind and another about precipitation. Think of that for a second, accumulated local weather observations for two, probably three decades! What a great statement that little volume would make today about global warming.

Webster's dictionary will tell you that a degree day is a way of indexing home heating oil consumption by tracking a day's "mean" temperature. No computers or Doppler radar needed here, folks. If you accept 65 degrees as the best possible average daily temperature, you have a starting point. You obtain your day's high temperature and the day's low temperature, and average them. Subtract that number from 65 and you have the number of "degree days" consumed for that day. Pretty simple, really.

Our area in Maine consumes some 7,500 degree days in an average season, July 1st through June 30th. There are weeks in July, August and September when not one degree day is consumed. There are a couple weeks in January and February when every day produces some 40-45 degree days. Those would be the days that "Hink" looked forward to... he was selling oil by the truck load, the brothers and I were slugging our way through snow drifts to find fuel plugs.

My stepfather "Hink" is gone now, so it's safe to tell you that one of the very few benefits to driving a fuel oil delivery truck would be the naps and "down time" spent on the side of the road somewhere. If my regular deliveries were caught up, and there was oil left in the truck, it wasn't uncommon to sit roadside in Richmond, or Topsham, or Dresden or Brunswick, and wait for a radio call for a special delivery. On some of these breaks I'd be doing school work, sometimes I'd be resting up from my weekend just past.

Once I took "Hink's" degree day book and did a Frank-style scientific study. The goal, I told "Hink" was to better predict the fuel oil delivery process and the amount of fuel we might need to purchase! It made perfect sense to me!

I found the heating year could be divided into ten parts each part getting 750 degree days. Sort of.

Using July first as the start date, I found it was November 1 (four months) before the average consumer used 750 degree days. By December 1, a second 750 degree days were gone and by Christmas, less than a month, another 750 degree days were gone.

January would consume 1,500 degree days and little February (only 28 days) consumed 1,500 more! March backed off to consume a surprising 750 degree days, April-May at least (at last) 750 more.

Yup folks, that mid-December to President's Day string of ugly winter days is fully ONE-HALF of our heating season. Aren't you glad that's over for another year?

"Hink" was always a tough guy to impress. My extensive research offered him no new insights. "Hey," says he, "Winter is winter, cold is cold. We get winter, it gets cold. We don't need science to study that."

Maybe "Hink's" right. But all these years later, on a cold and windy day when I'm glad I'm NOT sleeping in a truck on the side of the road, I still catch myself calculating the degree days, and smiling.

A list for Jadon

My son and daughter-in-law delivered a 7 pound, 6 ounce grandchild – Jadon Miles Connors – to this world December 5, 2006, and all are doing very, very well, thank you. I did say that just the way I intended it. This tiny young man is a "grandchild!" My grandchild! They can birth him, they can feed him, they can even raise him (as they should, and as they will) but let there be no mistake, this boy belongs to me, too!

I do stumble a bit over the idea that this little guy will always be a native of Rhode Island and not a Maine man. I could consider that an accident of birth, were it not all so very well planned. Then it occurred to me that Maine men are built, not just born. At this boys first Christmas, I hand-delivered a three-page list of things this little guy needs to do in the next few years of his life if he is to "grow up right," under the watchful eyes of his Grampie. Things like walking in the woods, fishing under rocks, canoe rides on the Cathance, even reading the right books. I expect him to tuck that list into the first book we gave him, *Lost on a Mountain in Maine,* and to start clicking off the items, just as soon as he can talk, and to get very serious about the list, just as soon as he can walk. Most of the items on the list will require oversight and coaching from an older guy.

When our son saw the list he laughed a little and told me it contained many of those stupid (and not so stupid) things he and I did when HE was a little guy. I didn't disagree. He then suggested a few things that might be added to the list, and we had a great laugh together. When Jane reviewed the list for something more than spelling, she shook her head and told me I can't remain a boy ALL my life.

We'll see.

I come to this grandfather's job late and inexperienced. Many of the guys around me already have two, four or ten grandkids, and several have GREAT grandkids. All that really means is that I have some catching up to do. Forgive me if I force you to look at pictures, or bore you with a story or two, when you next meet me on the street.

And there are the "other boys."

My daughter Abbie married this year, and FOUR guys came in that union, not the usual one. Her man George has three fine boys: Zack, Nick and Jake. That's right, we get to fast track the grandparent thing, from zero to four in one year! (In four months, really) I have to tread here a little more lightly, of course. These three are older and the train of authority just a little more cloudy.

But here's a warning to you, Abbie and George, I consider these guys to be fair game as well. I fully intend to inflict my knowledge and love of Maine on them, too, every chance I get.

And yes, time will generate another list or two.

Last fall, Zack, Nick, Jake and I spent an exceptional morning together, burning brush at one of my cemeteries. I showed them the precise art of throwing gasoline on a waning fire, and we talked of future projects that included smelt fishing, hiking and canoe trips, and I sensed a certain amount of enthusiasm. Abbie was kind of cool to, and startled by, the gasoline tossing thing, but she knows I am very careful. She and her brother both have all their fingers and toes, despite an adventure or two in her younger years. Abbie remembers more than one bonfire in our past, and no one ever got burned. She'll stay tuned.

But back to Jadon. Jadon was born on the full of the moon, and on my mother -in-law (Barbara's) birthday. I believe, and don't we all believe more deeply in something when we look at a new birth, that this little man is already blessed, already watched.

Jadon Miles Connors is not quite an armful yet. My fist is bigger than his head. But three weeks into his storied life, this little guy has already focused his clear, dark eyes on mine, and started the magic working. Not since our own children were born have I experienced such a profound feeling.

I think you all know what I'm talking about.

There is a new excitement, new expectations, and new meaning. You want a better world for this guy, and there is a new willingness and renewed energy to work toward it.

Is there a better way to start the new year?

The list

There is a fond hope, as Jadon Miles Connors is welcomed to this family circle, that many of the moments shared by his father and grandfather may be shared again with him. He must feel no pressure of completion, only the desire to have fun, and learn something about himself, and his family, while they wander together around Maine.

The List

- Find a live starfish
- Wade into the Kennebec where it leaves Moosehead lake
- Wade into the Kennebec where it meets the Atlantic
- Climb the fire tower on Kineo Mountain
- Climb Bradbury Mountain
- Wade through snow to Porcupine Mountain
- Climb the fire tower on Mount Ararat
- Cook (and eat) mac and cheese in a Cathance smelt camp
- Pick a bushel of apples
- Catch a smelt from a smelt camp
- Read, *Lost On A Mountain In Maine*
- Make a "poop" necklace for "Nannie" Jane AND Dina
- Find six hermit crabs
- Ride the "state Truck" the length of Swan Island
- Pee on a tree in a public place
- Walk across the Deer Isle Bridge
- Feed Grampie Frank's birds for a week
- List the birds you see at the feeder that week

- Touch the moose antlers at Abbot
- Canoe from Cathance Landing to Cathance Falls
- Walk, "the block," after dark, with a friend
- Read, *Charlotte's Web*
- Climb Borestone Mountain
- Meet six animals at the Gray Game Farm
- Walk across the Waldo Bridge
- Canoe up the Abbagadassett River to "head of tide"
- Walk across the Cribstone Bridge
- Pee in the 2nd Bowdoinham Privy, and understand why it's inferior
- Walk the Cathance River ice to the Middle Ground
- Drive Poppie's golf cart (slowly)
- Climb a lighthouse tower
- Visit the Maine State Museum
- Create a secret trail in Poppie's woods
- Fill Grampie's woodbox
- Find and fill a cup with sea glass
- Get a BIG rock for one of Nannie Jane's Gardens
- Walk the brook, from Center to Bridge streets
- Cook scrambled eggs and hot dogs on a camp fire
- Read any TWO Laura Ingalls Wilder books
- Retrieve three Monarch caterpillars and hold 'em to be Chrysalis
- March in the Celebrate Bowdoinham parade
- Collect six different kinds of tree leaves

- Sleep overnight at Nannie Jane's and Grampie's, WITHOUT "the" folks

- Shoot Grampie's 22-target rifle

- Swim "the length" of Poppie's pool

- Collect $2.00 worth returnable bottles out of a roadside ditch

- Canoe to Swan Island, hide the boat and track a deer

- Open a savings account at the Bowdoinham Credit Union

- Toboggan downhill at Grampie's

- Cut your own Christmas tree

- Ride the WW &F narrow gauge Railroad

- Gather cemetery acorns, and deliver them to the deer on Swan Island

This list may be added to, at any time, with absolutely NO notice.

Grampie Frank, Christmas, 2006

My mother's minced meat

This is the season where I really miss my mother's mincemeat. I grew up on the stuff. In my younger days, I could smell a freshly opened quart jar of the stuff two rooms away. I could sneak over, dip in a tablespoon, haul out a heaping quarter cup and down it before Ma even knew I was in the room. I was younger then, for sure.

There has always been that association to the Holidays for me and mincemeat. For years after we were married Jane and I would come home one late fall evening and find a quart jar (in a good year, TWO) of mincemeat on our kitchen table. Usually there would be a small red ribbon draped around it but never a card or notes. None was ever needed since no one makes mincemeat like my mother.

It's been several years now since that last jar. Mom is older now, is chronically ill, and just doesn't have the energy it takes to "do mincemeat." And it always was an operation. Fall came around and if someone in the house didn't get a deer a neighbor was always willing to pass on some venison quarters or a deer neck. (Sorry folks, but Mom preferred the neck meat.) Mom would boil the venison till the meat was "pickable" and I'd sit at the table, picking till I got a cup, then two, sometimes six, of the venison that so many folks considered scrap meat. Of course, you can use steak, you can also use hamburger. Heck, some of the faint of heart use green tomatoes! But be careful – the meat is very key.

I often helped peel apples for the "stew." I usually picked the seeds out of the citrus. Mom never let me touch the raisins. She always said they were too expensive and I ate too many. I usually plowed the big wooden spoon through that huge kettle, once, then again, then again and again. I never tired of the stirring job. Those smells were always just shy of magnificent.

This holiday season, Mom and I are sitting around and talking a lot. Whenever I can I steer her mind backward to times and events only she can remember.

Her body may be weak but her mind still has the same exceptional richness and variety of her mincemeat. She's told me of her bitterness and disbelief when her brother's body (a combat casualty) was shipped home on Christmas Eve, 1941. We've talked of my father's loss four years later in the same war. But most of all we've talked about the multitudes of moments when we were all growing up.

There has been funny stuff, crazy stuff and some stupid stuff…all the personal things that have us laughing and sad in the same breath. We take up old pictures, chat about them, and make notes on the back. My sisters and brothers come in and get caught up in the same discussions.

Mom has this habit of apologizing too much. I keep telling her that and usually she apologizes for apologizing. Last Wednesday, Mom apologized for not making new mincemeat this year. I took a deep breath, considering lecturing her again about being sorry, when it hit me.

Probably this year, Mom and I are brewing what will become the best batch of them all.

Mom's Marvelous Mincemeat

10 cups venison

35 cups apples

4 cups brown sugar

2 cups white sugar

5 cups raisins

6 oranges

11/2 cups sherry

1 t. salt

1 t. Allspice

2 t. cinnamon

Cook and grind the venison; peel the grind the apples; grind the raisins; peel, deseed and grind oranges and lemons

Combine ingredients; let set overnight in a cool place. Cook 3-4 hours very slowly in a heavy pan, in oven (low heat) or top of stove, very low heat. Stir at regular intervals with a broad, wooden spoon. Cook until apples are transparent.

Place in hot, sterilized jars and seal. Makes 10-12 quarts of really good stuff.

Many thanks to the plow guys

I was a plow guy for a while and frankly, I just didn't like it!

I suppose there's a sort of glow attached to driving a huge vehicle, on the darkest of nights, in the worst of weather, but that glow fades after the first couple hours and the boredom sets in. Snow plowing is tedious, cold, thankless, lonesome, and often dangerous.

I was Bowdoinham's manager when the job description included, "filling in" for contractors when they got tired or their equipment busted… or when there were holes to that needed plugging or when there were taxpayer complaints to answer. It didn't happen too much, but it happened too often, and it always happened when the weather was the worst.

We had a driver flip a truck on an icy road he was trying to sand one night, and the contractor wanted me to come help! What did he really think I could do? I drove my little pick-up out there, got soaking wet, cut my hand, ripped my jacket and made sure the driver was okay, then headed to town. It was 3 in the morning and I had to find another sand truck! You get the idea, not just another happy night.

There was another time, about midnight on a very icy, snowy night, when a resident called our house, woke both kids and told Jane's he'd been "partying" and needed to know what road was the safest route home.

Jane told the guy she had no idea what roads were sanded, or where I was, then she left him with distinct impression she really didn't care how he got home. You can bet that call was discussed at the next selectman's meeting! As luck would have it, I happened to be spreading sand on the Ridge Road when that taxpayer was offended that night. So, I have nothing but respect for these guys in the big red truck, pulling 12-hour shifts that start about the time I head to bed.

I give them room when I meet them on the road, I pass them with reluctance, I even wave at them when they blow another ton of white stuff under Norman and Barbara's mailbox. It's a thankless job, with little or no reward, ever.

Then we have the guys with the pick-up plow rigs who do driveways. Some are so excited they hook their plows on their trucks by Halloween, and they won't drop them till Easter. Some of them know what they're doing, some of them don't. Some of them care if you exist in their world, some of them don't.

We have a good plow guy. Our drive is perhaps 500 feet up the side of a hill and through a grove of pines. There's a great chance to mess it up, but he seldom does. The town plow always comes by an hour or two after the snow has stopped, and always make one last, sloppy attempt to block our drive and destroy our mailboxes. More often than not, our plow guy will clean up after they clean up, and this is all done for under $50 a storm. Don't you even think I should give you his name.

Norman had a GMC and a plow, back in the day. He used to plow driveways for friends and neighbors for $5 (and/or) a six pack, or for the fun of it, if he really liked you! He has trouble understanding that our plow guy is a good deal. Every fall, we talk about maybe buying a snowblower, maybe mounting a plow on my Ford Ranger, or just "shopping around" to see if we can find a better deal.

Early each season, Norman shows signs of panic when the plow bills start rolling in. But every winter, when we get that monster storm that dumps a dozen, wind-whipped inches in our drive in the middle of the night, I thank my lucky stars for our plow guy. I remember for a minute about rolling off an icy road in Bowdoinham all those years ago, and then I pull the quilts over my head and go back to sleep.

Skiing and me

When I was just a teen and a rookie skier, one of the lifts in front of the main lodge at Sugarloaf was a rope tow, and the skis under my feet really were boards. Wood anyway. Sugarloaf is now a world- class resort, most skiers have no idea what a rope tow was, and me...heck, if I tried to ski this winter Jane would probably disown me, and no doubt you'd find my bones under a tree sometime next spring.

Fact is, the last time I skied was nearly 20 years ago. My little boy Miles was a ski school instructor at Sugarloaf (the apple seldom falls far from the tree) and a student at Farmington, AND having his 21st birthday, so I drove up to spend the day on the mountain, just like old times. The first insult came when the guy in the ski shop laughed at my equipment, telling me "thong bindings" had been illegal since HE was in high school. Turns out he was a friend of my son, and he let me try out a pair of his "snap-ons," making me promise I'd buy a set from him if I ever came back.

Insolent little kid.

I taught both of my kids to ski, I introduced the sport to Jane, I did a stint with the ski patrol, and in High school my first flush as a columnist was a nasty little weekly piece in the old Brunswick Record we called "Slope Talk." You can say "back in the day." I was a very, VERY dedicated skier.

Anyone here remember Sky Hy? It was a great little ski area in Topsham with a vertical drop of two, maybe three hundred feet of ledge between the crest and Bradley Pond that could be a little hair-raising, but there were several trails that meandered through the woods that were fun, and if there was plenty of snow for padding, even the front slope was inviting.

I started off skiing the fields of Bowdoinham with my brothers. This would be long before the days of "cross country gear," mind you, but we literally did ski cross country for miles. Those were the wonderful days of night skiing. If you have not ventured out on a cold January night, on or near the full of the moon, folks, you have cheated yourself. You can see stars you had no idea existed. The moon is bright enough to create long, adoring shadows, and as you yodel your way along the shoulder of some clear, untouched ridge toward a frozen river, you'll start to understand what winter in Maine really is all about.

In those tenuous early days of my relationship with Jane, I once described her to a friend as, "perfect, if she only knew how to ski." There started a series of challenging dates on the slopes of Sugarloaf, Sunday River, Saddleback, and weekends in Strong.

You learn lots about a person when you try to teach them to ski. I suspect the long drives up and back did more for melding our lives together than did my coaxing and harassing on the sides of those mountains. I remember one day when Jane overheard me telling another skier we had to "light a fire" under our dates or OUR day of skiing was going to suffer. That was the day I learned just how good Jane's hearing was, and I was told for the very first time, where I might want to put my left ski. "I don't like being cold," she told me, " and I don't like being scared." Nobody's perfect, I know that now, and she's always willing to let me go by myself.

Miles took to skiing like a duck to water, Abbie, not so much. There was a night at Lost Valley in Auburn when she didn't come off the mountain with a gaggle of her friends, so I shot up the lift and did a sweep, just like in the ski patrol days.

Halfway down the mountain I spotted Abbie sitting on her skis on the side of the trail, feeling quite dejected. She was covered with snow, shivering, discouraged, and wishing she was on a beach somewhere. I told she could do this, and she did. That night turned into another night, twelve years later, when she became ski coach and teacher for her new husband and his sons. That's the kind of girl my Abbie is!

My career in the Ski Patrol was born of necessity. It was a free ticket to ski almost any mountain I wanted. There was lots of cruising on lots of slopes, with an occasional flush of excitement picking up wounded skiers.

As the first snows of 2013 fall, I find myself getting that old urge to ski once more, though my knees, my back, my wife, and my sensibilities seem to muster against it. Will this year be the year of my return to Sugarloaf? Miles thinks Jadon might like to ski, after all. In the mean time I have snowshoes I can pad around on, and manage not to hurt myself and in a couple years, I'll be able to ski free as a senior citizen.

When winter isn't

Don't you feel even a little bit cheated?

I mean, this is Maine, we've just seen the dead of winter... and no one died! Where is all the snow and ice, the cold and the misery? Are we ready to be satisfied with such a wimpy winter?

Jane thinks I'm crazy to write this column.

Jane says Gluskap or some other "less than kind" earth spirits with ties to our state will get us if we go and get to confident. She worries if we get too smug about an easy winter, we'll be putting baskets over our Daffodils in April, just to keep the snow off. But I say the signs are in place, and at least (at last?) this one year, the signs favor us.

January was a piece of cake, the sun is warming every day, we've done 4,000 degree days and I have yet (mid-February) to see a below-zero night on my thermometer. There was NO shadow in Topsham this Groundhog Day; and the bays, even the rivers, are more open than frozen. My smelt fishing buddies have moved their camps on and off the ice six times, and by now, disgusted, they have all but given up. One guy told me he was skipping the camp for the rest of the season, instead he's sitting on the ice, fishing through a hole and enjoying the sun. Another guy suggested he may just fish for smelts from a canoe!

We have turned the corner, folks. No one can take away those January days when the mercury climbed to 50 degrees. No one. I put a new roof on my chicken house last month It needed shingling, I had it on my mind for a spring project, but now it's done! It was just a small roof, and a minor project, but it's still done! That's pretty much like gaining a weekend in the spring, the way my little mind works.

Groundhog Day is a day I share with Helen. She's an old friend from The Highlands, and for a number of years, we have celebrated the day together. Or not. The general plan is to gather together at the Maine Lodge flagpole, watch the sun come up, check our lee sides for shadows and retire quickly to Frosty's where we eat glazed donuts, drink hot coffee and talk about the weather.

Helen always shows up, sometimes I don't. Two, maybe three years, I've left my Helen sputtering at the flagpole, shivering in the cold, wondering what happened to Frank. I take more pleasure in that than I should, Sorry, Helen.

This year we gathered together under the flag at 6:54 a.m., shivering together for maybe two minutes before observing the lack of sun. "No sun," says I, "early Spring," I predicted. The morning news said the Pennsylvania groundhog did see his shadow, but do we care? We went to Frosty's and did raspberry bismarks. Just another in a series of good signs, I say Helen and I ordered extra donuts.

Don't you think Maine should have its own resident groundhog? Who really cares about spring in Pennsylvania?

I'm starting to accept that this may be the first season in many when I don't get my walk on the river ice. I mean, the way this season has been, I wouldn't send my worst enemy across the Cathance!

The brothers and I used to haunt Swan Island all winter, never even wondering about the ice underfoot. We'd haul hay, acorns and stale bread over the Kennebec and give it to the deer. It really will be unbelievable if I have to pass on that trip this year.

Even the Valentine's Day blizzard, the one that dumped

several feet of snow on New York and Boston, was a no show in our area.

So here's my prediction. I'll stick it out there, and stick to it. We will get one last slammer of a snowstorm, maybe in March, maybe even April. There will be a foot plus inches of snow, just to appease ol' Gluskap. But, just deal folks! Snow is nothing more than a nuisance after February. It can't pack down and depress us for months, not like the same storm in December might.

Winter's back has been broken. I say that in print, with confidence. I'm not worrying about Jane's worries, or warning.

You read it here first. '05-06 will go down in the books as an open winter, with nothing old fashioned about it. Those who cry about global warming will have another bump on their graph to point toward.

Some of you may be wondering if I'm going to tell you who Gluskap is, and of course, the answer is yes! Gluskap is that mean-tempered Indian spirit-half man and half moose, (with wings) who inhabits the crags and cliffs of Mount Katahdin. His mischief is what is supposed to create the wild, unpredictable, and sometimes evil weather that shrouds Katahdin, and often torments hikers on that mountain's ridges. If you've climbed Katahdin more than once, you know who I mean. You've met him.

We'll just have to see if I'm right, or if it is Jane. Either way I expect I'll be dealing with Gluskap in July.

An affection for eagles

In that moment I willingly and willfully chose to break a Federal law. The kids and I were walking the river, it was all clear and frozen, a white and grand day. The feather was stark and dark against the snow. We stopped together, Miles, Abbie and me to pick it up. "Eagle" I uttered the words with not a little awe.

Abbie seemed almost to shy away, Miles looked to me for a signal. He wanted it. I picked it up, and brushed it against the kids flushed cheeks. "Feel the power," I said to them, and stuck it first into Abbie's blond curls. When Miles seemed ready to pluck it as his own, I raised my hand and told him to wait his turn. "Patience is a sign of the eagle," I said solemnly.

I've always felt a deep affection for eagles. I love to watch them as they soar in the sky over my head, or as they perch on the tall, dead trees along the river, or as they feed on the carrion that someone might have placed for them on the ice. They offer a power, an independence, a grandness that is unique in the wild world. They're big, they seem invulnerable and so far from reach.

One of my first missions as a young boy scout was to find an abandoned eagle's nest on Little Swan Island in the Kennebec River. Story was that it was the largest bird nest in Maine, story also was that it had been unoccupied for years. This was in the early '60's folks, people were just starting to realize that DDT was not a cocktail, and that Rachel Carson was not a crackpot.

We boys did find that nest, tried to climb the tree and failed. What a sad thing it was that eagles couldn't have babies anymore we all decided, and then we moved on to another merit badge.

But high school and then college showed me the beginnings of controls on toxic wastes, and we watched in wonder as the Bay and its rivers really did clean up. There was the stirring of an environmentalist in me, and so many other Mainers. Weren't those hopeful days?

Thank you John Cole, thank you Ed Muskie.

Then came the stories of those brave (if a little crazy) guys who were "seeding Eagles," remember? Eagle eggs were coming to Vacationland from Alaska and Minnesota, and were being hand placed in the place of damaged eggs. Young pairs were being released and finding they could again live even flourish in this area,

But my college experience was cut short by a draft board. It wasn't six months until I was a member of the 101st Airborne, and proudly wearing a "Screaming Eagle" on my uniform.

When Jane and I were courting there were many trips into the bay and its rivers, and the good trips often offered glimpses of eagles. I know we landed on Swan Island more than once, and stalked that nest above the gravel pit with some success.

My cemetery in Bowdoinham is on a ridge between the head of the Cathance River and Merrymeeting Bay. I can't tell you the number of times I've seen eagles from that yard, But I will retell the one moment when, during a burial, a grand, white-headed eagle landed in a spruce tree not 50 yards away. That tree limb swayed dramatically under the weight of the bird, while all talk and activity at the graveyard ceased. Every eye in that cemetery fixed on that magnificent bird!

When that minister finally managed to recover his tongue, his message was changed. Every person in the yard that day came away believing more deeply in the spirit world, and me, I had an undertaker asking me if I could get the eagle back for his next service.

But the ice walks are still the best. Fresh, crisp air is framing the day, me rounding a corner and spotting an eagle in the air, in a tree or on the ice. I just never tire of that sight, sharing that moment in the life of something so wild, so grand, so symbolic. It matters not that they may be feeding on the carcass of a dead deer. When that great white head turns, and the piercing yellow eye seems to be looking right through me, that moment is one that seems to cut through the layers of my soul. And I love the idea of sharing that moment with my kids.

The feather goes into my shirt, Miles accepts my promise of the gift when we get home.

So, I won't quite claim the eagle as my totem, but put me on record as glad that I can live in a place where I can still find a simple feather on the ice and keep it. I can know the story of these simple moments, and have the desire to share them. There lies the real treasure, the true spirit of the American Eagle.

Pre-pay? You don't say!

With all these spiraling gasoline prices we've had to endure the past couple years, who among us have also noticed the death of service station SERVICE? I'm old enough to remember 20 cent per gallon gasoline, and to recall the guy who used to come out, pump gas for me, probably washed my windshield, usually offered to check my oil, and still managed to lean on the car long enough to find out how my day was going, who my sisters were dating, and what my neighbors were doing.

Remember those guys?

I pretty much make a career of driving with my fuel tank on empty. When my gas gauge is more than half full, the truck tends to handle funny on turns, and lean to port on the straight stretches.

When I pull into a gas station, I'm there because I need gas. Once last month, I was emptier than usual when I pulled in to a pump (won't tell you where, but I'll bet the cashier remembers) grabbed the nozzle, pushed the appropriate buttons, and POOF, nothing happened. I took a breath, pushed the buttons again, squeezed the nozzle again, once more, nothing. The deep breaths stopped working. I punched the buttons again roughly, still no gas! About the time I'm considering kicking the pump, I hear this microphone voice saying, "pump number three, if you are paying with cash, you need to come inside and prepay…"

PREPAY! Folks, it is three in the afternoon, I know they have cameras watching every move at every pump. I'm dressed better than usual, I don't look like a flight risk or a terrorist. I'm here to tell you I'm put off by the whole prepay process. I took my $20 bill and stormed to the counter, then told the lady who had nothing to do with company policy what I thought of her company policy.

Then, I told her I wanted one dollar's worth of gas. Yup, says I, I expected $19 in change. She looked at me like I had three eyes, and handed over my money. Thank you, I said honestly, accepting a fist full of dollar bills, then I went outside and pumped my cup full of hard-earned gas. Then I drove to another station, where I hope they more appreciated my business.

Speaking of stations that DO appreciate our business, I'm reminded of the Dead River station on Bath Road, Brunswick. Tuesday and Thursday between 9 and 3 those guys still pump gas for seniors, and there is no extra charge for the service. That's a perk that People Plus negotiated for you several years ago, after Brunswick's last full-service service station closed its doors because it "could no longer be competitive."

People Plus went to a dozen gas stations in town, telling them there is a segment of their market that cannot, or do not want to pump their own gas. All stations dismissed our observation, saying manned pumps were, "a thing of the past," and would be hard, or impossible to staff. After a second visit, however, the Dead River people decided to try manned pumping once each week on an experimental basis. Guess what, three times they have expanded that program to keep up with the demand!

I want to add one more comment about this same station. Late one evening I was driving past and pulled in to refuel. It was a weekend, I'd been doing outdoor stuff all day, and mid-afternoon in response to dropping temperatures, I'd pulled a pair of long pants over my more fashionable shorts. I had pumped my gas, gone inside to the counter and reached for my wallet to pay. It wasn't there!

But it was there. My wallet was inside the inside pair of pants, belted and zipped safely away, out of reach. I looked at the cashier (male, thankfully) smiled, and said I could pay him, but first I had to drop my pants. He said nothing, he stared at me keenly. He stepped back one step, and I saw one hand go under the counter. "My outside pants," I promised.

For the very first time, it occurred to me how all this looked, and decided the only thing to do was to do the thing. I flipped my belt, the pants dropped down past my knees. I smiled. "See," I said, "two pair of pants!" I decided it would be good to leave soon.

I took $20 from my wallet and laid it on the counter. The guy did not move real fast to pick it up. I bent, grabbed my pants, reset them and turned without even belting the belt. I cleared the door, wondering if I was on their security tape. I didn't look back.

It must be interesting, working the night shift in a gas station. It's curious. Gas prices have dropped again to $2.20, and we're all thinking that the good days are back, and we can feel better about driving again. I guess they really do have us over their barrel.

A widow on war

Being a war widow with a house full of kids, one of the very few extravagances my mother allowed herself were her magazines. *Life, Look, Saturday Evening Post, National Geographic*...those arrivals in our mailbox were greatly anticipated, and their pages quickly opened and consumed.

Mom often got those magazines- like most everything else in our house- after we kids had plied them, and usually, late in the night. One of my lasting mental images of my mother will always place her at our wide kitchen table, relishing both her aloneness, and her magazines.

I guess I was a veteran myself before mom finally told me one of her deepest magazine secrets. She admitted to being a sucker for any magazine that carried text or photographs from World War II. She even confessed to an unthinkable luxury, buying a newsstand copy with grocery money, if that magazine professed to contain a "special section" about the war.

My dad was in Patton's armored infantry. He went through the mauling his outfit took in North Africa, he went to Italy for the push to Rome, he survived D-Day and the Normandy beachhead, only to be gravely wounded and sent home to die as his unit continued its push through Belgium.

Mom never got to a place where she would talk about what that war did to her or to her family. Her brother was killed four years before my dad died, so I can only tell you she took it very personally.

But there was also this fascination. She would spend long minutes, scanning published photograph after photograph, always looking, she admitted, for a glimpse of my dad. She confessed to me, it made her feel guilty. She guessed the chances were ever so impossible, but she continued her search for years. After her death last spring, my sisters found a collection of photographs she had ripped from the pages of some long-gone magazines, saved in a book because the image, the idea, gave her some sort of comfort, some sort of connection to my father.

Mom would have enjoyed, even treasured, the *WAR!* series Ken Burns played on PBS last month. She would have sat enraptured, watching every frame, thinking any minute, her treasured Alden might walk across camera and throw her a final smile, or wave.

If you didn't see that series, watch for the replay or buy the DVD.

There is an old family story, telling of a day my dad was driving his ammo track through a crossroads, "somewhere in France," only to be yelled at by his brother who was an MP directing traffic at that very intersection. That story made their hometown newspaper, and there was a photograph to record the moment. THAT is the very stuff that made the Burns series so special. It brings the war to a personal, more reconcilable level. It makes that connect between guys at the front and their families back home. It makes you think about the sacrifice, the commitment of these people, and to realize how hard that war, any war, was for so many people.

Burns also drove home the realization just who a veteran really is. You start to see the part played by a mother who sent off a husband, a son or two, even a daughter, toward mortal danger on a distant shore. You come to see the part played by a kid saving tin foil or string, and saving dimes and quarters to buy war bonds. You realize why women welded long hours in shipyards, and how housewives managed without refrigeration.

You realize this "big" war, like none other, made veterans of us all.

I didn't watch every frame. I was very young when my father died, and I'm sure I wouldn't recognize him with the gaunt, dirty face of a combatant. When I try to visualize him, I never give him that look.

I have to admit my own combat experiences in another war really make it hard to focus on Television programs like this one. I get restless. I walk to the kitchen for water. Sometimes I sweat, or feel my heart pound. I take breaks, step outside to look up at a beautiful night sky and take a deep breath. Once, I flipped the channel back to one of those reality shows! How stupid was that?

I returned to the Burns' *WAR!* Indeed, there was reality!

A friend dismissed the series as too noisy, too fractured, too confusing. I dismissed their criticism as coming from a person who'd never experienced the awful noises and deadly confusions of warfare.

I encouraged my kids to sit through the whole darned thing. While it is a far cry from "entertaining" entertainment, *WAR!* really should be on everyone's must-see list. The series is a fitting tribute to America's greatest generation, and, in a sobering way, a challenge to all generations that follow.

I wonder, could we meet a global challenge like that today?

Christmas in Florida

That Christmas in Florida wasn't really that great.

I was still a snip of a kid, five-years old and just counting, but with four older and younger brothers and sisters, I really wonder why I don't remember more.

Grampie sent us a Maine Christmas tree, I'm sure he didn't want his grandchildren putting balls and ornaments on a palm tree. That tree arrived on the train, rammed tightly and looking quite miserable in a thick paper tube and looking even more distressed when we pulled it through and stood it up. I'm guessing, but the temperature that afternoon had to be in the 70's...quite a distance from ideal tree trimming weather.

We stuck that tree in a pail of beach sand and water, and before long, it started to perk up and actually, finally, became quite serviceable.

Grant, Alden and I gathered and treasured the needles that fell from that tree, divided them and stashed them in our pillowcases, sleeping for maybe a week with that breath of Maine.

When mom discovered what we were doing, the air changed, immediately.

Mom had stashed a box of tree ornaments in the big box that traveled on the roof of our car from Maine. She saw to it that we all had at least one favorite decoration in that box. We also went to the Orlando Woolworth's for fresh supply of tinsel, each with 50 cents in our pockets to, "pick out any ornament we wanted." I got a reindeer with a bright red nose, but only because my sister bought the one I really wanted, a little metal sleigh filled with wrapped presents.

That night, we popped big bowls of popcorn in a borrowed popper, stringing some but eating most. Alden got caught eating some of the stringed stuff, and had to stand in a corner.

Mom put the angel atop that Bowdoinham fir, and we all placed our ornaments, one at a time. Sisters got the favored spots, always. We pitched tinsel, but paper chains and paper icicles. Shortly after my first argument with my older brother, that tree really started to look like something.

A couple days later, "THE" package arrived from Maine. It was so big, three of us had to lug it to the living room together. The Mailman came to the door, I remember him because he always wore shorts, and he had very hairy legs. He asked that we come out to his truck and give him a hand. That big wrapped box contained wrapped packages from Grammie and Grampie, a bag of apples, packs of cookies and some of Grammie's great caramel. And peanut brittle. Some of the stuff was wrapped in newspaper, and mom saved the wrapping to, "read, sometime later."

Perhaps the most festive thing we did that year was go around town Christmas caroling. There was not a base voice among us. Five sweet children, all shined up, dressed fancy, and walking in descending order. This was the only time that Grant got to lead our sisters.

We did "Silent night," "The First Noel" and something we liked to call "O little town of Bowdoinham," among others. I like to think we made quite an impression on those Southern folks, because throughout that winter, we were called back to sing at the Church, at the town's community center, and for friends in the neighborhood. Lots of people we sang for gave us cookies or candy, even a few coins. Cookies went in a bag our sisters carried, the cash went right in our pockets.

Christmas morning brought us a new bike, a used tricycle and a two-story doll house. Mom said the doll house was from Santa, but we kids caught her putting it together, late on the night before. There was hand-made furniture for the dollhouse, some from Uncle Phil, some from Grampie, and some from mom. There was huge pile of oranges and grapefruit from Santa, and everyone got a new set of clothes.

Christmas dinner was fancy and plentiful, and then we all piled into the car and headed for the beach. Mom said we'd all remember being at the beach this Christmas, because it was something that almost never happened in Maine. My brothers and I all got in the water, just because we knew Grampie would ask.

When we finally heard from the folks back home, the report was loaded with snow. Our winter in Florida was the year of the '51 blizzards in Maine. Mom was right, we would remember.

Coming Home   by John Gable

Picking a tree

I really have a hard time driving to a corner lot and buying a Christmas tree; I don't care what charity I'm supporting with the purchase.

I grew up in Bowdoinham, and we always take our Christmas trees very personally. First, there would be the obligatory walk in the woods with my sisters. The "FINAL" decision on the tree was never one that we boys could make, not without some sort of feminine supervision. You all know the implications of that. Boys just don't have the essential sensitivities, we were told.

My brothers and I spent long hours in the woods, year round. Hunting, exploring, hiding out…whatever the reason (if we needed a reason) we'd wander for hour after hour, week after week, season after season. On a good day my brother might say, "hey, that tree would be a great Christmas tree…" and of course, several months later we could always remember right where they were.

Sometimes we could be resentful of our sisters, and of the process we had to endure to get a tree. After all, we were the woodsmen of the family, what gave them the right to walk up to a tree we had already rated somewhere between "primo and perfect" and just flip it off too casually, saying there was a branch out of place, or the top was crooked, or doubled, or the north side was thinner than the south side? Usually, they wouldn't even offer a reason as they condemned our trees, they'd just say, "NO," or "YUCK," or just crinkle their pretty little red noses in open contempt of us and our trees.

We accepted the process as tedious and flawed, and we were not without our defenses. We knew they would reject the first two or three trees we offered, regardless of their worth or our presentation. So it was not uncommon for us to "tweak" the process. If we found a good tree within an easy carry of home, there was no way in the world we'd show it until we'd presented another tree, or three, farther from home, expecting them to be rejected. That always worked!

It also helped if we weren't overly enthusiastic about a tree. For us to promote a tree as perfect was a guarantee that they would absolutely reject it. "The kiss of death," we called it.

One masterful year, we'd selected a tree but took them to another not ten feet away. We left them to discover our tree as theirs, and to listen humbly as they told us why the tree THEY had discovered was so much better than any tree we had found. It was not unusual for us to cut scrub bushes out of the way, even mud the stumps and haul off the brush, just so they'd get the perfect look at their tree, as we walked past to present ours!

Once the tree was selected the girls considered their job done, almost. The logistics of getting the tree out of the woods was up to us; they'd leave us and head for the warmth of home. "Don't drag the tree," they'd command, "don't knock any needles off," they would say. "Remember last year's tree, you almost spoiled it by dragging it in the snow…"

Every year we'd have to cut the tree and hold it aloft for their inspection. This was yet another humiliation. It was their way of saying THEY were making a final inspection of the tree, noting where cones were, making certain it was perfect, and expecting us to accept responsibility for any damage during the haul out. God help us if it didn't look the very same when we finally got it home, shook it down and displayed it for all, outside the dining room window.

The haul home was never easy. Butt first and shoulder high was a must, for it would never do to bang the tree against another and snap a branch. And it always seemed like the best trees were on the wrong side of the swamp, on the back side of the ridge, or the farthest from the access road.

We always cut a tree right where our sisters pointed, and that was always some two or three feet longer, or taller, than necessary. When the tree was finally home, the first thing we'd have to do was cut away that heavy, excessive butt. We never quite understood why the extra wood had to be cut and carried, but we seldom questioned that process.

Finally, the tree was hauled into the house. "Be mindful of the falling needles," we'd hear three or four times, then we'd suffer the final indignation as we held the tree in the window and twisted it around several times, to be certain it was straight, true and perfect.

Now that I'm thinking about it, perhaps I'm not as resentful of lot trees as I am of my sisters! Perhaps this is the year I should get over one more childhood "thing." Maybe I should call my sister, get to a lot and pick out a tree.

Walking on the river

For me, walking on the river is a winter pastime. Pick a cold, crisp day, a blanket of snow on the land, a bright blue sky above…and just go, there need be no destination in mind.

Sure, the river should be frozen.

The fish and game people say two inches of ice is ample to support a guy my size. Me, I like to know there are six to ten inches in most places before I lead my family, my friends or myself onto the ice. If it's frozen under the bridge, that's even better.

Only once have I fallen through the ice to my waist, and found myself frightened, freezing, and kicking for my life. And once is enough, thank you.

I walk the Cathance or the Abbagadassett as a rule, the Kennebec or Androscoggin if I'm feeling frisky, AND if I know there's lots of ice. You will notice all these rivers are tidal, and I pretty much know the shores, "like the back of my hand." It is always a plus to know where the roads and bridges are, and, if you are walking with friends, to be able to point at "stuff" with a reasonable appearance of intelligence.

My favorite destination has to be my neighbor's Jon's smelting camp. There's nothing wrong with having a woodstove and a Molson somewhere in your afternoon's journey. As it works, Jon fishes on the "middle grounds," of the Cathance, in a small cluster of camps exactly one mile up river from Bowdoinham Village. It's a neat walk. There are bends in the river, you can park at the town landing if you're from out of town, and if feels like a "wild" walk. I mean, you get around the corner from the bridge and Jimmie's camps, you could feel like you're 50 miles from nowhere!

If you're lucky, you're going to see an eagle or two. There have been days when I've seen four, but those are really good days.

Some of the local guys place animal carcasses on the ice, and that seems to be a draw for the eagles. Also, the huge birds love it when fishermen throw waste fish and bait onto the ice. Seeing an eagle circle over your head, then swoop down and snatch a fish off mirror-like ice is an image many people can only imagine.

On the Cathance, I can show you right where to turn around and look at the Bowdoinham Town Hall steeple, some two miles away. That usually impresses the easily impressed. If I'm really leading a tour, I know where to cut off to Molasses Creek, and it's big, granite railroad bridge.

With my kids in tow years ago, we'd haul sleds or toboggans and a blanket of two. There would usually be a food bag on the back end of the toboggan, and always, we'd find an open sheet of glass- like ice, and "whip the whip" until I fell on my head or one of the kids complained of being dizzy. Sometimes if it was really cold, we'd find a sheltered cove, break some kindling off a spruce or pine, and build a tiny "finger fire." An old gallon paint can, with vent holes in it sides, is perfect for that.

On the Abagadasset, several friends have homes near the shore, and it's always fun to wave at them as they stand behind their living room windows. Being called in for a cookie is never against any rules. This same river is dotted with smelt fishing camps, both singles or small colonies, and, if you get upstream far enough, there's another railroad bridge on which to climb.

I consider the Kennebec or Androscoggin rivers to be

"destinations." I don't often walk them without a particular goal in mind. Swan Island, off Richmond is a favorite walk for my family, and Baxter's Island, off Bay Bridge Road, Topsham, is an Androscoggin trek of only a little consequence. I get a little unnerved on the bigger rivers, since currents, rot spots and open water areas are much harder to predict.

More years ago than I want to admit two cousins were here for a visit and we decided to walk the river one cold, clear night. It is always a delight to see the smoke curling from smelt shanty stoves, to see our shadows under the bright, muted moon, and to hear the muffled conversations of the fishermen as we walked through the two colonies nearest the bridge.

Up river maybe a half-mile, I reminded one cousin (let's call her Beth) that we were walking above tide water, and that the ice would be moving up or down with the tide, and she should not be surprised to feel a little "motion."

Beth was in the middle of a rebuttal lecture about how I shouldn't always assume she was a "big city girl" with no "outdoor experiences" when the ice up and down river made a correction not unlike a artillery explosion, and everything settled under our feet maybe two inches! I was a little surprised. Beth was on her hands and knees, scurrying like a rat towards shore! Conversation was pretty sparse on the road home that night.

An ice-sheathed river is a different world...white, cold, even alien to what most people seek out for entertainment. But if you want a real taste of winter, and really want to enjoy it, go walking on the river.

Winter night walks

Night walks are never "cooler" than the ones I do in January. The air is always crisp, the sky never more clear. It is most stimulating, if not even frightening, to bundle up, add hat, mittens, scarf, even extra socks, and just go. It's something we all should do a little more often.

I have talked of my night walks before. Yes, I have this near perfect, mile-long route that circles out Center Street, over Cemetery Road, down Pleasant Street, back up Main Street and back home. There are hills, both up and down. The Cemetery Road section is dark as a pocket, the Maine Street piece has all the urban benefits that beautiful downtown Bowdoinham can provide (six houses, two stores and five streetlights, more or less.) Sprinkled in between is a dark cemetery (yes, on Cemetery Road,) several neighbors with those darned motion detector lights, an on-coming car or two, chance encounters with wild animals, mean dogs and friendly (or not so friendly) neighbors.

But I want you to go find your own route, don't clutter up mine. Fact is, I've never had a walk that wasn't worth the effort. Most of us can walk a mile in a half hour, give or take a few minutes. It's not a bad idea to drive a route first, identify any possible hazards, getting the mileage, etc. It's a good idea to walk with a friend, if you have one, but I usually walk alone, for only the very best reasons. Always tell someone where you are going. You know, stay safe, be sensible.

Now, back to my January night. Wait for a fresh snow, a good moon, and clear roads. It is possible you will go through a whole January without ever getting the three all together, but the results of waiting will make the wait worthwhile.

A new snow makes everything a surreal unnatural white, washed in beautiful tones of a deep bluish purple. Shadows are exaggerated, depths are twisted, sounds are magnified. The air should be cold enough to feel like a burn when you gulp it. I just cough first and get it over with. That first step out on the spruce steps should produce a sound that snaps like a rifle shot. Snow underfoot will make a crushing noise. The interstate is a mile from our house, but some nights I can hear the truckers playing their radios. If a dog barks it could be a neighbor's or it can be a mile away.

My route passes a brook. Sometimes the water passes swiftly, unheard, under the ice, sometimes it's still open. There is always one place where I hear that sweet babble, unless it has been one of those cold heartless months and the snow is feet deep.

Soon enough, I'm in the dark section. No houses, no street lights, no nothing. The first sign of civilization is the cemetery, and it's some 200 yards away. Here is where I find the wild stuff. One night, a flash of white caused me to make a VERY wide circle. I had no idea why that skunk wasn't hibernating and I chose not to ask.

Another night, a faint, hollow, "clacking" caused my crisped ears to perk...I froze, listened, heard nothing, I moved again, heard the "clack" again. Turning quickly, I noticed a deer had emerged from the brush behind me and stepped onto the pavement not ten feet away. It was a small deer, probably a yearling. The moon on its coat made it appear a strange, albino color. We stared at each other for seconds, the both of us finally exhaling crystal wind. In seconds, the deer bounded over the snowbank on the other side of the road and was gone, offering what was a snort of contempt as it leaped and crashed in the underbrush.

When I want a real detour, and the snow's not too deep, I've been known to cut off the road and walk a lane in the cemetery that is parallel to the street. Yup, sometimes I say "hi," to the folks in the yard...Charlie Hinkley, Captain Curtis, T.T. Rideout, Richard Green to name only a few... There are dozens of folks in there I entertain with what I'll call passing relationships...

The Community School has many more lights than it needs, but I really am tired of complaining to the principal. Just past the school I walk through a cluster of houses, walk down a long hill, cross the railroad tracks and join the river. Right here I stop and listen to see if the ol' Cathance is doing what I call "tide grinds."

Before winter really locks the river down tight, the tide and current moves the ice around with a crisp, hollow grinding that you gotta' hear to really enjoy. From here the road can get busy, maybe I meet a car. I pass a couple stores, the little credit union, several homes and a church. Hard to believe, but this is the least exciting piece of the walk. Most of my neighbors go to bed before I do, I guess, at least they pull their shades.

When I get home, usually there's a cat to greet me who wants to get inside. I open the door and it runs past fast, and Jane usually hellos the cat, and sometimes suggests the cat is smarter than I am.

Jane doesn't like to be cold much, and perhaps she is right, but remember she didn't see the little deer, did she?

Smelt fishing

My neighbor Jonathan thinks smelt fishing makes winter worthwhile. Just yesterday, he was looking at his thermometer and crowing about these sub-freezing days being "ice making weather," and saying, "it won't be long now!" Usually by mid-September, Jon is saying "smelt fishing is coming," and if he's not on the river by January first, well, he starts to claim "something fishy is going on here."

Perhaps you have never been smeltin'. First, you gotta' get yourself a camp. Usually the basic (or typical) smelt fishing camp measures something like 8 x 8 feet. (Yes, there is a direct relationship to a single piece of plywood.) There has to be just enough room for a 12-inch by 8-foot hole down one side (some camps do have holes on both sides), then a woodstove with chimney, a singular bait board and two or three chairs. Sometimes the serious fisherman will lose the chairs and sit on their five-gallon fish buckets.

Camps can be made from plywood, aluminum foil, or anything in between. The operative word is "cheap," even disposable, and lightweight. Formed over a simple, bareboned wooden frame, some look like little houses, some like camps, most like shacks. Add them to the list of unique and "functional Maine architecture."

No one ever said they had to be pretty.

The smelt is a silvery little fish, a member of the herring tribe, I'm told. They school in the cold, salty Atlantic, and come to Maine's brackish, fresh-water tidal rivers to spawn. A "keeper" can measure six inches in length, a "real one" can be nine, even ten inches long. Four or six of them make a good meal, or a "mess" as my grandfather used to say. They're best if you roll them in beer and flour, and cook them just as they come out of the water. You can go light on the flour, but never on the beer. When we fish, we like to add a fry pan to the list of essential equipment carried up-river, then we avoid the whole, nasty prospect of carrying the fish home and "smelling up" Jane's kitchen.

Last season my friend Henry introduced me to baked smelt, rolled in a heavier flour and some spices he wouldn't identify. There are some possibilities there Henry, but I still think you need to use more beer!

Yes, there are fishermen I know who consume beer when they fish. Some might even use fishing as a reason to consume beer. The snap of that first flip top can is certainly not an uncommon sound among the shantytowns on the river. But hey, it's all good for the local economy.

It's a tough sport. You sit there in a cramped camp, two feet from a raging wood fire, two feet from the hole where your six or more lines enter the water. Probably it's night, certainly its cold outside, maybe it's quiet. Usually you are fishing with a friend, maybe two, but the talk closes down after a while. You know how guys are.

My favorite fishing expeditions came when our kids, Miles and Abbie, were young. Usually, we'd tie them together with a four-foot piece of rope (Jane insisted, always adding that if one of them went in, I should save them, then jump in and drown Myself)

Often my brother Grant would come with one or three of his kids, and we'd have a time! Grant and I spent most of our time re-worming hooks and untangling lines, but these were great moments for the kids, and better for us. We'd cook macaroni and cheese by the pound, wash our plates in the river, all the while creating stories and telling jokes.

Every child should smelt fish.

If the tide was slow, or wrong, or the fishing bad, there were walks on the river. "Tom Cod" and other "trash fish" get thrown on the river and always attract sea gulls, and sometimes a bald eagle. I can tell you that both of our kids saw their first eagles by looking out a smelt camp door. If the snow is sparse, there will be an acre or two blown clear for skating, sliding, or spinning on sleds. It was always a short walk over to where the railroad tracks run beside the river and crossed Shingleman's Creek, crossing a bridge that everyone needs to explore.

I didn't know it then, but that was some of the best "real time" that I spent with my kids. Jane often stayed home, so the three of us had good times, cooking, talking and laughing…or just becoming better friends.

There are a dozen places in Bowdoinham, or Brunswick, Bath, Topsham or Dresden where camps can be rented. $10-12 per tide is the usual fee. You do NOT need any special skills or licenses to be a successful smelt fisherman. I stand as proof of that.

You will have to bait a hook, but if you can get past that, you will almost certainly catch a fish, or six. Take a friend, take a kid, or take a kid you want to have as a friend.

It WILL be a good time!

Two cents worth of frozen gold

Grant called the other night and wants to go cut some ice.

Years ago, when the kids were smaller and we were a little less smart cutting ice on the Cathance or Abagadasset rivers was a deep-winter family tradition. My brother Grant would take his three kids, I'd gather my two, a couple friends would donate a few more, and off to the frigid, ice-locked river we'd go.

It was a day that gave a few mothers (and grandmothers) some premature gray hair. We tried to disguise the day as an historical society event, thinking it would give us more credibility if child protective services showed up. Besides, all the tools we were using were 150 years old, and had been placed in the custody of the Bowdoinham Historical Society, and my barn.

We'd hit the river during the heat of the day, everyone bundled warmly and ready to work. Linwood Rideout would show up with his snowmobile (our only concession to the modern world) pulling a sled with a large woodbox strapped aboard. Usually, that same box would carry a treasure trove of cookies, hot chocolate, and blankets, and as soon as the wood was off-loaded, Linwood's high-speed rides, hauling three, maybe four kids at a time, would begin.

Grant and I would scrape a foot or more of packed snow off the river ice, clearing an area about the size of our living room. Next we'd take a fire axe and whack a hole maybe six inches wide.

Our old ice saw came from a loft in Vernie Tourtelotte's barn, inherited from the tool shed of Anson Percival Morrell Given. Did we need more history that that? Including the wooden handle, this saw stood some seven feet tall. One tooth was larger than two of my fingers, and this crude if intimidating tool had maybe 36 teeth!

About the time that the end of that saw was inserted into the water-filled hole, I would be busy trying to convince Grant that he was older, smarter and stronger than me, and that only he seemed to have the proper "rhythm" to make that saw sing. He'd start to saw, I'd continue to dump snow.

Grant really does have the knack. A wide, circular motion-shoulders, body and saw working as one- and soon there would be a rusty, arrow-straight line in the ice some 25 feet long. Thirty minutes later, Grant would be working in his t-shirt now, there would be an equal and parallel line in the ice. By then I might have a bon-fire burning in a tub on a pile of snow, or Linwood could have towed a smelt fishing camp, complete with a toasty, cheery-red stove into the area. Maybe we'd be roasting hot dogs, maybe we'd be stirring a pot of mac and cheese, maybe sparks are burning little holes into the kids outer garments, but everyone was having a good time, in spite of the bitter cold.

I step up with a bustin' bar, offer my best grunt to Grant, and the block work begins. A bustin' bar is nothing more than a massive chisel with a flared, shaped end, maybe five feet long and weighing 25-30 pounds. A rope through the handle goes around my wrist, if I slip and the bar goes in the river, I'm supposed to go with it. Grant suggests I put the rope around my neck...everyone seems to like that idea but me.

Unless you have cut ice, you may not know how similar the process is to cutting glass. Clear river ice looks just like a cube of ice from your refrigerator, and it will break with the predictability of a piece of scribed glass. We start popping these cubes, we prefer to call them cakes, or blocks, up to the surface, creating an open channel of cold, coffee-colored river water about 24 inches wide. The rush of the tide creates a little rippling of the surface that always strikes fear into the hearts of young mothers.

Kids get roped together at their belts.

I step up and tell all who will listen about the "glory days" of cutting ice, "back in the days just before Grant was born," I suggest. I often preface my talk with a comment about how once in a while, the ice cutters of old would find fish or frogs frozen in the ice, and they'd take the little critters home and thaw them, only to watch them swim away when the process is complete! Kids always love that story, and it makes them focus on the emerging 75-pound blocks of ice, rather that the open channel.

Maine's Kennebec and Cathance rivers really were centers for the harvesting, storing and selling of "frozen gold," 150 years ago, before modern refrigeration came along to spoil what some people considered a perfect business—selling a natural resource (ice) that Maine always produced in ample quantities. It's interesting to note that through that entire era, ice was taken from acre-sized fields, the work being done by great crews of men using saws and bars just like the ones Grant and I had inherited.

One year we tried storing ice from our tiny river harvest, with the expectation of chipping it and tossing it to excited children along the parade route during our town's July 4th celebration. The reasons that plan never worked are pretty funny, and offer fuel for another story.

I can tell you with a great deal of pride that we never lost a kid (or an adult) during the years we were cutting ice on the rivers in Bowdoinham. But I do have to add, considering my brother's standing, mid-winter invitation, that I'm not absolutely sure I want to go out and tempt the fates one more time.

It's SAD!

The Farmer's Almanac tells me that in Maine we lose 58 minutes of day's length in November, and that comes hard on the heels of the hour lost to Daylight Savings Time late in October.

Cumulative, ain't that enough to knock the daylights out of almost anyone?

I have nothing against darkness. I walk in it, sleep in it (even whisper in it. But I do hate to work in it.

If I'm driving to work and the sun isn't up, I tend to drive slow. Real slow. I've even been known to stop and watch the sunrise. If I'm REAL under motivated by the lack of light, I've been tempted to watch the sunrise in my side view mirror, since that requires less neck work.

On the other side of the day, just let the sun get really low, or disappear from my Noble Street window, and I definitely start to lose interest. I yawn, I repeat myself, I start to nod, it just ain't pretty folks, and I tell you, it's not really my fault.

My Jane craves light like I crave chocolate, but this time of year, the light is just NOT there. We add wattage to the bulbs in every room, we add lamps where they never used to be, we leave lights lit when we should shut them off. What else can we do? I mean, we always rise before daylight , and it's dark when we quit work, we can't seem to avoid it. Some days, I almost forget what my house looks like.

My daughter Abbie told me the other day if we (her folks) didn't live here, if her grandparents weren't still here, if her cats weren't here, she wouldn't spend two more days in Maine. I'm a lover of the Pine Tree State; to hear that from the mouth of my daughter ... it hurt. But I don't blame her. Can't.

But it's sad.

Professionals call it "Seasonal Affective Disorder," SAD for short. I'm (not being a professional) might call it "Seasonally Affected Disorder"...It makes November seem all gray, gross, or worse, and it makes December all cold, barren and useless. Think of it friends, two thirds of our day in darkness!

No wonder they put Thanksgiving and Christmas in the months of November and December. How else would they have saved that whole, ink-black bottom of the calendar?

For those who like such detail, Daylight Savings Time originated in Britain as an economy measure during the First World War. The United States followed the British lead in 1918. The U.S. Congress repealed the law in 1919, (bet too many people didn't like it) even though many major cities continued to follow the times saving program. After WWII began, Daylight Savings Time gained widespread use, but it was still implemented on a state by state, even city by city basis. It wasn't till 1967 the U.S. Congress acted again, making daylight savings official from the last Sunday in October to the last Sunday in April. Even that 1967 law allowed individual states to stay on Standard Time, if the local legislature so decreed.

I'm sorry, but I think we should just leave it alone. We should take that hour back, and cancel Daylight Savings Time.

The government must have numbers that prove lack of daylight contributes to loss of productivity, increased consumption of alcohol, pet abuse, an increase in smoking, more depression...you name it, I'm sure there's a bunch of bad stuff related to darkness. It's just another carefully guarded, government secret.

The only good thing, really, comes at the end of December,

when the daylight does start to stretch, minute by minute and we see feeble signs of a new season.

Abbie still isn't happy, of course, because it stays cold for two more months, but me, I take the cold because my daylight is coming back.

I smile more, I cease to suffer from SAD.

Making cooking fun!

One of the things we "inherited" when Jane and I moved into her folks' home was her mother's extensive collection of cookbooks, and the crown jewel of that collection was Barbara's original edition of "Cooking Downeast." In its new-printed state, this yellow, hard-bound book was maybe an inch thick and brim full of Marjorie Standish's recipes, wit, and wisdom.

Today that book looks like a book that may have survived a library bombing, and if you were to boil its pages down, I'm guessing there would be enough food stuffs splashed and dried on them over the years to make a pretty tasty and firm broth.

You do need to see Barbara's edition to believe it.

The binding of that book was splayed, perhaps as early as 1970, and today this food-stained, thread-bare book is one of a kind. Barbara's habit was to make notes behind a good third of the recipes, telling the world (and reminding herself) what she thought of the recipe. Maybe she thought it needed less sugar, maybe if she didn't think the "Delicious Banana Cake" was that delicious, she'd say so. If Barbara found a recipe that tasted better, sounded better, even looked better, she'd just tape or glue it in the book, anywhere she found a white space.

I have to say right here that if you still have one of those yellow first editions from the '60s, consider it to be worth its weight in butter, and if you ever want to sell your copy, just give me a call. There is still a spiral bound edition of the Standish "Cooking Downeast," at book stores today, and the book is worth the read.

I don't think I ever met Marjorie Standish, but this is a woman who made the world a better place. For many years Marjorie wrote a cooking column in the Portland Sunday Telegram, appropriately called "Cooking Down East." She was originally a Home Service Advisor for Central Maine Power, took the column on because she was asked, and published the book as a labor of love.

I've been told my mother-in-law, Barbara, and Marjorie were contemporaries, Marjorie played basketball at the Farmington Normal School, class of '31 (plus or minus), and took her degree in Home Economics. Barbara, "Fish," as she was called in those days, would have been a cheerleader at the Gorham Teachers College, at about the same time. Marjorie was a Holbrook, of the Cundy's Harbor Holbrooks, and (here comes the connection, folks) Barbara and Marjorie's sister Doris taught together at Brunswick's Longfellow School for years.

Marjorie produced a second book in 1973, "Keep Cooking the Maine Way," with more recipes from her column and repeating some of the best from the first book. This was a lady who knew that butter was a good thing, and a little more butter was even better. She used salted pork as a base in her chowders and would tell you that a number of vegetables could be improved by pork flavoring as well.

My Jane says Marjorie tends to use a little too much sugar, but who among us can call that a fault?

The cookbooks of Marjorie Standish are a representation of the way Maine used to be. She cooked for men who worked hard all day and came home hungry at night. Those guys never had to worry about counting calories, where their cholesterol numbers were, and if their waists were expanding, or retracting. It remains for us to make the adjustments.

We learned at People Plus years ago that the best way to run an event is to throw some food at it. Finally, with the help of nutritionist Anita Huey, and Claudia Adams, and the University's Extension Service, we're moving closer to "Maine-lining" food at the Center. In the coming months there will be many new and exciting ways for us, and for you, to explore food. We want to make cooking for one fun and interesting, and we want you to come to luncheons and share a meal with 50 or 60 of our best friends.

If the process is going to work, however we all have to recall what the Marjories and the Barbaras have already done for us. Cooking needs to be FUN!

Personal thrift?

I've learned to accept that I'm never going be rich, and part of my response to that reality has been what I like to call personal thrift.

Yup, I save stuff, I reuse stuff, I borrow when I can, do without when I can't. I'm willing to try something myself, rather than hire someone to do it. I like to think I received some of those traits from my grandfather, but today, as I watch and wonder as my own grandsons grow, I'm finding it tougher and tougher to transfer these same habits to our next generation. I mean, it's just not as easy as it used to be.

When I was a little, little kid, I used to walk the roads, search for bottles and turn them in at the local store. The nickels would add up to quarters, and after I'd treated myself to an occasional soda (10 cents) or some penny candy (that actually cost a penny) I'd make a stop at the post office where Fred, the postmaster, would greet me and open a drawer as I came into the room. "Here for a stamp?" he'd ask, and I'd nod yes. Those stamps would accumulate in a book till I had enough to trade in for a bond and yes, Fred was personally involved when I got that bond.

If I want to buy a bond for my grandsons, I can't do that at the post office and now I can't do that at a bank. I have to go on line and order it electronically. They try to make me believe that process is easier, but Fred the postmaster at the Bowdoinham Post Office and I would both disagree. More importantly, I fail to see a good way to teach thrift to a child using that process.

I don't remember ever having a regular allowance, or ever really missing it. Daily chores were something all of us did in our house to keep a large family functioning. I did occasionally iron my brother's shirts for a dime, or do odd jobs for neighbors, and when I decided I could work for real money it was weeding Prout's fields or picking his carrots, radishes, beans or squash.

When a credit union opened in Bowdoinham, my account was a two digit number, and it was exciting to sit at the "treasurer's" kitchen table, give him a couple bucks to add to a book and have him look over his glasses at me and tell me how much interest I'd accumulated in a month. Today that credit union has left my hometown, and their sterile new offices down the road look like a fancy doctor's office. Banks everywhere seem more intent on forming clubs for little kids, giving them silly prizes and useless gifts rather than inspiring them toward real thrift by offering them a little simple interest on a savings account.

Both of my grandsons have had accounts opened to help them with college expenses. Here, finally, there still seems to be an opportunity to help prepare them for the future. Grandparents can send checks and lobby against the day when their kids confront crushing debt to get a college education.

But there really is something missing. In these days of corporate bailouts, seven or eight digit deficits, and monthly mortgage payments of a few thousand rather than a few hundred dollars, the opportunity, even the motivation, for personal thrift and savings seems lost. How are we going to fix that?

Greatly missed, long remembered

Turns out, I've known Norman Marriner longer than I've know his lovely daughter (my wife) Jane. When I was a fourth string basketball player (and manager) at Brunswick High, Norman was the school board member always sitting on the top row bleachers, always the perpetually optimistic fan, always blaring out encouragement and advice, even when there was little or no hope for what was then just a ho-hum team. In the 40-plus years, from those days to this, I never took it personally that Norman didn't tell me back then that he had a daughter. I bet he had his reasons.

Dying last month at the age of 96, Norman would have been the very first to tell you he had lived a wonderful life. There was no surprise when his childhood in Topsham was compared to an episode from one of the old Walton's TV shows. His stories from his early days: working in the Daggett Brothers farm fields, playing basketball in the old Brunswick Town hall, hooking mail with his uncle at the old Rogers farm, chasing his brothers down Winter Street on sleds, or chuting onto and across the Androscoggin River, certainly reflected a different age.

Norman worked hard every day of his life. He didn't go to college, but he made certain his kids had the opportunity. He took two, maybe three pills a day. In his ninth decade his blood pressure was better than mine, and most of his days his mind was as quick as mine. (Okay, sometime quicker.) Most nights he could eat more than me at supper. He was a navy veteran from the "BIG" war, plying the Pacific on a sweaty old repair ship. It took a visit to the WWII memorial for him and me to come to terms about my "little" war, but we did it.

Norman was a patriot. He loved this country of ours without

question, the old fashioned way, and he felt the same way about his community. His was an old-fashioned Republican mind. It was his pleasure, and usually his delight, to issue Republican logic to the misguided Democrats who seemed to encircle him.

For the past two years, Jane and I shared his home and his life. This was the place he and "Barb" bought when he came home from the war, and he never wanted to be anywhere else. He never doubted for a minute, these last years, that our presence was the difference between him staying in his home or going to "one of those facilities..." Most days, I think he was grateful. But most days, sharing the house with him meant just as much to us. Experiencing him in his last days was a period neither Jane or I would ever change.

Today there is a huge bowl of condolence cards on our dining room table, and their common theme reflects on the spirit that was Norman. "Always there" said one, "made the world better for the rest of us," said another. "Dandy of a family patriarch...Warm and welcoming, always...smartest Red Sox fan I know...an anchor...one of a kind." And there was this. "He was the likes of which we will never see again."

I need to suggest, at least from my point of view, that we lost more than a man here. Norman was my local connection to the last century. He was one of the reasons I'm walking confidently into this century. He was our family's last connection to the greatest generation.

In his own favorite phrase, I'll say, "here we go!"

I salute you, Norman, and accept the obligation no, the challenge, of trying to live life to your standards.

Caskets under the bed

The decline in John's health was so dramatic and rapid that Ellen knew it was time for her to make the call to their kids. In the year just past, John had suffered increasingly from a debilitating illness, and in the last month, a fall had broken several bones and punctured a lung. Now he rested quietly, Ellen at his side, refusing "extraordinary treatment," and calmly awaiting what was next. John and Ellen had been married more than 50 years, nurturing daily the love and the bond that had carried them through all the difficult days of his illness, and prepared them for this day.

The boys immediately answered their mother's call, visiting their dad at the hospital, coming home to busy themselves with leaves, mowing, carrying out and stacking up. It was an important time to find projects, and their mother was eager to please. "Go up to our bedroom," she suggested quietly, "and bring down one of those wooden kits you'll find under our bed." Eager to please, the boys bounded up the stairs, only to return in five minutes, faces ashen, expressionless, carrying a pile of pine and instructions to assemble a casket.

The story is that John and Ellen, years ago, had visited a carpenter's shop and decided, "it would be useful to be ready," so they purchased two casket kits, carried them home and slipped them under their bed. "There was just never a time to tell the kids," Ellen explained simply.

That same night, with the family gathered and John resting comfortably at the hospital, there was a family meeting and Ellen, the boys, their wives and their kids developed a united front to be sure that John final wishes could be met. They planned a final celebration of John's life, and managed to share the joy, with the sorrow, of his passing.

I'm reminded of a time when Jane and I took her parents on one of our extended annual trips. We were outbound, driving through Freeport and headed for Michigan, Jane flipped out two folders and announced to her folks, "before we come home, I want to know all there is to know about your hopes and plans for your final days." My knuckles went white on the steering wheel, and we were through Portland before I even dared a glance in the rearview mirror.

Jane's mother, Barbara, opened first. She wanted to be cremated, she said, she wanted to be buried with her son, she wanted to go quickly and she didn't want any fuss. Norman stayed quiet, offering advice when it was asked. I bet we drove more than 100 miles as we chatted over Barbara's obituary, learning stuff about this gracious woman that I suspect her husband of more than 50 years didn't know. Norman's comfort level increased as the days wore on, and I think they penned their signatures onto a formal directive as we drove down Pleasant Street, almost home. We had chatted on and off that whole trip, planning a certain future, and noting details of two storied, and busy pasts. It was a wonderful, enlightening experience.

And I'm reminded of another discussion with an old friend named Caroline, who I once gave a hard time for pre-planning her funeral and erecting her own gravestone. She was quick to say, "You don't die a second sooner, just because you're ready," she'd say, and then add, "and think of the work I'm saving my family."

When you think of it, it has everything to do with family. First, life is made infinitely easier for everyone at a time of sorrow and crisis. Second, everyone has a sense that things are done in a process that everyone can embrace. Jane and I redid our wills this fall, her advance directive is finished and mine is almost done. Thanks Ellen, for the motivation.

"The $40 guest room..."

When Jane and I sold our rambling old place in Bowdoinham to move in with her dad, we did so knowing space and privacy would quickly become an issue. We were right, of course. We wanted Norman to retain his lifestyle as close to the way he has enjoyed it for more than a half century, but, we knew we would be needing breathing room too. The general expectation was for Norman to stay in his space downstairs, with some of our stuff. "Sprinkled in," and we would take over the apartment we'd fashioned upstairs. Ah, but the apartment was designed for our daughter, back before she was married, and there are two of us, and then there is me, with my baggage.

The ace I always pushed forward as the permanent solution soon became a project I affectionately called the "master's bedroom."

The upstairs front gable end of Norman's house was an unfinished attic for the first 100 years the place existed, and when Jane lived there as a teenager with her folks and brothers, Norman finished the area into two smaller rooms, smartly dressed out with knotty pine he harvested from their woodlot. When we started eyeing the space, the two old, cold, rooms were filled with the cultch of two or three generations of Jane's family, and there was a history of the rooms being too small, too cold in the winter and too warm in the summer.

Now, almost two years after the first visioning, we're excited to move in.

Remember, this project started while we were still rooted in Bowdoinham. While we were sorting and tossing from our house of 36 years, 'upland," in Bowdoinham, we also tried to focus energy on doing the same for this space. Results were mixed, and wicked slow. There were old beds, more boxes of stuff, books, pictures by the pile and built-in shelves and closets full of clothes. I remember it was months before we discovered one of the rooms was carpeted wall to wall.

I climbed into the attic, intent on the reuse of 6-8 inches of nasty, 1940 style blown-in insulation. "This I do for your next husband," I told Jane, "this stuff could kill us both." She smiled, saying nothing. We bagged the insulation and used it to double the r-value over the main house. Then we tore out the ceiling so the new room would have a new and more spacious headroom.

The closet partitions that created the two small rooms went away next, exposing our new and spacious room for the first time since the days of the attic. Others started to see through the dust and agree the room had the potential we envisioned. The four rackety windows were replaced with wood sashes with low-E, low-glare, high-efficiency glass. Rigid insulation went on the sloped walls, R-45 insulation overhead. Even Jane started to believe my prediction that the place would be warm enough with body heat and a couple candles.

We tore out the floor, put in new reinforcing stringers, then we added more insulation, replaced the old flooring, added a layer of underlayment plywood, and a new naturally finished pine floor, NOT from Norman's lot, but Norman really liked that.

Norman doesn't climb stairs real well any more, but he has made a point of visiting every month or two, "just to see what the noise is all about," he'd say. Several times, I've had to stop pounding nails and go say, "hi," because he would be downstairs calling, "come in!" The low ebb of those tours came the day he looked around at my reconstruction and said,

"Can't hardly see anything of the work I did years ago." It reminded me that after 40 years, I am still a visitor in his house. Mostly, Norman loves what we have done. The floor is great, the walls are wonderful, "It looks like a $40 guest room," he told me once. That is a compliment I'll take to the bank.

After years of working all sorts of projects in old houses, this room, when we move in this month, will be the first room done, "soup to nuts" BEFORE we moved in. Rugs are down, pictures are on the walls, curtains in the windows. DONE! It's pleasant, it's warm, light and well ventilated. Most important of all, I'm pretty sure the "master" is pleased.

Kids having kids

You have to realize I'm still pretty new to this grandfather thing. I still think of my thirty something year old son and daughter as kids, thank you very much, so it does get complicated and befuddling when I try to get my mind around my kids having kids. And this time folks, it was my one little girl doing the parenting!

Silas Alexander Morin joined the party on this earth late in the evening of January 26. I'm assured there were no serious complications, even though he arrived nearly two weeks before his due date. (Who sets a due date, anyway?) Little Silas is my Abbie's first child, and pardon me while I brag a little and say she made it all look easy. Abbie worked an eight hour day that day, went to an already scheduled doctor's appointment about 4 pm, and was told quite matter of factly to go home and get her bags, the birth was underway. There was a two-hour labor and Silas was born at 10:06 pm. "Piece of cake," the doctor announced.

Me?, of course I was in Bowdoinham doing a historical society thing. I got home that night about 8:30 to an empty apartment and a note on the bed, "Abbie's having our baby, get to the hospital."

Jane didn't sign it, she figured I'd figure it out.

I booked it down that icy driveway, finally glad I lived in Brunswick (Jane keeps telling me this would happen) and not more than four miles from the hospital. It was still a long ride, me thinking all the time about my little girl having a baby.

There was no record in the Emergency room, so the nice nurse told me to get right up to maternity. I vaulted the stairs, double-timed down that long hallway, and very soon was confronted by two locked doors. Two nurses-aides in a nearby waiting room told me the maternity ward was always locked down, security, you know, and I should push the little white button on the wall. This I did, and a slightly excited little voice came over the speaker suggested I take a seat, there was a baby being born next door. I tried to convince the nurses' aides to let me into the ward, (they admitted they knew how) but they guessed they would be in lots of trouble if they gave in to my sad story. They suggested I take a seat.

Less than a half hour later, the little voice was back over the little button looking for, "Mr. Connors?" When I answered yes, she suggested I come in and meet my grandson.

Silas weighed just under seven pounds at birth. He feels like a football when he cuddles under my neck. He already has this little habit of pulling his knees up when I cover most of his back with one of my hands. I told Jane he was smiling at me, she told me he probably was having gas. Undaunted, I took that little guy in both hands, held him up where we all could see him and said, "Silas, the world will be a better place because you are here."

My son Miles, Dina and Jadon visited that first weekend, of course, and it was interesting to watch four-year old Jadon visit with his new cousin. He was very tentative as he approached the little guy sleeping in the same cradle that had once snuggled his mother. There was genuine curiosity, then he started to giggle. "Mom," he said, "When he gets bigger, he can be just like me!"

But it was great grandfather Norman who stole the show. At 95, he seemed to look into little Silas' soul and a tear came to his eyes. "Precious," he said, "our world will go on."

Must do's and wanna do's

Me, I work best from a list. It's not uncommon to find me on a Friday night mapping out my weekend with a list of must do's, can do's, should do's, might do's, even a few wanna' do's. Of course I pay close attention to adding things that Jane might suggest, (usually, they're at the very top of my list) and then I check the calendar to see what's coming, and, if I'm real sharp, I'll add a thing or two that didn't get done the weekend before.

I wasn't born yesterday, so I'll admit the list always includes a ringer or two, something simple that I can whack at early in the weekend and draw a quick, thick line through. You know, "go to the bank...get gas in the truck..." Effortless, routine, mindless items that guarantee quick and unconditional success. Few things work better than an early sense of accomplishment.

Maybe you recall my consternation four years ago when I realized my first grandson was about to be born a native of Rhode Island. Part of my response to that malady was to produce a list of things that I and this little guy could do to enhance his status as an adopted, or exiled Mainer. I can tell you with a certain amount of pride that this list remains an active and fruitful one. We've done some of it, we've added to it, and now, it will be a delight to rework and turn this same list loose on my second little grandson, who is coming any day now, and being born on the proper side of the old Piscataqua River.

You have to be careful with the wording of any list. If there are four cords of wood waiting out back to be stacked, or several lawns to mow, the list should say, "stack wood," or "mow lawn." Then, if Sunday's sunset comes and you have only put a half hour into these projects, you still get to cross them off you list. "Mow THE lawns," is too specific. "Stack a cord of wood," is a trap. "Stack all the wood," is certainly an even bigger mistake.

I also have to admit I can sometimes be sneaky. If I know I have to paint the house, I must mow some lawns, or the garden needs weeding, but I'd rather be canoeing, I might put, "canoe on the Cathance," on my list. Of course casual is a rule. It needs to be somewhere near the bottom, and certainly well below the mowing and weeding. Jane takes an active interest in most of my lists, and she's almost certain to pick up on canoeing, hiking, snowshoeing, or the like, if any of them appear too high, or too obvious. But seeing them on the list is like planting the seed. She likes to canoe and/or snowshoe too, after all. More than one wonderful weekend adventure has started after I posted the hint on my list.

But now I'm thinking a master list might be in order. I'm not as young as I used to be, you know.

There are some things I want to do once, or once more, while I can. There are no black motives here, folks, I'm not secretly sick, and I'm not the one retiring, not yet. But I know what motivates me, and I'm sure if things appear on a list somewhere, there is a slightly better chance I'll get to them and get them done. Sort of my own bucket list, if you saw the movie.

I want a camp, or a yurt, where I can sleep overnight with my grandchildren. I want to cross Katahdin's Knife edge with my son. (Grandsons) I'd like to visit Vietnam again, and not be shot at. The house needs a new roof, and a coat of paint, while I'm agile enough to get it done. I want a hive or two of bees. I'd like to write a history for Bowdoinham, I'd like to visit the top of Sugarloaf or Saddleback and not ride down on the chairlift…you get the idea…MAJOR stuff! Stuff that borders on dreams, or lots and lots of effort.

So, one of my plans for 2011 is to work from and watch TWO Lists. There will be the "effortless list" the one I sink or swim with each weekend, and the "wonder list" that I plan for, hope for, dream about, and add to my life's work.

Wish me luck!

What's in the name?

Yup, my little girl is having a baby. Her due date is early next month. Tests have already told us that this child, Abbie's first, is a boy. Other tests confirm the little guy is "thriving," that his weight is perfect, that our daughter is doing just great, that we're headed for a 'perfect landing,' and that Jane is authorized to do most of the worrying.

Is it any wonder that those who can are focusing interest on this young man's name?

Names are never to be taken lightly in my family. My son Miles was named for my Grandfather, my daughter Abbie, the focus for all this questionable garble, is named for Jane's great grandmother (or the Abagadasset River in Bowdoinham) depending on who you ask and if Jane's in the room.

My eldest sister was named for my mother's favorite elementary school teacher, my elder brother proudly bears my father's mother's family name. My sister Ruth is named for my grandmother, and I was named for my mother's brother, who had just died in the war, back in 1941. My younger brother, born several months after our father's death, is named for my dad. My two younger sisters, born 15 years after me and when my mother had remarried, assumed their names are "reflections of their father's name" (Allison Lynn, and Marilyn). Marilyn likes to think our mother's admiration of Marilyn Monroe came into play with her name. That's a reach! Allison also theorizes that most of the "good family names" were taken when kids numbered six and seven came along, and that mom's imagination might have diminished at least a little. I like that Allison speaks frankly, too.

All my brothers and sisters polled agreed that mom picked names that were 'resistant' to becoming nicknames. She didn't like nicknames, she even disliked it when Grampie called me "Frankie!"

Early on there was a bunch of family chatter about picking the name of Abbie and George's firstborn. George, a true (and clever) gentleman, backed off just a little and suggested the decision should be Abbie's. Smart move, George! Maybe it was Thanksgiving when Abbie patted her bulging belly and suggested if the child was a girl, she would be named Sadie, if it was a boy, probably Silas.

BAD move, Abbie!

"Uncle" Henry, from away, (way away) puckered his nose at both. He allowed Sadie, because it was a family name, but he just couldn't abide Silas. "SILAS!," he flailed both arms, "Who ever heard of a name like SILAS?! No one in New York, obviously, but Henry, this ain't New York! Silas just happens to be a wonderful old New England AND family name. Henry immediately started a drumroll for William, just so you know the level of HIS imagination.

Since that outburst, Abbie has become quite silent about the process of name calling, Yes, she is still taking suggestions. (I gave her a couple more last weekend) At the same time and in the interest of full disclosure I told her I had this secret desire for a little granddaughter, but a grandson would be just fine, thank you. I did add, just so she knows how pleased I was with the "Sadie" reference, that if this little guy happens ever to make me upset, I might just call HIM "Sadie!" How's that for a nickname, mom?!

But rest assured folks, my little girl has her head on straight. "Dad," she told me last week, "when I see this little guy, I'll just know what his name should be."

You go girl, you are so right!

Remembering Grampie

You need to know that my dad died when I was less than a year old, and the "male influence" in my house during my formative years was my grandfather, Miles Hilton.

Miles and a couple neighbor guys (let's call them Phil and George), handled my upbringing when my mother was distracted, frustrated or simply figured I needed that "male touch." Grampie Miles was an Aroostook potato farmer who brought his family south during the Great Depression. The story is they got here with what they had in their car, but were thankful for it.

In Bowdoinham, Grampie always kept a small farm as a second job, worked at BIW during the war, worked at Sagadahoc Fertilizer every spring, worked at whatever he needed to work at to make lines balance at the end of the year. Guess that was one of his first lessons for me. He was the guy who convinced me that working the soil was a noble endeavor, not a dirty job. I bet I was 5 or 6 when he roped off a corner of his massive home garden, showing me how I could raise radishes as a cash crop and walked with me around the neighborhood when it was time to make the sales. He taught me to drive wheelbarrows and then cars. He told me bees would never sting unless they were threatened. "People are like that, too," he said more than once.

I have two brothers and two sisters, and I don't ever remember Miles raising his voice, or his hand, toward any of us. If there was disciplining to do, he would take a firm grip on our arm at just below the elbow, pull us out of whatever we were doing and utter the words, "That disappoints me, Frank" and the correction would be made.

When my first grandson, Jadon was born four years ago, I gave him a couple Maine books for his first Christmas, and attached a 4-page list of stuff he and I needed to do, "before I got too old." We've crossed off several lines from that list already, and have added still more items to be concluded. I have to consider that list is a constant work in progress, and realize that living the list is helping me to stay young.

When Silas, grandson number two, came along in January, the impulse was to create another list. Soon however, it was obvious that these two boys would need to share the love, and the obligation, that follows having me as a grandfather. There's a vision shaping in my mind of the three of us becoming a troupe of musketeers. I just can't wait to get the two of them together for a hike across a blueberry- laden field, and yes, now I have to figure a way to get TWO boys over Katahdin's Knife Edge, and still get their grandfather home alive.

Last month, Jane, Abbie, Silas and I went to a local greenhouse, seeking flowers for the new season. Silas was awash in one of those belly baskets (my name for a complicated, multi-strap thing that attaches him to my chest, facing out). Arms and legs are swinging, he's smiling at every young clerk that comes over to say "HI,"and I'm remembering when we did the same with Jadon. I think Miles would have been impressed.

All this is a tribute, and a challenge, to the fathers of the world, and a statement to my kids who now have to deal directly and constantly, with a grandfather who wants to inject himself into the lives of THEIR children. I hope they always see my actions as coming from a quiet place of love, and respect. I hope they stay gentle and kind to their kids and to me. I don't want Jadon, or even little Silas, to feel any pressure, but Silas will be 6 months old when I turn 65 in July, and when I'm 70 in 2017, Jadon will be 10, so we don't have a lot of time to waste!

And I just hope when my run is over, someone compares me to my grandfather.

ABOUT THE AUTHOR

A Maine native and life-long resident, Frank Connors likes to describe himself as a "pointman" for the Baby-boomer generation.

A former reporter-photographer for the Bath-Brunswick Times Record, Bowdoinham Town Manager, home designer, and truck driver, he still busies himself as a cemetery sexton, local historian, gardener and canoe paddler. He loves to talk and tell stories and is working on his listening skills.

He is passionate about his home town of Bowdoinham, his grandsons Jadon and Silas, his military service in Vietnam, and most everything else he happens to focus on during a given day.

Connors and his wife Jane are restoring the saltwater farm in Brunswick, where she grew up all those years ago.

ABOUT THE ARTIST

John Gable is a painter and muralist living in Maine. His career has covered an amazing range of subject matter from images of Maine life to commissions for America's Cup crews, rowing regattas and classic automobiles at Pebble Beach. His murals and paintings of Senators, notable families and historical figures can be seen in Washington D.C. And the Smithsonian Institution.

John has endured a long friendship with Frank Connors, and they have collaborated on many projects together. The artist lives with his wife, also an artist, in a 200 year-old farmhouse on Maine's Montsweag Bay.